LIFE BY THE BOARD FOOT

Roy O. Martin and the Martin Companies

By

James E. Carter

Edited by Maggie B. Martin, Ph.D.

Copyright, 2004
by
Roy O. Martin Lumber Company

ISBN 1-57980-985-5

Published and for sale by
CLAITOR'S PUBLISHING DIVISION
3165 S. Acadian at I-10, P.O. Box 261333
Baton Rouge, LA 70826-1333
Tel: 800-274-1403 (In LA 225-344-0476)
Fax: 225-344-0480

Internet address:
e mail: claitors@claitors.com
World Wide Web: http://www.claitors.com

Dedicated

In honor of and to the memory of

ROY OTIS MARTIN, SENIOR

And

MILDRED BROWN MARTIN

Without whom none of the other

would have occurred

TO ROM

They said he came from Michigan
Not many years ago;
That he went forth to brave the world,
And his own row to hoe!
Instead of plow he chose an ax,
And worked with might and main;
Until he won the crown he sought,
And vict'ry he did gain.

They say he's rough at times! Alas!
His drive is strong and fierce,
That mighty men oft quake and fall,
Before his eyes that pierce.
But many know that 'neath the steel,
Beats one Big Heart of Gold –
This fierce upstart from Michigan
With mighty words, and bold!

And now he drives a Cadillac,
And whizzes past, you bet!
But harried salesmen know the will
When once his mind is set!
"A hundred here – a hundred there. . ."
And then they all relent;
But no! this man with keenest mind,
Deducts his "two per cent"!

Paul Bunyan swung a mighty ax --
Least history books all say;
And carved a niche for Paul to last
For many a weary day.
But here's to him from Michigan
Who SAWED his way to fame;
He's one strong guy with heart of gold.-
Roy O. Martin is the name!

      Les Evans, 1954

TABLE of CONTENTS

Preface i

Foreword iii

Prologue v

I. Forestry 1

II. Founder 19

III. Foundation 67

IV. Function 113

V. Fundamentals 145

VI. Family 187

VII. Fortune 233

VIII. Future 249

Roy O. Martin Companies 295

Roy O. Martin Trademarks 296

Index 297

Endnotes 309

Appendix A – Glossary of Terms A-1

Appendix B – Calendar of Significant Events B-1

Bibliography C-1

Preface

A board foot is a standard of measurement. Measuring twelve inches long, twelve inches wide, and one inch thick, a board foot is the standard of measurement for both raw timber and finished lumber. Although both timber and lumber are now often bought and sold by the ton, a board foot is the traditional standard of measurement for both timber and lumber.

You will never see a board foot, unless it is a lumber salesman's sample. Just as you will never come upon a barrel of West Texas crude oil, neither will you ever find a board foot.

For those persons and families who lived in the context of the forest-products industry, life, too, is sometimes calculated by the board foot. Several years ago, Ed Kerr wrote an article, "Success by the Board Foot." Published in Forests and People, official publication of the Louisiana Forestry Association, this article focuses on Roy O. Martin, Sr., who was then president of Roy O. Martin Lumber Company. The title of this book, Life by the Board Foot, is a twist on the title of that article and is used by written permission of the Louisiana Forestry Association.

For Roy Otis Martin, Sr., and his family, life has literally been by the board foot. Timber and its manufacture into lumber and other forest products has accounted for their livelihood since 1923. Actually, it goes back even farther than that, since Roy O. Martin, Sr., worked for the Cyrus C. Shafer Lumber Company in South Bend, Indiana, and the Nickey Brothers Lumber Company in Memphis, Tennessee, before he moved to Alexandria, Louisiana, to buy a small groundhog sawmill on Fenner Street. From that meager beginning, the present Martin Companies developed.

While I could not claim to have known Roy O. Martin, I did meet him. When I was a student at Louisiana College, Roy O. and Mildred were members of First Baptist Church in Pineville, Louisiana, as I was. Although we did not visit at church, I knew that was Mr. Martin sitting in the congregation across from me. My closest encounter with this formidable businessman resulted from the rather informal transportation system that existed for male college students at Louisiana College during the early- to mid-1950s. If a student wanted to go into Alexandria, he would stand at the bus stop on College Avenue in Pineville. People regularly stopped, picked up the student (generally male), and gave him a ride into town.

Coming back from Alexandria to Pineville, the student would stand at the Walgreen Drugstore at the corner of Murray and Third Streets, and people would give him a ride back to the college.

I rode with Mr. Martin twice. Each time, he identified himself.

In telling this story to Norman Martin, son of Roy O., he remarked that I was unusual. Most people would not ride with him but once.

This writing assignment came at the invitation of Jonathan E. Martin, president of Roy O. Martin Lumber Company, and his wife, Dr. Maggie Martin. We were neighbors on the Cane River where I live and where they then had a camp. When I lived in Alexandria, we were also fellow members of Calvary Baptist Church. Maggie served as the editor and technical consultant for the work on this book.

This assignment has been a pleasure. I could not have asked for better support and cooperation from anyone than I have received from the Martin family and the Martin organization. They have been supportive, cooperative, and helpful in every way.

I trust that you will find the book as informational and as enjoyable as I found the research and the writing of it. For the Roy O. Martin Family, life has truly been by the board foot as the forest-products industry gave them sustenance, employment, definition, and the base for their significant contributions to their community.

James E. Carter

Cane River

2002

Foreward

Why a History of Another Family Company?

Certainly the principals managing any successful family-owned company feel that their family is unique. And most probably, they would be correct because every family possesses traits that particularly define them. Naturally, then, those who own and operate a closely held enterprise create an equally unique business as they integrate their distinguishing familial traits into their corporate structure.

However, this book did not develop simply from the premise that the Roy O. Martin family is an exceptionally different family, although it probably is. Indeed, the story of its forefather Roy O. Martin, Sr., could be viewed as a twentieth-century version of Louisiana's Horatio Alger. Born into a poor family in Elkhart, Indiana, in 1890 and becoming a lumber salesman in South Bend by happenstance in 1914, he ultimately made his way to Louisiana. With $65,000 in the bank and a dream in his heart, Roy O. Martin determined to find a way to control the destiny of himself and his family. Thus, in 1923 his entrepreneurial spirit brought him to Alexandria where he purchased his first sawmill. Eighty years, and more than that many descendents, later, the company he founded owns almost six hundred thousand acres and operates four manufacturing plants, now guided by third-generation Martins.

Neither did this book necessarily develop from the premise that the Roy O. Martin Lumber Company is a unique business, although it, too, may be. Eighty years later it operates from the same principles and similar genetic traits evidenced in its founder. Its story, then, is one of a highly successful business guided by strong-willed, impetuous people who are so performance oriented that they sometimes inflict tension onto those who love them best.

These two factors, a unique family who created an extraordinarily successful business, indeed contributed to the writing of this book, but they are not the primary premises behind the process.

The first reason for this book is quite personal. Because Roy O. Martin, Sr., died in 1973, more than half of his eighty-seven direct descendents were never privileged to know him. This book, then, is their introduction to him and his wife Mildred. As they get to know their ancestors, these family members most assuredly will come to know themselves better. After all, DNA is definable and indisputable. And, as the story of their heritage unfolds on the written page, hopefully they will come to appreciate even more fully than before the sacrifices that were made to provide them a life of privilege.

The second reason for this book is much more public as it chronicles the story of a key player in the economic development of Louisiana. Yet, few in our state know the contributions Roy O. Martin Lumber Company has made, and is continuing to make, to improve quality of life for its neighbors. Dr. William Slaughter, SSA Consultants of Baton Rouge, expresses well the second reason for this book: "Until I began consulting with ROM, I was unaware that the company even existed. Johnny Martin's response was 'the Martins like being low profile.' My feeling about that was that in Louisiana, we receive much exposure about all our shortcomings and that we need to do a better job of sharing our successes. Therefore, the state needs recognition for a company like ROM, which is and has been a great success story and contributes in many positive ways to our state."[1]

This book, then, is for you, Martin family, and for you, general public. May each of you come away from its pages with a greater appreciation for Roy O. Martin, Sr., and the company that proudly bears his name.

Maggie B. Martin, Ph.D.
2004

---

[1] Email to Maggie Martin from Dr. William Slaughter, February 21, 2004.

PROLOGUE

In 1912, at the age of twenty-two, Roy Otis Martin wrote his sister Cora Belle Stevens, requesting a loan of fifty dollars to enable him to move from South Bend, Indiana, to Memphis, Tennessee, to seek a job in the lumber industry. In her reply to him, Cora Belle indicated that the family was disappointed in him. He had been out of high school for four years, but still was unable to make his own living.

When he boarded a steamboat at Cairo, Illinois, to travel the Mississippi River to Memphis, he put his sister's letter in an envelope, sealed it, and wrote on the outside of the envelope, "Do not open this letter until you are making $5,000.00 per year." A few years later when he achieved that goal of earning $5,000.00 annually, Martin returned the letter to his sister with a note thanking her for her encouragement and advice.[2]

The business career of Roy Otis Martin got off to an inauspicious start. But from that meager beginning, Roy O. Martin ultimately became quite a successful entrepreneur, building a multi-faceted business that is still thriving eighty years later.

---

[2] Roy O. Martin, <u>Roy O. Martin: An Autobiography of Roy Otis Martin</u>. Charles H. Jeffress, editor. Alexandria, LA: Printing Department of the Roy O. Martin Lumber Company, 1961, 20-22.

*"The cultivation of trees is the
cultivation of
the good,
the beautiful,
and the ennobling in man."*

(J. Sterling Morton who initiated the first Arbor Day in 1972)

Life By the Board Foot: 1

1.

FORESTRY

... I saw, and behold a tree in the midst of the earth, and the height thereof was great. The tree grew, and was strong, and the height thereof reached unto heaven ... hew down the tree, and cut off his branches, shake off his leaves. .. (Daniel 4:11-12, 14).

The Golden Age of Forestry in Louisiana ended before Roy O. Martin founded his Roy O. Martin Lumber Company. He had missed the Golden Era of the lumber industry in the Bayou State, those first two decades of the twentieth century.[1]

The peak years for lumber in Louisiana were 1913, 1916, and 1917 when production exceeded four billion board feet. Those were years of bountiful--and unquestioned--supply as lumbermen sent loggers into Louisiana's virgin forests to retrieve the biggest and the best trees that Nature grew. With virtually no thought for tomorrow's supply, woodsmen eagerly plundered the state that would continue to yield more than three billion board feet of lumber annually through 1925.

This did not mean that the lumber industry was dead in 1923 when Roy O. Martin, Sr. (Roy O.) came to Louisiana. It was just diminishing from its zenith. Opportunity still existed for success in the state's forest-products industry if a person were industrious, hard working, and visionary. Roy O. was all of these. He would join the ranks of those in Central Louisiana who already fit this category. Fortunately for his personal gamble and for the state's general economy, a few conscientious, forward-thinking industry leaders had already begun to realize they could not continue to cutover precious land without contributing to future timber crops. They were beginning to experiment, albeit tentatively, with measures to provide forests for the continuance of their lumber industry.

LIFE BY THE BOARD FOOT

Early practices of reforestation

CHAPTER 1 - FORESTRY

Hence, early, fledgling steps toward reforestation began with a few landowners replanting the cutover land, but only as they saw fit and only as excess capital allowed.

In the meantime, the industry continued to prosper. As late as 1929, manufacturing of forest products still accounted for 38,000 jobs. However, only one hardwood mill in Louisiana, the E. Sondheimer Company, operated off timber it produced from its own lands. Instead, the more common arrangement was that of independent loggers who bought timber from landowners and sold logs to surrounding mills. Competition for the available wood was strong.

By the rip-roaring 1920s, Alexandria had become both a railroad center and a lumber-manufacturing center. This relatively small Central Louisiana town had access to six railroad lines: the Missouri Pacific, Texas Pacific, Louisiana Railroad and Navigation Company, Louisiana and Arkansas Railroad, Southern Pacific, and Rock Island Lines. With their main-line tracks and branch lines, these six railroads, which came through Alexandria, covered 2,200 miles of railroad within a one hundred-mile radius of the thriving town. Their competitive freight-rate structure made it economical to go as far out as one hundred miles in any direction to ship logs to Alexandria.[2] This preponderance of rail lines allowed easy transport of raw materials into local mills while simplifying shipments of manufactured products to customers. As a result, the city boasted five hardwood mills and two pine mills operating in and around Alexandria in 1926. This area was truly at the center of Louisiana's forest industry: railroads criss-crossed this Central Louisiana town that was surrounded by lush, wooded acreage just waiting to be harvested, or so it seemed.

In this setting, with the Golden Era ended and the area's timberland receding, the thirty-three-year-old Roy O. Martin founded Roy O. Martin Lumber Company in Alexandria, Louisiana, in 1923. This humble lumber mill would be the foundation for all future Martin business enterprises, the foundation for the success of Roy O. Martin, Sr. and his company. Even though he may have missed the Golden Era of lumbering in Louisiana, Roy O. would create his own era of achievement and success in Louisiana's lumber industry.

LIFE BY THE BOARD FOOT

LUMBERING IN LOUISIANA

The American lumber industry began in the northeast part of the United States. Until the 1850s it operated primarily in Maine. Antiquated techniques, limited transportation, and relatively stable markets restricted this agrarian industry. However as the nation grew, especially after the Civil War, lumber manufacturing was induced to expand. Like other aspects of life during these early years of America's industrial revolution, it, too, began moving westward. First, it moved to New York, then to Pennsylvania in the 1860s, and on to the Great Lakes region as far as Wisconsin in the 1870s.[3]

Technological advances also accompanied its westward expansion. New saws, modern harvesting techniques, and lumbering railroads combined to create an effective--and a progressive--industry. It was so "progressive" that, in only twenty years after reaching the Great Lakes, lumbermen were already running out of trees.

Unfortunately, this lumbering march westward left a swath of destruction in its wake.

Utter Devastation from Clear-Cutting Timber

CHAPTER 1 - FORESTRY

Timber resources then were looked upon as something to be mined or harvested, not as crops to be cultivated. The United States was still an agricultural society until well after the Civil War. Most often, trees were seen as a nuisance. Their removal cleared the way for farming, which was viewed as the nation's road to prosperity. Also, common knowledge dictated that it took one hundred years to grow a tree. Investors did not feel they could wait that long. This "attitude echoed a truism in American agriculture: when a field played out or was damaged by weather, a replacement always lay ready just a few steps into the wilderness. Conservation and artificial regeneration were not only arcane and expensive; they were believed to border on the imbecilic."[4] This cut-out-and-get-out philosophy was rampant and destructive.

Consequently, lumbermen began to look south. In 1876 Congress repealed the Southern Homestead Act, which opened up millions of acres of federal lands for private ownership, particularly in Alabama, Arkansas, Florida, Louisiana, and Mississippi. Investors, many of them northerners or foreigners and many of them in syndicates, bought up vast tracts of this land, often for as little as forty cents per acre. State governments also became involved by offering state land and low-tax deals to railroads that would expand into their local areas. Between 1880 and 1890, railroad trackage in Texas, Arkansas, and Louisiana increased by 211.4 %. Additionally, per capita income in the South was about one-third of what it was in the North. The South was covered with small farms largely worked by indebted tenant farmers. A ready supply of cheap labor existed. Bargain land, vast forests, willing local governments, and cheap labor all combined to make the South attractive to the lumbering industry.[5]

Until the advent of railroads in Louisiana, lumber production progressed slowly. Most lumber manufactured by these modest sawmills was for local use. Those few small parcels of lumber that left the state were shipped out of the Port of New Orleans. Incidentally, the first steam-driven lumber mill in the nation was built in New Orleans in 1811. The primary reason for this slow development of the lumber industry in Louisiana was a lack of transportation, not a lack of resources. During this era, more than eighty-five percent of land in Louisiana was covered by trees. In all areas of the Bayou State (except its sea marshes and southwest prairies), virgin forests of pine, cypress, and tupelo gum were available for harvest. More than seventy varieties of trees could be found in these lush forests. Amazingly, Louisiana contained more timber than any other state in the union with the exception of those in the Pacific Northwest.

LIFE BY THE BOARD FOOT

Perhaps even more amazing, considering this great natural asset, in 1869 lumber production in the South was its lowest in Louisiana at seventy-six million board feet annually. But with the coming of railroads also came northern capital—and subsequent local prosperity. Louisiana's lumber production almost doubled itself each year until the Bayou State passed all others in the South in 1904 with an output of nearly 2.5 billion board feet of lumber.

Louisiana Virgin Cypress

In fewer than ten years, this production was almost doubled again. Movement of lumber out of Louisiana began in 1881 from Lake Charles when the Southern Pacific system connected its various lines. Peak production was an all-time high of 4.1 billion board feet in 1913. The state's largest producer was Great Southern Lumber Company, Bogalusa, which was the first mill in the world built of steel. With four eight-foot band mills, this company turned out one million board feet of lumber every twenty-four hours. [6]

CHAPTER 1 - FORESTRY

Great Southern Lumber Company
Bogalusa, Louisiana

In Central Louisiana, lumbering began in a big way in 1891 with the establishment of J. A. Bentley Lumber Company at Zimmerman, seventeen miles northwest of Alexandria. This mill, built by J. A. Bentley and E. W. Zimmerman, burned in 1906. To capitalize on a still-booming industry, the owners rebuilt it immediately.

Henry E. Hardtner began cutting in the Urania forest north of Alexandria in 1896. Additionally, Hardtner organized Urania Lumber Company at Urania in 1898.

One of Hardtner's competitors, C. T. Crowell bought a tract of virgin longleaf pine timber about thirty miles south of Alexandria and established a mill with A. B. Spencer at Long Leaf, Louisiana. That mill was incorporated as Crowell-Spencer Lumber Company in 1897.

LIFE BY THE BOARD FOOT

Two years later in 1899, Crowell organized Bodcaw Lumber Company in Stamps, Arkansas. A short time later he sold it to William Buchanan who also operated Pine Wood Lumber Company, Springhill; Minden Lumber Company, Minden; Grant Timber and Manufacturing Company, Selma; and in Central Louisiana, Trout Creek Lumber Company, Good Pine Lumber Company, and Tall Timber Lumber Company, all in LaSalle Parish.

In addition, Hillyer-Deutsch-Edwards Lumber Company operated a mill at Oakdale. Industrial Lumber Company had mills in Oakdale and Elizabeth. This was a time of promised prosperity, a time of "wheeling and dealing" for those willing to launch into the high-stakes lumbering game in Louisiana. Its major players may have been few, but they were influential.

In 1903 Bentley organized Enterprise Lumber Company, which depleted its supply of wood twenty years later. But Bentley Lumber Company continued to operate a mill at Zimmerman until the middle of the twentieth century.[7]

Lumbering and the forest products industry were significant economic factors in Central Louisiana when Roy O. Martin began his lumber company in 1923. Local lumber businesses were already well

CHAPTER 1 - FORESTRY

established with experienced and prospering players in the field. Only time would tell if it had room for yet another budding entrepreneur.

THE LUMBERING PROCESS

During this era, trees necessarily had to be moved from the woods to the sawmills. In some cases, particularly in mill-towns where a sawmill was located in the midst of a forest, lumber companies built railroads, cutting essential paths into dense woods. Shorter tramlines were then built to reach various locations where timber was being cut.

At other times, lumbermen floated logs down waterways to a mill.

LIFE BY THE BOARD FOOT

Martin's earliest mill received logs from shipment either by railroad or by trucks.

Logging crews worked in virgin woods to cut and bring out massive trees. Filling their ranks with flatheads, filers, muleskinners, bullwhackers, swampers and scalers, these early log crews worked hard and long hours in sometimes dangerous operations. Tree cutters, known as flatheads, who worked with two-man crosscut saws, often cut gigantic trees.

CHAPTER 1 - FORESTRY

Saw filers kept crew saws clean and sharp and supported the flatheads. In many cases on smaller crews, the flathead was also a saw filer. Each flathead, then, was responsible for keeping his saw in good working order. Teamsters, muleskinners or bull whackers who handled either mules or oxen, necessary logging equipment in those days, also supported the flatheads. Logs were loaded either onto large wagons with big, fat wheels to keep them from sinking into the mud or onto two-wheeled, brace-type carts where one end of a log was placed and the rest dragged along the ground.

By these methods, logs were moved to places where they were loaded either onto railroad cars or onto trucks for shipment to various mills. Swampers were those men who scurried around the teamsters, clearing ground of debris or freeing logs from potentially dangerous snags on the ground. Scalers calculated the board feet contained in each log.

Prior to the introduction of cranes to load felled trees, logs were skidded onto cars or trucks. Two skid poles were leaned against the railroad car as a ramp. Mules were unhitched from a wagon and led to the opposite side of the car. Then a chain was run up and over the car and snaked under the log. A chain then was attached to the mule team on the other side of the car. As the mules walked away, the chain tightened and gradually rolled the log up sometimes-rickety skid poles and onto the car.[8]

Saws used in sawmills went through an evolution as mechanism impacted the industry. The original pit saw was, by today's standards, an archaic method of sawing lumber. In this cumbersome process, a log was first roughly squared by using a broad axe. Then the log was placed either over a pit dug in the ground or on top of an elevated trestle. Two men, one above the other, pushed the saw up and down and sliced a piece of lumber from the log. This method was also called whip-sawing.

The sash gang-saw was the next step in the evolution of sawing. With it, a vertical saw blade was fixed in a frame, giving more much-needed stability to the saw. Powered by water and later by steam, a sash saw made one hundred twenty strokes per minute and could produce from 2,000 to 5,000 board feet of lumber each day. Some minor changes in the sash saw resulted in what was called the "muley saw."

CHAPTER 1 - FORESTRY

Sash Gang Saw

The circular saw came next. A continuous-cutting model of the circular saw appeared in the 1840s. A further development of this sawing mechanism was the use of curved, inserted teeth, which was substantially more practical for sawing lumber in quantity.

The band saw was introduced in the 1890s. This saw is a continuous ribbon of steel with teeth on one edge. Its steel band was usually about fifty feet long, fourteen inches wide, and one-eighth of an inch thick (50'x14"x1/8"). This truly innovative endless saw was mounted on two large wheel-like rollers, which were eight feet in diameter. One roller rotated on a shaft overhead while the other roller was below the cutting-room floor. Its engine, which was usually powered by steam, powered the lower roller. A saw traveled vertically in one direction only, at a high rate of speed. Rollers positioned the saw, aligning it with the carriage and its log, then moved to a head-saw, which made the first cut on the log. The band saw cut a small kerf, or saw line, which reduced waste. With this saw, a skilled sawyer could cut almost twice as much timber a day as he could with a circle saw. Seated in an elevated position near the saw, he could oversee the whole operation. He would carefully manipulate levers while controlling all movement of a carriage that sent the log into the saw. The carriage was propelled back and forth on a track by a device called a shotgun feed, which was a long and fast-acting steam cylinder and piston. Steam filling the cylinder and then being discharged after the stroke produced characteristic sounds of those early mills. This cyclic booming echoed constantly during their hours of operation. Roy O. Martin, Jr., (Roy, Jr.) observed that at one time a person could drive from Alexandria to Monroe and never get away from this rhythmic sound of a sawmill. Certainly, technology greatly increased the production of sawmills.[9] An astute businessman, Roy O. must have realized the potential benefits of this machinery when he bought his Fenner Street mill, which utilized the band saw.

Subsequent development of kilns to dry lumber was another technological step forward for the lumber industry in the South. While drying prevented the bluing of lumber, it also reduced its weight and moisture content. This technique allowed southern lumber to compete with other woods in the northern consumer market.[10]

During that Golden Era of lumbering in Louisiana, many sawmills were located in mill-towns, which generally could be found in the midst of great virgin forests, often pine forests. True to their name, these tucked-away, corporate villages were complete communities with housing, commissaries, physicians, schools, and churches. Roy O. Martin never operated a mill-town. Establishing and maintaining such a community was immensely expensive. One also required owning large tracts of timberland, something that Roy O. did not have initially.

Since, in 1923, the prevailing philosophy of lumbermen in Louisiana (and elsewhere at the time) was to "cut out and get out," Roy O. surely practiced at least some of those logging principles. For the first two decades of his business, he hired loggers who knew little else but to cut all standing timber on a tract or in an area, then to abandon that site for another lush site. Like his peers, those early lumbermen, he practiced neither selective cutting of trees nor reforestation of land. Selective cutting would have required going back to that part of the forest later. Using temporary lumbering railroads to harvest timber and tram lines to connect to commercial railroads, this seemed impractical. Generally, lumber operators saw standing timber as the only item of value on a tract of timberland. They were in the business of turning timber into lumber in order to yield a fair return on their stockholders' investments. Growth rings on trees they cut often indicated an age of seventy years or so.

CHAPTER 1 - FORESTRY

Huge Sweet-Gum Log

These early lumbermen, however, did not realize that marketable timber could be grown in thirty years. But even if they had realized it, they were not willing to wait thirty years for another crop to grow. Quite simply, reforestation was an idea whose time had not yet come.

In writing about a large sawmill operation in northeast Louisiana, William T. Childers observed that "lumbermen predicated the life of their mills and equipment on the amount of timber they owned, and to extend their operation for much longer periods would mean expensive overhaul and retooling of their mills."[11] For them, cutting all available timber from a site and then either abandoning their temporary mills or relocating them seemed to be the best practice. They got all the money they could for standing trees and took their chances at disposing of the cutover land at the best price they could get.

So prevalent was the practice of "cut out and get out" that an Abandoned Mills Report issued on October 23, 1935, from the office of the Rapides Parish Clerk of Court, listed seventy-eight major mills that had shut down in Region Eight of Kisatchie National Forest, which is in Central Louisiana. Each of

LIFE BY THE BOARD FOOT

these mills was capable of producing a minimum of 25,000 board feet of lumber daily. Of course, at that time, some mill closures were undoubtedly due to the Great Depression. Others, however, closed because their operators had clear-cut the abundant land, following the common practice of cutting and getting out.

Mill	Location	Dates of Operation	Mill	Location	Dates of Operation
Iatt Lumber	Verda	1903-1909	Manistee Lumber	Manistee	1895-1914
Bell Lumber	Loftin	1904-1908	Clark Brothers	Simms	1903-1909
Lone Pine	Colfax	1903-1910	Lee Lumber	Tioga	1900-1925
Frost-Johnson	Campti	1905-1915	J. F. Ball & Brother	Ball	1898-1910
South Arkansas	Jonesboro	1900-1911	Alexandria Lumber	Pineville	1906-1914
Hodge Hunt	Hodge	1910-1925	J. A. Bentley Lumber	Alexandria	1900-1918
Guest and Lagrone	Quitman	1904-1910	Long Pine Lumber	Alexandria	1900-1913
Sulphur Timber & Lumber	Winnfield	1905-1908	Rapides Lumber	Woodworth	1892-1925
O. C. Butler	Gaw Mill	1916-1930	Harrington Creek	Forest Hill	1895-1901
Edenborn Lumber	Menefee (Winnfield)	1919-1923	Crowell-Spencer	Longleaf	1892-1950
Edenborn Lumber	Gulf Crossing	1923-1926	W. M. Cady	McNary	1911-1923
Doyle Lumber	Womack (Chatham)	1909-1913	Louisiana Saw Mill	Glenmora	1912-1927
Antione Lumber	Chatham	1908-1910	Phillips Lumber	Blanche	1895-1900
Bruine Lumber	Gulf Crossing	1920-1922	Beering-Conrad	Pawnee	1893-
Tremont Lumber	Eros	1901-1916	Louisiana Central	Clarks	1902-
Macon Lumber	Eros	1925-1927	Urania Lumber	Urania	1898-
Cook Brothers	Chatham	1930-1932	Standard Lumber	Standard	1899-1934
Frazier Lumber	Cartright	1905-1908	Smith & Adams	Castor	1899-1905
Frazier Lumber	Eros	1932-1934	Zenoria Lumber	Zenoria	1914-1930
Frazier Lumber	Choudrant	1904-1909	White Sulphur	White Sulphur	1907-1917
Tremont Lumber	Tremont	1900-1906	Lee & Beal	Georgetown	1902-1907
Willhite Lumber	Clay	1930-1935	P. F. Rogers	Linean	1894-1906
J. M. Lagrone	Ruston	1908-1910	Ball Lumber	Howcott (Georgetown)	1913-1916
Dubach Lumber	Dubach	1897-1922			
Robinson Lumber	Middle Fork	1915-1917	Fish Creek	Fish Creek	
Eunice Lumber	Bernice	1919-1922	Sand Spur	Sand Spur (Pollock)	1905-1913
Silverthorne Lumber	Randolph	1900-1909	McMain & Brannon	Antoine (Pollock)	1896-1905
O. W. Farmer	Jonesboro	1927-1934	Good Pine	Good Pine	1907-1935
Hardy Cox	Wyatt	1918-1920	Tall Timber	Good Pine	1914-1938
Calvin Lumber	Calvin	1902-1904	Grant Timber & Mfg.	Selma	
Dodson Lumber	Dodson	1917-1919	Comaine & Boyd	Atlanta	1905-1925
Alberta Lumber	Alberta	1903-1915	Tremont Lumber	Rochelle	1902-1938
Horn and Petty	Robertsville	1887-1896	Wyatt Lumber	Wyatt (Jonesboro)	1902-1912
Louisiana Long Leaf	Victoria	1882-1922	Tremont	Pyburn	1901-1906
Black Lake Lumber	Campti		Pine Tree	Pine Tree	1901-1906
Hart & Adams Lumber	Bentley	1906-1913	Hall & Legon	Tannehill	1902-1912
John Harper Lumber	Stay (Bentley)	1900-1905	Woods Lumber	Winnfield	1904-1907
Big Creek Lumber	Pollock	1892-1919	Murray Northern	Moore (Winnfield)	1904-1907
Lee & Beal Lumber	White Spur	1895-1915	Wright Lumber	Sardoni	1905-1907
Clark Brothers	Simms (Pollock)	1903-1909	Whitford Lumber	Whitford	1904-1910

Unfortunate, but true, Louisiana's landscape was devastated following this practice of clear-cutting. Those original stands of virgin timber, which had been park-like, quickly no longer existed. Gone was the canopy of limbs and leaves overhead, which had sheltered ground clear of underbrush. Archer H. Mayor described the devastation:

> The once serene and towering trees fell, one by one, in slow, rushing crunches to the slicing of the saw . . . . All that effort had a dramatic impact on the forest. Like a huge, slow-motion scythe ripping through tall grass. As the trees fell, the filtered light disappeared, replaced by the harsh glare of an unforgiving sun. The once lawn-smooth ground became buried under the flammable debris, abandoned treetops, limbs, and powdery sawdust. When the loggers left a site for the last time, it resembled a battlefield, torn up and blasted.[12]

CHAPTER 1 - FORESTRY

Devastation from Cutting Out and Getting Out

Since Roy O. originally owned no land other that on which his sawmill sat when he began his business, he was not as blatantly and personally involved in the cut-out-and-get-out practice as those saw-millers who had large land holdings and mill-towns. He either bought timber off another's tract of land or he bought timber someone else harvested. However, because selective cutting was in its infancy, hardly practiced at all, certainly some of the land from which he took timber was likely as devastated as Mayor described. That was simply the practice of the time.

Thus was the milieu in which Roy O. began Roy O. Martin Lumber Company. Fortunately, for him and his company, the forest-products industry was well established in Central Louisiana even though it had passed its Golden Age. Nevertheless, logging was hard and dangerous work. Sawmills were a major source of employment in the area, but the lumbering process left all cutover land barren and bleak. A problem for Roy O. in finding a mill to purchase was that pine was the timber of choice in Central Louisiana; his experience was with hardwoods. Typifying the Martin business psyche (daring to be different and finding success through that difference), Roy O. sought and located a hardwood mill to own and operate in the midst of an area known for its production of pine lumber. Most of the Martin family would agree that Divine Guidance, rather than fortune, fate, or happenstance, led him to Alexandria where the Fenner Street hardwood mill became the foundation of subsequent business enterprises of Roy O. Martin.

Life By the Board Foot: 2

2.

FOUNDER

And he shall be like a tree, planted by the rivers of water, that bringeth forth his fruit in his season; his leaf also shall not wither; and whatsover he doeth shall prosper (Psalm 1:3).

Roy Otis Martin was born to Albert Andrew Martin and Susie Belle Kittell Martin on April 24, 1890, near Elkhart, Indiana, also birthplace of his father Albert Andrew Martin. Known as Buster, the older Martin had been born on December 7, 1859, and lived until June 6, 1930. With his seven siblings, Buster grew up about four miles north of Elkhart, near the Michigan-Indiana state line. He first married Lottie Bishop who died shortly after their marriage. They had no children. Buster then married Susie Belle Kittell who was born on September 20, 1865, and died on September 20, 1950.

Albert Andrew and Susie Kittell Martin
1911

LIFE BY THE BOARD FOOT

The third of four children, Roy O. had two brothers and one sister: Albert DeWitt Martin (Bert) who was born on September 3, 1886, and died on February 16, 1916; Cora Belle Martin Stevens who lived from August 12, 1888, until April 12, 1946; and Wallace Beardsley Martin whose lifespan stretched from December 4, 1895, to January 4, 1985.

The Albert Andrew (Buster) Martin family
Seated, left to right: Susie Belle Kittell Martin, Albert Andrew, and Wallace Beardsley
Standing, left to right: Albert De Witt, Cora Belle, and Roy Otis

CHAPTER 2 - FOUNDER

EARLY LIFE

At the time of Roy O.'s birth in 1890, his father owned three acres of land on the banks of Simington Lake, about three miles north of Elkhart, Indiana. A good fishing spot, Simington Lake attracted people who not only traveled there by horse and buggy to fish but others who also built cottages along its banks. Buster built extra stalls in his barn, ostensibly for renting them to people who would leave their horses in his care while they were at their cottages. He also built a pier that extended into the water about eighty feet. This pier had a wide boathouse at the end.

One of Roy O.'s earliest scrapes happened at that pier. When he was about five years old, he fell from a boat into the lake. His older brother and sister, Bert and Cora, pulled him from the water and saved him from drowning. Because his mother was away in town and his father was working away from home at the time, his brother and sister bathed him and changed his clothes. His parents presumably never knew of this close call, which may have been a portent of the daring and adventurous spirit that would guide him toward success as an adult. Perhaps even then he did not want his peers telling him what to do (sit in the boat) or how to do it (sit still), two traits that would define his character as an adult.

Cora, Roy Otis and Bert Martin

Along with his livery business, Buster operated a marina with rental boats, fishing tackle, baits, and cushions. As a first step toward his entrepreneurial spirit, Roy O. and his brother Bert kept their dad's boats clean and ready to rent. Seemingly never idle, even as a youngster, he also dug worms and kept a large box of these wriggling creatures to sell to fisherman for five cents a dozen.

Buster also performed odd jobs around the community where they lived. Having a circular saw driven by a small steam engine, he cut up broken rail fences into twenty-two-inch lengths and delivered them as firewood to bakeries in Elkhart. From all indications, that was where Roy O. got his first smell of sawdust.

During cold, winter months, Buster butchered hogs. Having all the tools necessary for slaughtering hogs, he created a rather successful business catering to people in a fifteen-mile radius from the Martin home. Buster would slaughter and butcher hogs, rendering lard and making sausage. Roy O. later observed that his father must have made a million pounds of lard for neighbors and acquaintances. His work day would often extend from 4:00 or 5:00 a. m. until 9:00 p. m. after which he would drive home in a wagon or sled in all kinds of weather on trips that would frequently take as long as two hours.

Later Buster built a gristmill. Farmers would bring their corn to his mill to have it shelled and their corn and oats to have them ground. At the age of eight, Roy O.'s job was to feed corn and oats into the gristmill as well as to fasten sacks onto its accompanying grain elevator. Buster also converted the front room of their house into a little store, which his wife ran in the winter when he was butchering. Susie churned butter and baked bread, cookies, and pies to sell to people living in cottages along Simington Lake. This strong work ethic evidenced in both parents undoubtedly influenced their young son.

These years in Elkhart were not easy. As a young boy there, Roy O. "knew poverty" (a phrase which turns up frequently in his reminiscences), and he didn't like it. Perhaps that is why he was so determined to succeed. Reflecting on his childhood some fifty years later, he was considerably more cavalier about his early days: "Well, it was a long time ago! Poverty, yes, but millions of others experienced it, too, and to many it is a blessing. It keeps your feet on the ground—teaches you sound economy."[1]

"'We never went hungry,' he recalls, 'but we weren't far from it on several occasions.'"[2] Retrospectively, then, Roy O. recognized hunger and deprivation as motivation that fueled his later success.

He additionally recalled two specific circumstances from that early period, which, at least in part,

CHAPTER 2 - FOUNDER

further determined the course for his adult life. One of these memories was that his mother always tried to make time every day to read her children a chapter from the Bible. Each week, she also did everything she could to send them to Sunday school, which met in the building where they attended school. Their walk from home to school was two miles, a difficult journey for children in Indiana's wintertime. With that background, church attendance and involvement were always important to Roy O.

The second significant matter that shaped his character was the building of a saloon a block south of their house. Roy O. stated, "I soon learned the effect of liquor on human beings. I am very happy to state, that, although we were exposed to liquor, no one in my family used it. We learned its evils at a very early date."[3] Roy O. neither smoked nor drank.

About 1900-1901 Buster rented a ninety-acre farm about three miles from where the family lived. By this move, he was able to curtail the amount of time he spent butchering hogs in the winter. He also moved his family away from the despised neighboring saloon.

After a couple of years on this rented property, the elder Martin bought an eighty-acre farm on time about a mile north of the Indiana-Michigan state line. With this relocation, again of three miles, the Martins left Indiana for Michigan. Buster built a small storage building on the place, then later moved a barn there. Until they built a house two years later, the elder Martin along with Bert and Roy O. slept in that meager barn. The three of them, with help from a carpenter, built the family house themselves.

May Street
Edwardsburg, Michigan

LIFE BY THE BOARD FOOT

Roy O. was born to work. He grew up in a hard-working family during hard times. With few financial resources, his father labored dawn to dark to support his wife and children. This work ethic was instilled in Roy O. at an early age. Not only did he maintain that strong work ethic all of his life, but he also expected it of those who worked with him.

YOUNG MANHOOD

Roy Otis Martin graduated from Edwardsburg High School in Edwardsburg, Michigan, when he was eighteen. He immediately took and passed the examination for a teacher's certificate. By that time, anxious to enter a profession and become self-sufficient, he had already committed to teach at Calvin Center, Michigan. While there, Roy O. taught all subjects and grades from beginners through eighth grade, earning forty dollars a month. Even though he had to buy clothes, pay room and board, and provide for personal expenses, he managed to save sixty dollars by the end of the school year. Saving money was integral to his personality, born from his early experience with poverty.

Roy Otis Martin, Sr.
age 18

During his summer break after teaching school, he attended South Bend Business College in South Bend, Indiana. With only the sixty dollars he had saved, he needed other employment. Thus, he found work at Kables' Restaurant, first as a dishwasher and then as a waiter, and at Spiro's Clothing Store two evenings

CHAPTER 2 - FOUNDER

a week while attending business college. After returning to Calvin Center for another year of teaching, he again returned to South Bend Business College for a second two-month session.

Following that summer of study, he had a brief fling of about thirty days selling Occident Flour to homemakers. This was followed by a career of nearly the same duration selling Oliver Typewriters.

Then he worked for a brief time at Studebaker Corporation, which made wagons. While employed there, Roy O. was in the same group as Mildred Brown. The two had first met during the second summer he attended South Bend Business College. From Hartford, Michigan, she, too, had been a student at the college. And, after finishing summer school, she, too, had taken a job with Studebaker, where their paths crossed once again.

Mildred Brown
Circa 1910

LIFE BY THE BOARD FOOT

Born on February 21, 1892, Mildred was the daughter of Henry and Nettie Brown of Hartford, Michigan. These hard-working Browns were pioneers in southwest Michigan, having descended from settlers who came to America on the Mayflower. Henry was a farmer. Later he had a threshing machine and worked on farm equipment. He had a good singing voice and a love of music, which his daughter inherited. A devout deacon in Hartford Baptist Church, Brown and his family lived their faith, daily practicing morning devotions at home. [4]

Not only did the properly raised Mildred and the ambition-driven Roy O. work in the same group while at Studebaker Corporation, they also dated some. However, all indications suggest they were not in a serious relationship at this time. Apparently Roy O. felt he needed to prove himself as an adult of potential substance before he could court a lady.

Mildred at Studebaker Plant
Circa 1910

In 1910, Roy O. thus asked his teachers at South Bend Business College to help him find suitable employment. From these business college contacts, he received an offer to teach bookkeeping at New South Business College in Beaumont, Texas. He wired an immediate acceptance of the offered position.

Traveling on a fifty-dollar loan from his father, the twenty-year-old Roy O. arrived in Beaumont on a Sunday night and began teaching on Monday. Teaching both day and night classes in bookkeeping, he would often work until 9:00 p.m. Living at the YMCA, he would then go to his room and prepare lessons

CHAPTER 2 - FOUNDER

for the next day, staying just one day ahead of his unruly students who were not much younger than he. He averaged only five or six hours of sleep a night because, as part of his job, he had to travel to surrounding towns on Saturdays and recruit students for the business college. Not only was he a teacher (the job which he had accepted), he was also a salesperson (a position which he had not envisioned). His work schedule was arduous; his social life was minimal. The only lasting contact he made while in Beaumont was with J. Elliston Thomas who would become a lifelong friend.

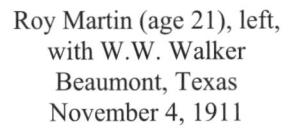

Roy Martin (age 21), left,
with W.W. Walker
Beaumont, Texas
November 4, 1911

Unlike his experience at South Bend Business College where he had studied, many students at this business college were little more than juvenile delinquents who had been expelled from school. Rather than make them work, apparently their parents had sent them to business school as a means of keeping their aimless sons out of trouble. Unfortunately, since trouble defines juvenile delinquency and since Roy O. necessarily interacted with these miscreants in his classes, he eventually encountered trouble, literally coming face to face with it. During a scuffle with four unruly students, a particularly errant one knifed Roy O., inflicting two gashes on his torso. Only a pad of calling cards in his shirt pocket kept him from being stabbed in the heart. With those experiences and the impression that the president of the

LIFE BY THE BOARD FOOT

business college was not too happy with his work, after he completed the nine-month session at Beaumont, Roy O. resigned and returned home.

WE FURNISH EMPLOYERS STENOGRAPHERS FREE OF CHARGE
SHORTHAND COURSE — LILIAN HURT
Shorthand, Correspondence, Punctuation, Manifolding, Spelling, Office Practice, Court Reporting, Penmanship, Touch Typewriting
COMMERCIAL COURSE — ROY O. MARTIN
Bookkeeping, Commercial Law, Commercial Arithmetic, Banking, Business Forms, Penmanship, Rapid Calculation, Spelling, Business Practice
A PREPARATORY COURSE IS MAINTAINED
INVESTIGATE OUR STANDING
NEW SOUTH COLLEGE
BEAUMONT, TEXAS   1911
COME TO NIGHT SCHOOL. CALL OR WRITE FOR CATALOGUE

Upon returning to Indiana, he first visited his mother who was sick in a hospital in Elkhart. Roy O. then went to his family's Michigan farm and worked there for about six weeks. Then he went to South Bend, Indiana, to find a job. For about a week he again sold Occident Flour door-to-door, but his pay was less than his expenses.

Roy Otis Martin
(Fall of 1911)

This time could have been a low point in his life but for a chance encounter with that attractive young woman from Hartford. One Sunday while attending First Methodist Church in South Bend, he spotted Mildred Brown sitting a few rows ahead of him. Acting on the attraction he felt, he invited her to lunch that day at the YMCA where he was staying. She accepted. Their lunch lingered into an afternoon

CHAPTER 2 - FOUNDER

together, which led to their returning to church that night to attend the Epworth League meeting. Roy O. later observed, "I must admit that I had a warmer interest in Mildred when I returned than I had before."[5]

Now, more than ever, he needed permanent employment so that he could properly court a young lady.

Consequently, one Saturday in 1911, he went to an office building in South Bend and began knocking on office doors, one floor at a time. On either the fourth or the fifth floor, an office door opened and a man asked what he wanted. When Roy O. replied that he wanted a job, the man invited him into the office of the Cyrus C. Shafer Lumber Company. Although he had no prior experience in the lumber industry, Roy O. was hired to work at Shafer Lumber Company for twelve dollars a week. When the brother of the man who hired the inexperienced lumber salesman heard of the proposed salary, he thought it was excessive and abruptly reduced it to ten dollars a week. Surely disappointed by his salary reduction but thankful for an employment opportunity, Roy O. began work with the Shafer Company early the next Monday morning. He wrote, "Here was where I got my first taste of the lumber business."[6]

Roy O.
at
Shafer Lumber Company
1912

LIFE BY THE BOARD FOOT

Later, Roy O. said about his life's work that he entered accidentally,

> There was nothing premeditated about it because I had knocked on several doors in the same building before I got to Mr. Shafer's office. But you know how it is on a Saturday, nobody in; it just happened that Mr. Shafer was, and he had a job for me when I asked. If it had been an insurance agency or finance company, instead, I'd probably be in that business today. I wasn't particular what it was, I just needed work.[7]

Ellis Martin (Ellis) asserted that his father "got into the lumber business by starvation. His decision was to make enough money to get married."[8]

Thus Roy O. Martin got a rather inauspicious start in the lumber business. The Shafer Company was a lumber wholesaler. In addition to his duties, Roy O. also helped the bookkeeper two or three times a week, a learning experience that would bode well in his journey toward financial independence.

Shortly after Roy O.'s return to South Bend and his employment with the Cyrus C. Shafer Lumber Company, Mildred returned to Hartford, Michigan. On the one Sunday a month that Roy O. took off from work, he would go to Hartford to visit the attractive brunette. She later took a position with a stock brokerage office in Grand Rapids, Michigan.

Roy O. and Mildred
(circa 1911)

30

CHAPTER 2 - FOUNDER

When time came for Roy O.'s vacation after working for the Shafers a year, he asked if he could go to their office in Cairo, Illinois, for his vacation week so that he could learn more about lumber. Roy O. apparently wanted to learn as much as he could about the business in which he had become involved. With his ambition to succeed, he must have wanted to be as well prepared as possible. This pleased his employers greatly. Shafer's local manager in Cairo asked for him to stay an additional week, which he did.

Roy O. Martin
at
Shafer Lumber Company
Cairo, Illinois

This stay in Cairo obviously led to his transfer there. Unfortunately, some time after his transfer to Cairo, his once-good relationship with the manager soured. He thought Roy O. had been sent there to report on him. Recognizing their working relationship was beyond repair, Roy O. regrettably resigned his position. Because he thought he had failed in his mission, he declined an opportunity to return to Shafer's South Bend office.

While in Michigan and Illinois, Roy O. had continued to correspond with J. Elliston Thomas, his Beaumont roommate whom he described as "the dearest friend I have ever had."[9] When Roy O. left the Shafer Company, Thomas was working in the office of a lumberman in Memphis, Tennessee, which was then the biggest lumber center in the South. Thomas invited Roy O. to visit him in Memphis and check out job opportunities there. Desiring the opportunity, but lacking the capital to act, this was the time that Roy O. asked to borrow fifty dollars from his sister Cora. He got the letter, the lecture, and the fifty dollars.

With that borrowed fifty dollars, he made the trip by steamboat to Memphis. There, he met with his good friend from Beaumont who gave him the names of three or four lumbermen he could petition for a job. The third lumberman he contacted had no available positions, but he gave Roy O. the name of the

LIFE BY THE BOARD FOOT

Nickey Brothers who were opening a new company. Roy O. immediately pursued this lead and located the Nickey Brothers' office.

Memphis, Tennessee
1912

When he met with their general manager, he asked for a job as a lumber inspector. After learning that job was not available, undeterred from his mission, he said that he could keep books. But a bookkeeper had been hired that morning. The general manager then asked him if he could sell lumber. Roy O. replied, "Yes. I can sell lumber" even though he had never sold a stick of lumber in his life.

At sunup the next morning, Roy O. began his work with Nickey Brothers at a salary of eighty-five dollars a month. He never worked fewer than twelve hours a day. He wrote his own letters, made his own contacts, and spent time on the lumberyard so he would know the stock. In less than two month's time, he knew more about the lumberyard than any of the other employees. Chances are his knowledge also surpassed that of some of the owners.

Working hard in Memphis but remembering the attractive brunette in Grand Rapids, Roy O. would arrange lumber selling trips to the north to include Michigan so that he could visit with Mildred.

After a year Nickey Brothers sent him to Rockford, Illinois, to open a sales office there. By that time, Roy O. and Mildred were already engaged to be married, awaiting the time they could afford to marry. Roy O's reassignment from Memphis to the Rockford, Illinois, office, provided that opportunity. He and Mildred could finally set a wedding date.

CHAPTER 2 - FOUNDER

MARRIAGE

Roy O. and Mildred married on October 8, 1914, at the Brown home. About forty people attended the wedding, including Roy O.'s parents, brothers, and sister. The local Baptist pastor officiated, and Mildred's sister sang one of two solos. <u>The Hartford Day Spring</u> of October 14, 1914, described Mildred: "The bride wore a dainty hand-embroidered gown of white voile and carried bride's roses. She is a popular young lady of Hartford, interested in church and educational work. The groom," the article continued, "holds a responsible position as northern salesman for a large house in Memphis."[10]

Mr. And Mrs. Roy O. Martin, Sr. (seated)
Albert Andrew and Susie Belle Martin and Henry and Nettie Brown (standing)
October 14, 1914

The newly married couple took a short wedding trip to Chicago, which was interrupted by business responsibilities. Interruptions of personal trips or vacations by business concerns are a consistent Martin practice. Even today, Martin executives frequently incorporate business calls into personal trips.

33

LIFE BY THE BOARD FOOT

Roy O. and Mildred returned to Rockford, Illinois, renting a small apartment with one bedroom and a kitchenette.

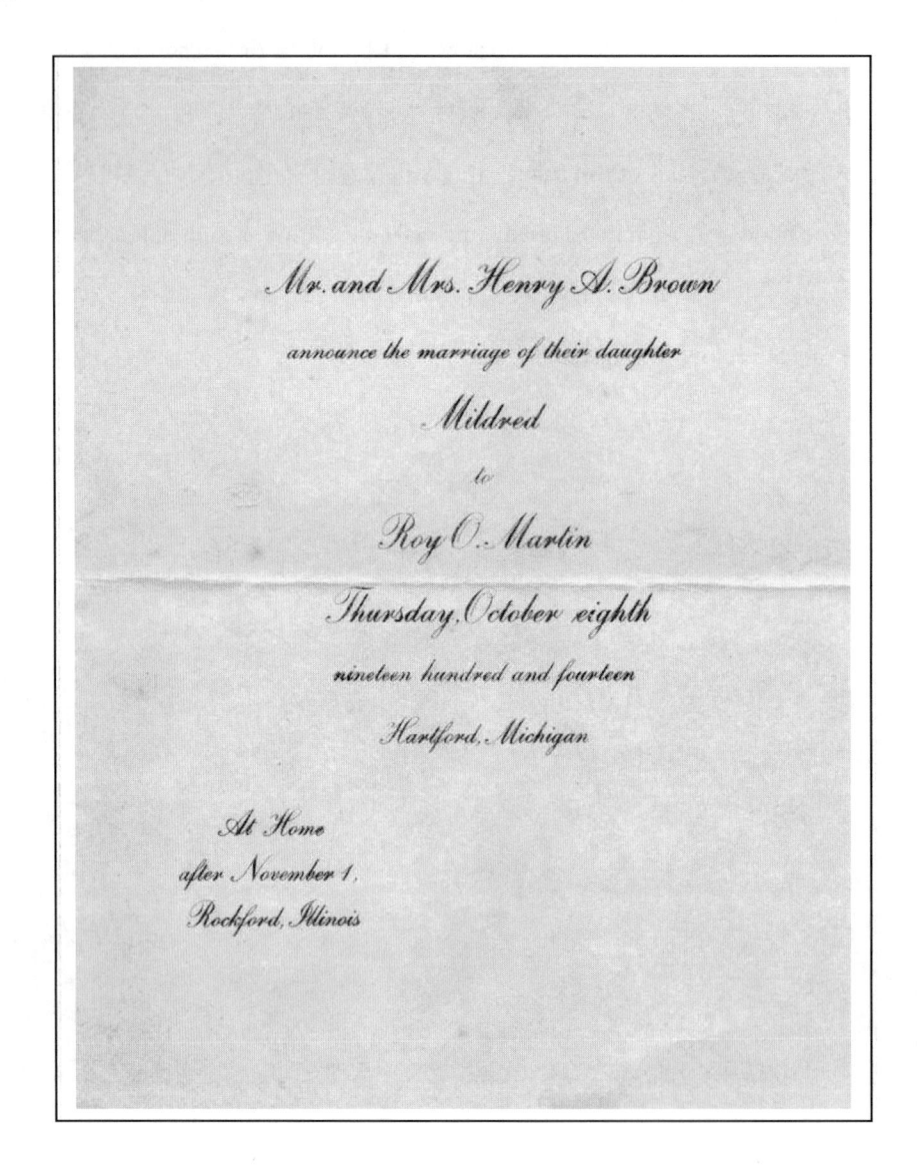

> Mr. and Mrs. Henry A. Brown
>
> announce the marriage of their daughter
>
> Mildred
>
> to
>
> Roy O. Martin
>
> Thursday, October eighth
>
> nineteen hundred and fourteen
>
> Hartford, Michigan
>
> At Home
> after November 1,
> Rockford, Illinois

The office Roy O. rented consisted of one room with a typewriter and a telephone. Mildred watched the office when Roy O. was away on selling trips. Seven weeks after his marriage, Roy O. prepared a monthly statement. On November 24, 1914, he computed his net worth to be $371.49, as evidenced by an advertisement for The First National Bank of Chicago, an institution that would become Roy O.'s lender of choice.

CHAPTER 2 - FOUNDER

Today he would have to write it in the millions

(A TRUE STORY)

"MY PERSONAL net worth is $371.42 this November 30, 1914", wrote the young clerk in the lumber yard. He was seven weeks married and he was toting up things to see where he stood. Some day he meant to own his own business. He would be making monthly statements then, why not begin now? As you can see, he was a young man with a Plan. He has always been. And the results are written today in millions of dollars in net worth.

We believe every businessman will be interested in how The First National Bank of Chicago became a part of his Plan and why.

First, our young friend taught himself to *save* money. It took twelve years to save enough to buy his first business—a small sawmill and six acres of land. Next he learned how to *borrow* money. Let him tell how that fitted into his Plan, and what the results have been.

"We have always been large borrowers of money and have always paid our debts. Because of our banking connections this parent company and eight subsidiaries have never missed a discount on purchases since they have been in business. That discount ability has enabled us to buy to better advantage and more than paid the interest to our banks over a period of thirty years. We believe in carrying good balances in our bank, more than the normal banking practices require. I believe that a good cash position, even if it is borrowed cash, is a prerequisite to successful operation. We have always laid our matters before our banks, giving them a clear and concise understanding of our operations, whether they were profitable or unprofitable."

In the bad times of the 1930's, it was rough to stick to that Plan. Lumber prices tumbled to half what they had been, doubling the company's indebtedness in terms of lumber. But strict economy and lots of hard work enabled the company to squeeze by, reduce their debts, take their discounts.

It was then that this lumberman came to us. He wrote us about that the other day, "I came to The First National Bank of Chicago without introductions," he says. "I had heard so much about what you had done in our industry and how highly you are regarded. We urgently needed a stable and reliable bank that could help us not only in good times, but in hard times."

"*I learned then, and since, the advantages to a customer of your Divisional setup, organized, as it is, by industries. We found officers who were specialists in lumbering, who not only had the authority to make decisions on loans but did so immediately. They were also able to give us technical advice because of long experience in handling other concerns in the same business. We are proud of the fact that from such men we have always received the loans we asked for.*"

The italics are ours. They make a point that is important about our relationship to industry: we are uniquely equipped to help, and we do so promptly. Our ten Divisions cover all the basic industries.

Well, that original sawmill and six acres have grown to nine properties with a net worth of five million dollars, with sales of 50 million feet of lumber a year. Their reforestation program is growing five trees for every one they cut.

"If my descendants carry on, this mill can run for hundreds of years," our friend proudly writes. "My three sons feel about The First National Bank of Chicago as I do, and I am sure will pass that knowledge on to their sons."

Can you use the kind of help you are reading about here? A phone call, a wire, a letter will bring us together. Whatever your business or wherever you are located, we'll be glad to acquaint you with the Division that serves your field.

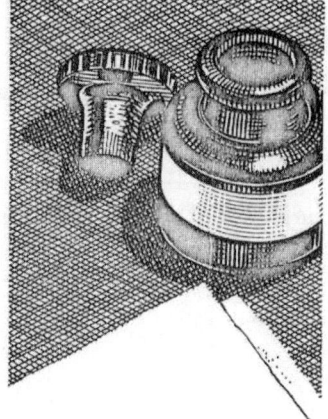

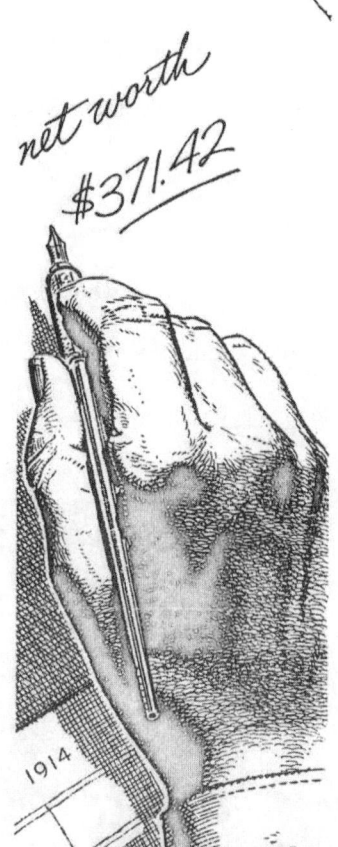

The First National Bank of Chicago

Building with Industry since 1863

MEMBER FEDERAL DEPOSIT INSURANCE CORPORATION

This advertisement appears in the January 15, 1954 issue of U. S. News & World Report

(Advertisement from U.S. News & World Report, January 15, 1954.)

LIFE BY THE BOARD FOOT

As this article indicates, our young entrepreneur, as early as 1914, already had a plan for success. Each methodical turn put him another step closer to achieving his vision of fiscal independence for himself and his family.

After about nine months in Rockford, he received a telegram requesting that he return to Memphis immediately. Expecting to be fired, Roy O. instead was made general manager of their Memphis office, including sales.

MEMPHIS

After Roy O. and Mildred had been back in Memphis for two months, the general superintendent of the outside work of the company was fired. Welcoming this opportunity to gain greater professional experience, Roy O. then managed the mill, both inside and outside.

That first year in Memphis, Roy O's professional life moved in a demandingly upward spiral, certainly an exciting time for the young businessman who achieved so much responsibility so quickly. Struggling amid hard hours and working through long days, he found himself rapidly reaching the top of his professional heap, even confidently beginning to sense that success was within his grasp.

Roy O. Martin, Sr.
Nickey Brothers
Memphis, Tennessee
Circa 1915

CHAPTER 2 - FOUNDER

However, while his professional life may have been flourishing in the midst of purposefully committed work, his personal life with his young bride likewise demanded some sacrifices, most notably that of lacking a home of their own. Not uncommon for the time, they shared an apartment with Elliston Thomas and his wife that first year in Memphis. Then in 1915 they bought a two-bedroom house at 288 North McLean Street.

Roy O. Martin, Sr., and Roy, Jr.
288 North McLean
Memphis, Tennessee
(circa 1921)

The three oldest Martin children were born while they lived there. Roy O. and Mildred had five children, all who are still living (2004). Mildred Virginia Martin (May 27, 1916), Ellis Spencer Martin (October 14, 1917), and Roy Otis Martin, Jr. (June 3, 1921) were all born in Memphis, Tennessee. The two younger children, Norman Kittell Martin (August 29, 1926) and Esther Louise Martin (August 27, 1927) were born after the family moved to Louisiana.

By the time he had worked for Nickey Brothers for ten years, Roy O. earned a salary of $20,000 a year—an income of substance in 1922. During his decade with Nickey Brothers, he had also become a stockholder in the company and a stockholder and director in the DeSota Oak Flooring Company. Perhaps more significantly, he had saved $65,000. This thirty-three-year-old budding entrepreneur knew the time had come to consider the options for his future.

LIFE BY THE BOARD FOOT

His decision first led him to purchase a larger home to accommodate his growing family. He bought and Mildred renovated a larger two-story house at 305 North Montgomery Street in Memphis.

305 North Montgomery Street
Memphis, Tennessee

The day after moving his family into this larger house, Roy O. resigned his position with Nickey Brothers.

This decision could not have been an easy one for him to make. He would later recall, "Sam Nickey was my friend, my boss, my business advisor, and always treated me as a son."[11] Principal owner Sam Nickey respected Roy O, having made him general manager for Nickey Brothers. Ever the realist, though, Roy O. knew that he could never become its president. Because the company was family owned, he faced a hard truth: his future with Nickey Brothers was tenuous at best. Sons and nephews who were far less qualified than he would receive those key executive positions to which he aspired. One relatively inexperienced Nickey nephew had already been brought into the business. Roy O. did not agree with many of the nephew's business decisions, but he was well aware that this nephew was a part of the owners' family. As a result, his influence would supersede that of a non-family member. In addition, Roy O. had a run-in with one of the Nickey brothers who actually struck him. Working under sometimes-strained

CHAPTER 2 - FOUNDER

circumstances and knowing that ultimately he wanted to head his own business, Roy O. resigned from the company that had honed his skills in salesmanship and increased his knowledge of manufacturing.

Roy O. stated, "When I started to work for Nickey, I resolved that I'd never borrow money from anyone for my personal needs and that I'd save twenty-five per cent of my salary even if I had to wear old clothes and get along on two meals a day. I frequently did both, but by strict adherence to that policy I saved $65,000 in ten years and was prepared to move when a business opportunity presented."[12] He had further saved money by riding a bicycle to work even after he became general manager. This personal and financial discipline that Roy O. exhibited throughout his life was developed early in his business career.

BUSINESSMAN

Roy O. went into business for himself when he left Nickey Brothers. He rented an office on Front Street in Memphis, equipping it with a desk, a typewriter, and a telephone. Then he began telephoning some of the people to whom he had sold lumber for Nickey Brothers. In addition to a lack of capital with which to operate, he ran into two major obstacles. The first obstacle was that it was difficult to get customers to switch from Nickey Brothers to him personally. The second, and totally unexpected, hurdle was that, often after placing an order with a lumber company, his wholesale suppliers would "dope" the grade and send a lower quality lumber than Roy O. had sold. Because of that, repeat business was difficult. With those problems confronting him regularly, Roy O. began to look for a sawmill that he could buy. He wanted his name on a mill--and he wanted to control the grade of lumber he sold. Not only did he like to control those enterprises with which he was involved, he also wanted credit for the good work that he did. Egotistic? Perhaps in a way, but he had great confidence in his abilities.

Just as Roy O.'s entry into the lumber business was seemingly by accident (getting his job with Cyrus C. Shafer Lumber Company) so was his move to Louisiana seemingly by accident (purchasing his sawmill in Alexandria).

He looked for a sawmill to buy in an area where lumber was reasonably inexpensive. His search took him to mills in Mississippi and to mills in Delhi and Plaquemine, Louisiana. A salesman for a

LIFE BY THE BOARD FOOT

wholesale sawmill supply house introduced Roy O. to J. F. Hopkins who told him of a mill for sale south of Alexandria, Louisiana. In company with Hopkins, Roy O. took a trip to Alexandria. That mill, it turned out, was unavailable.

J. F. Hopkins and Roy O. Martin
1924

But he learned of another mill located on Fenner Street in Alexandria. This mill, Creston Lumber Company, could be bought for $40,000. J. M. Peel, who owned the mill, was not operating it because he had run out of money. Roy O. negotiated the price, buying the dilapidated mill for $32,000, paying $10,000 cash with $10,000 due the first year, another $10,000 the next year, and $2,000 the third year with a 6% interest rate. His purchase included the plant, office and equipment, stacking sticks, tools, and supplies. The only thing on the mill premises that was excluded was the lumber, which was mortgaged. No timberlands were included.

CHAPTER 2 - FOUNDER

Original Office of Roy O. Martin Lumber Company

Roy O. and Hopkins returned to Memphis in the interval between signing contracts in October and taking possession of the property in November. While in Memphis, Roy O. arranged for the Memphis Bank of Commerce and Trust Company to continue as his major source of financing. He also ran into Otis A. Felger who was a major stockholder in the bank and a lumberman from Grand Rapids, Michigan. Felger expressed interest in Martin's venture in Louisiana and accompanied the young capitalist when he returned to Alexandria. Felger would become a stockholder in his company.

Roy O. took possession of the mill on November 5, 1923. The Roy O. Martin Lumber Company was underway.

Five days later the company was legally organized and incorporated. Stockholders were listed and officers were elected for the Roy O. Martin Lumber Company. Roy O. Martin was president, with six hundred of the one thousand shares of stock. Felger was vice president, with two hundred shares of stock. Hopkins served as treasurer, owning one hundred shares. Mildred B. Martin was secretary, owning one share of stock. Records show that nine hundred one of the one thousand authorized shares were bought at par value of one hundred dollars a share.

LIFE BY THE BOARD FOOT

The sawmill was a six-foot, band-saw groundhog mill. "Six feet" indicates the diameter of the wheel or pulleys pulling the saw. A "band saw" is a saw that is an endless steel belt running over pulleys. "Groundhog" means that the mill was built on the ground; it was not elevated. Consequently, the mill often operated in mud.

Fenner Street Sawmill
Alexandria, Louisiana
1923

According to Roy O.'s description, the mill was in poor condition and badly worn. He testified that it took a good mechanic and one or two helpers to work all night so the mill could run the next day. Roy, Jr., recalled that his father had poor mechanical aptitude. Fortunately, Hopkins was a good mechanic. He kept the mill running. According to Roy O., Hopkins also could handle a mill crew splendidly. He knew logs

CHAPTER 2 - FOUNDER

and knew how logs should be cut to get the best grade out of them. Of Hopkins he said, "He was just the man I needed because he was strong where I was weak."[13]

Amazingly, Roy O. paid off the mortgage on the mill in two years. In its first full year of operation, the sawmill made $23,000 (1924) and made $75,000 the next year (1925). From its beginning, the Roy O. Martin Lumber Company was a profitable enterprise.

ENTREPRENEUR

With the sawmill in Alexandria an immediate success, Roy O. was soon looking for ways to expand his operation. He became quite an entrepreneur, although all his ventures were not as successful or as satisfactory as the Alexandria sawmill. Some were terminated; others were sold—the Martin version of "cut and get out" (of an unprofitable operation).

Roy Otis Martin
1924

In January 1925, the board of directors authorized Roy O. to buy or build another sawmill in order to increase production. The company thus bought a small band mill at Meeker, Louisiana. After operating this mill for four months, Roy O. sought a larger line of credit from the Bank of Commerce in Memphis. That request was refused. Because money to expand the operation through the Meeker mill was not

43

LIFE BY THE BOARD FOOT

forthcoming from the Bank of Commerce, this mill was soon sold to Felger who then sold his shares of stock in the Roy O. Martin Lumber Company to the other stockholders.

After selling the Meeker mill and paying off his loan with the Bank of Commerce, Roy O. again approached the Memphis bank about expanding his line of credit. This time the bank agreed.

Later in 1925 Roy O. bought another mill in Alexandria. In receivership at the time of purchase, competing Commercial Lumber Company had an eight-foot band mill on the Missouri Pacific Railroad, five blocks from the Roy O. Martin Lumber Company. Since W. I. Wilkie had joined the company as a log buyer about the time of this purchase of Commercial Lumber Company, Roy O. and his directors formed a new corporation, Martin-Wilkie-Hopkins Company. This mill operated as a #2 mill. Roy O. was its president; Wilkie bought logs for both mills. All lumber produced by the #2 mill was sold through Roy O. Martin Lumber Company. In July 1927 the other partners bought out Hopkins. Company officers then changed the name of the company to the Martin-Wilkie Lumber Company. A year later this company and Roy O. Martin Lumber Company consolidated as Roy O. Martin Lumber Company, Incorporated.

The Meeker mill and the Martin-Wilkie enterprise had not been Roy O.'s only venture in the short time since his move to Alexandria. In May 1926, he formed the Roy O. Martin Lumber Company of Eunice for the purpose of partnering with the May Brothers of Memphis to purchase Newell Lumber Company of Eunice, along with fifty-seven acres of land. This partnership operated under the name of the Eunice Band Mill Company. Not the majority stockholder in that corporation, Roy O. realized rather quickly that he was not happy as its minor partner. Consequently, he sold his stock in that company to the May Brothers, vowing never to buy stock in a company he could not control. He liked to be the person in charge, the one calling the shots—what will surface as a notable DNA characteristic among subsequent Martin leaders.

In 1929 his company made its first significant land purchase. From Southern Bag and Paper Company in Hodge, Louisiana, it bought 6,560 acres of land with timber in the Black Lake swamp area near Castor, Louisiana. This deal included timber rights on an additional 720 acres. The first undertaking for the company after this purchase, and not a small undertaking, was to build an eighteen-mile railroad spur into the area to get the logs out. The next logical move in 1933 was to build an eight-foot band mill at Castor. Wilkie transferred to Castor to run that north Louisiana mill. Operating with a solid timber base, that sawmill was the foundation for Martin Timber Company, which was formed the same year.

CHAPTER 2 - FOUNDER

Also in 1929 Roy O. purchased from Long Pine Lumber Company 26½ acres of land across the railroad track from his Alexandria sawmill. Long Pine Lumber Company's mill had burned and subsequently closed. That additional land allowed an expansion of the Fenner Street operation.

In a venture unrelated to lumber, in 1938 Roy O. became a partner in a corporation called Safetygas, Incorporated. Obviously, he had forgotten the vow he had made to himself that he would never again buy stock in a company he could not control. Safetygas was to buy, sell, transport and deliver, and manufacture liquefied petroleum gas, as well as sell heaters and appliances that used butane. He lasted about six months in that venture until he sold to the other partners, again cutting his losses and getting out.

From 1934 until 1941 the company operated a store, Fenner Mercantile Company, at the Alexandria sawmill. Milroy Mercantile operated a similar facility at the Castor mill. Due to government regulations that a company could not operate an emporium in which the employer made a profit off the sale of merchandise to employees, the Alexandria store was closed. In 1940, the Milroy Mercantile Company at Castor was sold to Roy, Jr.

Howard Lumber Company in Natchitoches, which was incorporated May 7, 1946, was the first of what would be several retail lumberyards Roy O. formed. The name for this particular lumberyard came from Mark Howard, Virginia Martin's husband and thus Roy O.'s son-in-law, who managed the business. Ultimately, the company operated thirteen different retail stores in three states: ten in Louisiana, one in

LIFE BY THE BOARD FOOT

Magnolia, Arkansas, and another in Beaumont, Texas. These lumberyards provided an expanded market for lumber produced by Martin sawmills. At one time, about thirty percent of Martin's total lumber production was sold through their retail outlets.

During this same period, the company also acquired a small mill in Pineville, an oak-flooring mill in Alexandria, and, during World War II, a mill in Pleasant Hill. They had a ready-mix plant at their retail yard in Alexandria to provide concrete for foundations, streets, and sidewalks. After World War II, they began aggressively buying timberland. And for a period of time, they had an oil and gas company to extract minerals from their land holdings.

Roy O. built and sold small houses to employees on land close to the Alexandria mill. But the first subdivision developed by the company was Martin Park in Alexandria. The Grundy Cooper subdivision in Alexandria was also a Martin expansion in Alexandria. Later, Martin Park subdivisions were developed in both Natchitoches and Minden. With the integrated operations of sawmills, retail yards, and subdivision developments, the company used the motto "From Forest Farms to Cheerful Homes."

In 1956 Roy O. purchased a rather large tract of land from the Edenborn Estate in Shreveport. A treating facility, then known as Colfax Creosoting Company, was included in this transaction. Originally located in Colfax, this plant had already been moved to Pineville where it continues to operate as the

CHAPTER 2 - FOUNDER

Colfax Treating Company. Dura-Wood Treating Company, formerly known as Kopper's Plant, was also purchased in 1986. That plant was sold to RailWorks Corporation in 2000.

Roy O. retired from the business in 1970. With an entrepreneurial spirit, he had expanded his business from one "groundhog" sawmill with no timberland to an inclusive forest products enterprise that stretched from growing trees to building houses. He was personally involved in its operations throughout his active lifetime. He had forged his place in Louisiana's lumber industry. And he did so because he

> had dared to gamble all his energy and his meager bank account on an area's future timber supply when countless others believed the venture carried a stacked deck against him. He entered as an infant into a field of giants where none but the strong could survive—the field of rugged, vicious and unrelenting competition which strikes at a lumberman both from within the industry and without.
> It took sound judgment to do it. When others retreated during the depression, Martin advanced, spread out more and established the company as a leading contender in the lumber market.[14]

PHILANTHROPIST

Humbled by his success, Roy O. contributed personally to his community with the same energy that he ran his business. Not content just to take from the community through his business interests, Roy O. was also interested in--and ardently practiced--giving back to his community.

Because he was a Christian and an active church member, one way that Roy O. gave back to his community was through his church. He and his family not only attended religious services regularly, they also followed the tenets of their faith, annually giving a tithe (the bibilical ten percent) of their income through their church.

When they married, Roy O. was a Methodist; Mildred was a Baptist. For many years they attended the Methodist church. In fact, he was a member of the building committee when the Alexandria First Methodist Church (now First United Methodist Church) built an educational building on their former site at the corner of Jackson and Sixth Streets. His name was on the cornerstone of that building.

In 1937 the family moved from Alexandria to Pineville when they bought property on Edgewood Drive. The Martin family first referred to this twenty-acre property as their "country place," a place for their children to play in a wooded, rural environment with squirrels and geese rather than wandering the streets of Alexandria with rowdy kids. Their purchase of this Pineville property may have seemed like that of many other Alexandria families who had second homes on the Pineville side of the Red River where elevations were higher and temperatures were cooler in hot and humid Louisiana summers. Ever ones to buck the prescribed social norm, however, the Martins decided to make that little cottage on the "country place" their permanent dwelling. They would enlarge the small structure and make it their family home.

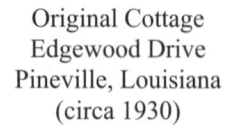

Original Cottage
Edgewood Drive
Pineville, Louisiana
(circa 1930)

About a year after the family moved "across the river," that is, across the Red River dividing Alexandria and Pineville, they began attending First Baptist Church in Pineville. Not only were many acquaintances of Roy O. and Mildred members of this church but their children also attended the adjacent Pineville Elementary School, where some of the younger Martin children attended. Since Pineville First Baptist Church was much nearer to their new home than Alexandria First Methodist, the spiritual move from Methodist to Baptist seemed a logical one.

Shortly after the Martins began attending First Baptist, their new church held a revival, featuring legendary evangelist Eddie Martin. As was customary in that era, the local pastor took his visiting evangelist to witness to those who had visited their church. During such a visit to the Martin home, Roy O.

CHAPTER 2 - FOUNDER

professed his faith in Christ. He was baptized in First Baptist Church in 1940. From that time on, he and his family were actively involved in the Pineville First Baptist Church. Roy O. and Mildred both were members of that church until their deaths. Through their church involvement, they made a continuing contribution to the community – and beyond.

Their commitment and support often went far from their local church. Through monetary gifts and physical goods, these early Martins aided numerous church-related causes, especially other less-fortunate churches. Norman related that country churches in the area would appeal to Roy O. when they had a building program. In many of these instances, he would respond by giving them lumber.[15]

Louisiana College, a Baptist college in Pineville, was also a recipient of Martin's generosity. The fine arts building on campus was originally a wood-frame building. In 1942, Martin helped in the reconstruction and redecoration of the building, which was named the Martin Fine Arts Building. All interior decorating and the furnishings for the building were given in memory of Martin's mother, Susie Belle Kittell Martin.

Martin Fine Arts Building
Louisiana College
Pineville, Louisiana

About this same time, Ware Hall, the girl's dormitory, was also renovated. Roy O. was involved in that project as well. A second-story assembly room was constructed as a consulting room with space for a group of sixteen people. A two-room apartment was created and furnished from a larger room. The apartment was remodeled for and given in honor of Rosa Dunwoody, widow of one-time head of the music department at Louisiana College.

When Roy O. and Mildred established the Martin Library in Pineville, it was understandably recognized as a major contribution to their community. Prior to this generous gift, Pineville did not have a public library, a situation that particularly displeased Mildred who was the first president of the Rapides Parish Library Board. Rather than housed in its own building, the branch library in Pineville was simply a room in Pineville City Hall. Because that room also served as the city's only courtroom, the library necessarily was closed when court was in session. The major problem, though, was that the city's jail cells were across the hall from this courtroom/library. Early in 1943, one particularly foul-mouthed inebriant made his presence known while Mildred happened to be in the library. That incident encouraged Roy O. and Mildred to begin the process of donating a library to Pineville, a topic they had already been discussing around their breakfast table.

The first step to having a local library was the purchase of a piece of property facing west on Shamrock Street, adjacent to the United States Post Office. After Roy O. and Mildred bought the lot, they donated it along with $14,000 to the city. The City of Pineville was to pave the street in front of the library from Central Louisiana State Hospital to Main Street. The two Martins selected ten people to serve as members of the Board of Directors of the Pineville Library Commission. Upon the expiration of Mildred's term as president of the Rapides Parish Library Board, she was no longer on the Martin Public Library Board of Directors. The charter was then changed so that Roy O. and Mildred would always be board members and that, upon their deaths, two succeeding Martins should serve on the board of the Pineville Library Commission. The arrangement was that the Rapides Parish Library Board would provide books and staffing for the library; the City of Pineville would provide all basic maintenance.

Unfortunately, the library commission could not immediately proceed with construction of the building. World War II intervened. Building restrictions were imposed; all non-essential construction was prohibited. Disappointed but undaunted, the Pineville Library Commission placed the Martin's original monetary gift as well as other funds in U. S. Treasury Bonds to earn income until the library building could be constructed.

CHAPTER 2 - FOUNDER

Architectural plans for the library building were completed in 1948, and construction finally began shortly thereafter. With exception of the doors, all wood in the building was cut from Martin-owned timberlands and was finished and kilned at the company's mills. Proud to showcase some of their products, they supplied Louisiana magnolia, hackberry, maple, and wild cherry for the interior structure. Dedicated on September 12, 1950, the Martins left a lasting and useful mark on their community. Former Louisiana Governor Sam Houston Jones delivered the dedicatory speech, declaring, "You have builded [sic] well and you have builded [sic] timely."

Martin Public Library
1950

At the fiftieth anniversary celebration of the Martin Library, Louisiana College history professor Thomas Howell, a Pineville native, quoted Roy O. as saying, "'This edifice will, no doubt, be my largest contribution to this community's betterment. The planning of it all, and its construction has done something to me – has enriched my life, has enlarged my horizons, has given me a greater interest in people.'"

Howell concluded, "The gift of the Martin family indeed has kept on giving, decade after decade, generation after generation – to paraphrase Roy O. Martin's words, enriched many lives, enlarged many horizons. The Martin family has never faltered in its support, providing for an expansion to the present configuration in 1975 and renovations in 1996."[16]

If Mildred relentlessly sought to create a local library, Roy O. was equally passionate about another community effort—the Salvation Army. Because he had stayed at a Salvation Army facility when he had first gone to business school in South Bend, Indiana, he knew, from first-hand experience, the importance of this organization. His personal acquaintance with the Salvation Army thus gave him an avenue of community service, one that continues today. Roy O. served on the board of directors of the Salvation Army in Alexandria for many years. Roy, Jr., followed him on that board. At the present time, Roy O. Martin III (Roy III) is on the local Salvation Army board.

Roy O. rendered further community service by serving as board member for Rapides Bank and Trust Company, now merged with Bank One. He was a bank director from January 13, 1953, through January 14, 1964. When he resigned from that board of directors, Roy, Jr., was elected to succeed him. Roy III presently serves on the local board of Bank One. Of Roy O's service as a bank director, Robert Bolton, whose family started Rapides Bank, said,

> He was a valuable director. He pushed everything he could here. He attended all the functions. He would always come to the branch bank openings. He did everything he could to promote the interests of the bank. . . . He attended the board meetings regularly. . . . He was always involved in board discussions. . . . I have a lot of respect for Roy O. Martin. I appreciated him as a person and as a businessman.[17]

Roy O. expanded his community involvement through membership in the Kiwanis Club of Alexandria where he was an active member, faithfully attending meetings each Thursday at Hotel Bentley. He participated in the club's service projects, although he was never a top officer of the club.

Undoubtedly, Roy O. profited from the community of which he was a part. But he also significantly contributed to that community. Through his business interests, his church relationship, his community involvement, and his philanthropic activities, Roy O. was very much a part of his local community.

CHARACTERIZATION

Attempting to characterize an individual as complex as Roy O. is not easy. Indeed, he often seemed to possess contradictory human characteristics, contradictions in character that somehow worked together for a success that defied the odds.

Intelligence. By his own admission, Roy O. had difficulty in school. He credited the assistant principal of his school with helping him to get the passing grades that enabled him to graduate from high school. But that does not mean that he was not an intelligent person. He passed the teachers' examination

CHAPTER 2 - FOUNDER

that earned him a teaching certificate following graduation from high school. He taught school for two years. He completed a prescribed course of study at a business college in South Bend, Indiana. And he taught in a business school in Beaumont, Texas, albeit for only one school session. His business success indicates that he had the intelligence necessary to succeed. Richard Landry, an Alexandria lumber broker who once worked for Martin, said that Roy O. was the most intelligent man he had ever known.[18] Others characterized him as a smart businessman.

Roy O. made decisions quickly. In the case of business decisions, he usually made the right decision. Long-time Martin forester D. B. Sanders illustrated that characteristic while describing an incident that occurred when he was involved in buying a small tract of land near Pineville. One of the owners had an undivided sixteen-acre interest in a forty-acre plot on which he was dealing. Because that area had a small gravel pit on it, this particular owner wanted twice as much for his land as was paid to the other owners in the forty-acre plot. Sanders took the deal directly to Roy O. After hearing the details, Roy O. told Sanders not to let the sun go down without getting that man's signature on the deed. The deal was made. The gravel from the gravel pit on that land "paid for the land many times over." Sanders said. "He knew a good deal when he saw it."[19]

Focus. Roy O. was a very focused individual. Since he was a bookkeeper, he had a bookkeeper's eye for detail. He was focused on his business and its success. Other matters would not divert him from his goal to achieve professional notoriety. Even after dementia due to his illness took over and he could no longer recognize his own children, he still went to the office each day where he read reports and signed checks. His sons indicated that he did not have good mechanical aptitude, nor was he good at operations. But he hired capable people who could do those things. His business college training stuck with him. He always paid attention to business.

Roy O. admitted that he never learned how to relax or to play. He did join a newly formed country club when he lived in Memphis. But he said, "I was never meant to be a country club man, as I preferred to work hard and save my money and help rear our children in an economical way and interest them more in our church work than in country club attractions. I resigned about two years after joining. I tried to show my children the virtues of economy and the value of saving in every way possible, without being penurious."[20] Those qualities stayed with him all his life.

LIFE BY THE BOARD FOOT

Vision. More than one person cites Roy O.'s vision as a positive attribute and as an explanation of his business success. In D. B. Sanders' words, "He was visionary. He could see. And he was persistent."[21]

At the time that he came to Louisiana, most of the state's dramatic lumbering days were over. Forestry writer Ed Kerr observed, "Central Louisiana's timberline had already receded dangerously close to the point of timber famine. Amid the vast cutover pinelands of that day, any talk of the timber business was pessimistic at best. Starting a sawmill at that time without owning any timber at all was a daring, almost reckless, undertaking." [22] But even in those conditions Roy O. could see the possibility of success in the lumber business. He pursued it persistently.

In two other areas, at least, Roy O.'s vision came into play. One area was the purchase of timberland. When he bought his first mill in Alexandria, no timberland went with the purchase. Following World War II, his company began to aggressively purchase timberland. Most available land in Louisiana at that time was in scattered, smaller tracts with only a few large tracts up for purchase. Sanders pointed out that most of the land Roy O. bought was on the open market and sold by competitive bids. Quite simply, he successfully bought land because he was willing to pay more for it. Roy O. had the vision to know that he could not operate indefinitely without owning land. To operate continuously meant he had to own trees; to own trees meant he had to own the land.

Another visionary area was in reforestation and timber stand improvement (TSI). Early on, Roy O. pursued both those areas. Norman claimed that they were the first in the area to practice timber stand improvement by deadening unwanted hardwood trees in a pine tree area. Sanders commented that they pursued timber stand improvement more aggressively than anyone else.

Illustrating the importance of vision in these two areas, Richard Landry recalled a company picnic in 1959 or 1960 when all the employees gathered around a long table set up in the pine shed at the Alexandria mill.

CHAPTER 2 - FOUNDER

At that picnic, Roy O. told the gathered employees that they had enough timber to cut for one hundred years, then they could go back and cut timber for another one hundred years. Owning the land, reforesting the land, and practicing good forestry management procedures provided for that. And Roy O.'s vision made it possible.

Drive. Roy O. had tremendous drive. Whether the drive came from his fear of failure, his determination to succeed, his early days of poverty, his energy level, or a combination of all, he showed relentless tenacity. He was willing to work and to work hard for what he got. Through that drive, he accomplished business success.

His impatience was also related to that drive. Time was his enemy. He was always in a hurry. He had something to do, and he wanted to get it done.

He was especially notorious for the way he drove an automobile. This, too, was related to his impatience. He did not have time to wait for traffic lights to change or for traffic congestion to clear out. He wanted to be on his way.

LIFE BY THE BOARD FOOT

Roy Otis Martin, Sr.
by his car

Roy, Jr., reported that at one time his father and the town marshal in Pineville had a running feud. When the family was clearing land at their Pineville property, Norman, who was then about four years old, fell into a pile of brush and ashes and burned both his arms and his knees. Roy O. grabbed him up, put him in the car, and started toward the hospital in Alexandria. While he was blazing through Pineville, the marshal tried to catch him--but never did.

He was also known to run traffic lights, even to drive on the sidewalk, to get around people. He would calculate that by running one traffic light he could catch the next two lights. Once, when he was behind a slow-moving car crossing the bridge over the Red River, he pushed the bumper of the car in front of him, much to the consternation of the passengers in that car. He simply was in a hurry and wanted to get across the bridge. At one time he missed a curve on a highway returning to Alexandria from Eunice and hit a cabin, scattering over the yard its inhabitants who had been gathered on the front porch. Fortunately, no one was injured.

Gene Howard, son of Virginia, recalls a childhood experience involving Roy O. and his frenetic driving. One Saturday morning, Gene and his dad Mark were on Fulton Drive en route to the Fenner Street

CHAPTER 2 - FOUNDER

mill. In those days before construction of a railroad overpass at that location, they found themselves waiting in line, about tenth in succession, for a train to pass. As soon as the caboose of the train began crossing the intersection, they noticed a car a couple of spaces ahead of them pulling out of line and arriving at the railroad barrier gates just as they started to lift. The driver was none other than Roy O. He went under the gates before the other cars in his line or in the oncoming line started to move, thus gaining a few seconds time. Gene remembers, "Dad and I just shook our heads after observing this. I thought, 'Yep, that's Grandpa Martin.'"[23]

Yes, he was always in a hurry. But, he also took time to offer a ride to those Louisiana College boys who wanted to go to Alexandria from Pineville.

Giving a ride to a recently graduated college student resulted in one of the most loyal and long-tenured employer-employee relationships in Martin's history of affiliated companies. Ellis related that one day, as he and his father were going home for lunch, Roy O. mentioned that he needed someone to help out in the office. Ellis happened to see Ralph Kees standing on a street corner thumbing a ride. Apparently aware that Kees had just graduated from college, Ellis said to his father, "There's your man right there." Roy O. stopped, picked up Kees, hired him, and, in Ellis' words, "He was a key player from then on." At the time of his retirement, Kees was in charge of all the Martin retail lumberyards.

Roy O.'s drive and his resulting impatience were reflected in the way that he often related to people. He knew what he wanted done. He knew how he wanted it done. And he expected those who worked for him to do it that way. Roy O. respected, however, those who would stand their ground and stand up to him if necessary.

Charles Jeffress, who served as company printer, pilot, and lobbyist, among other duties during his eighteen years with the Martin companies, related that he respected Roy O. and that Roy O. respected him. Once, when Jeffress was fairly new on the job, he was standing outside Roy O.'s office waiting to see him. Roy O. was "reading the riot act" to one of the employees; the man was shaking in his boots. When he went into the office, Jeffress thought that Roy O. was going to start in on him. In what one may have considered a bold move, Jeffress said to Roy O., "Mr. Martin, you are not going to talk to me that way. I will do whatever you want. If I have done anything wrong, you tell me. But you are not going to talk to me that way."

Roy O. said, "Well, come in and sit down." Jeffress reported that from then on they never had any trouble. If Jeffress got mad, he told his boss. And Roy O. would listen. They never had any confrontations. Certainly, he did not treat everyone that way, but Roy O. and Jeffress deferred to the other with mutual respect.[24]

John Munsterman, the first forester employed by the company, said that in differences of opinion Roy O. was never angry afterward. They each said what they thought. Recalling one time they had an argument, Musterman said Roy O. followed him out to the front porch and said, "That's all I have to say about it." He then turned and walked off. They never discussed that topic again. Munsterman observed that Roy O. could be overbearing to employees who would allow him. However, he would respect the person who stood up to him.[25] And he never carried a grudge.

Trained as a bookkeeper, Roy O. became manager and chief executive officer of a large business enterprise. His only formal training was from business school. He never attended executive training seminars. He had no management training. Since Roy O. had worked as both bookkeeper and lumber salesman, one might assume that he looked over the shoulders of those who worked for him in those capacities. Former employees replied that he did not. Rather, he gave people responsibility and expected them to fulfill their delegated tasks. He watched company finances carefully and kept up with details of the operation, but he gave his employees the freedom necessary to carry out their jobs. Then he made them accountable for doing just that.

Frugality. Roy O. was a very frugal person. That he saved $65,000 during his ten-year tenure with Nickey Brothers is a strong indication of his thrifty nature.

As another indication of his frugality, Roy, Jr., indicated that when his mother, Mildred, passed the one hundred-year mark, she was still mad at Roy O. for regularly taking those two-week trips selling lumber and leaving her at home with five children. Not only did he give her responsibility for their home and children but he also did not want to spend the additional money necessary for her to accompany him on those business trips.

That strand of frugality ran through the way he operated his company. Paul C. Hood, retired partner with the accounting firm Payne, Moore, and Herrington who handled the Martin account, said that one day he was auditing at the Alexandria mill toward the end of Roy O.'s professional life. The room that

CHAPTER 2 - FOUNDER

he was using was near Roy O.'s office. Hood would get up and momentarily leave the room to get something. When he returned, the overhead light would be turned off. He would turn the light on again. Then after awhile he would get up to get something else. When he returned, the light again would be off. He finally realized that if Roy O. would see the light burning in a room where no one was working, he would go over and turn it off.[26]

In those early Martin offices, "scratch" paper (notepads) was never bought. Rather, the blank side of discarded paper produced all scratch paper they used. Sheets of paper were cut into two parts and glued at the top to make a kind of recycled notepad. Before the days of computers and copiers, carbon copies were made of all correspondence. Offices of Martin companies, as was customary, used a thin yellow sheet of paper for making carbon copies. In that era, correspondence was meticulously saved for five years. Each year someone would clean out all five-year-old files. If a sheet of yellow carbon paper had been used on only one side, the paper would be pulled out, the original message would be crossed through with a cross sign noting the page, and the clean side would be used again.[27]

Another evidence of Roy O.'s sound business practice (some might call it "penny-pinching") was his practice of taking a two percent discount on all the bills. Chester O'Quin, an accountant who worked for the Martins for nearly forty years, remembered that, if an accountant or bookkeeper missed taking the two percent discount, he would be looking for another job. Many companies would give a two percent discount if the bill was paid by the tenth of the month. Roy O. automatically took that discount whether the billing company gave it or not. He never missed a discount, and he always paid the bills on time.

All bills had to be verified before being paid, however, something this young employee learned the hard way. Shortly after graduating from Northwestern State University in Natchitoches, Louisiana, O'Quin began working with the Martin Company. Soon thereafter he paid a bill to Southern Chevrolet Company in Alexandria. Since the statement had come, O'Quin thought he had acted correctly--and efficiently--by sending payment. He quickly learned that Martin company policy was to pay a bill only when an invoice accompanied the bill.

Roy O.'s office was next to O'Quin's office. Almost before the bill and check hit Roy O.'s desk for signing, he bounced out of the office and asked O'Quin why he had paid that bill. O'Quin replied that they received the statement and he guessed that they owed them, so he paid it.

LIFE BY THE BOARD FOOT

Roy O. demanded, "How do you know that we owe them? Do you have anything to back this up?" He answered that he did not. So Roy O. said to him, "I want to tell you something, son. Don't ever pay a bill by statement unless you have an invoice to back it up. If you do, you had better look for a job." O'Quin never forgot that lesson.

Roy O.'s penchant for frugality permeated his business.

Since one's work habits and personal habits are usually seamless, this trait also pervaded the Martin home. A particular instance of family frugality was Roy O's practice of managing his household finances the same way he managed his company finances. Monthly, Mildred had to balance their household account--to the penny--justifying every expenditure she made. One granddaughter remembers seeing Mildred's carefully detailed balance sheets among boxes of old papers stored in the Edgewood Drive attic.

That he was frugal in nature seems an understatement. However, an obvious contradiction of that frugality is his purchasing of an airplane. Perhaps giving in to the temptation to be seen as one of those "wheeling and dealing lumber men" of an earlier era, Roy O. persuaded his board to purchase a plane to use both for checking for fires on increasing company acreage and for making trips. Charles Jeffress was its pilot as well as state lobbyist for the company.

Company Airplane

Personal Life. In the words of Keith Peterson, long-time insurer of the Martin companies, Roy O. was a "clean liver."[28] That is, he neither smoked nor drank. Nor was he terribly tolerant of those who did. He would sometimes test a prospective employee by placing an ashtray on his desk to see if that individual

CHAPTER 2 - FOUNDER

would use it. When he wandered into someone's office and found cigarette butts in an ashtray, he would question that employee. He was known to fine employees two dollars if he caught them smoking on the yard. All Martin company facilities are smoke free at this time. While an occasional "damn" or "hell" might slip out, he was not given to profanity.

Neither was he a big socializer. In fact, he spent little time socializing. When the Martins lived in Alexandria, they lived in an area of the city where other lumbermen lived. But they did not have much to do with them socially. Peterson observed that Roy O. did not associate with the lumber crowd, or with any other crowd; he just worked. Eighteen-hour days were not at all unusual for him. This hard-working entrepreneur himself commented on his propensity for work:

> My contribution to this business has been 30 years of incessant work. During these years the welfare of the business has been with me every waking hour, for I regarded my leadership as a solemn duty that could only be discharged by the most conscientious devotion. Such devotion has left me scarcely any time for play or diversion of any sort—my childhood was the same.[29]

From this retrospective vantage of having gained the success he envisioned three decades earlier, he seemed to view his role as something akin to a spiritual calling, one that he assumed seriously and dutifully. And well he should have because when he made this statement in 1953, some 650 employees worked directly for various Martin enterprises. Roy O. solemnly realized that 650 families depended, in great part, on how he personally performed each day.[30] Every decision he made, every action he took directly impacted the jobs, hence the lives, of everyone working under him. God had richly blessed him; subsequently, he viewed his primary task as continuing the flow of financial security to those in his employ.

In devoting so much time to work, he and his family necessarily made personal sacrifices, a notable one being lack of time in developing an intimate circle of close friends. One Martin daughter expressed the opinion that she did not feel her family was ever really accepted in the Central Louisiana area; the other daughter agreed. The consensus was that, if this were true, the fault did not lie with the community but with the way the senior Martins positioned themselves in their community. Roy O. and Mildred did not move in the social circles of Alexandria. They did not belong to a country club. They did not throw big parties. And they did not attend many significant social functions. Virginia Martin Howard observed that they moved to Alexandria right after World War I, in the Flapper Era. She said that her mother was raised on a farm where everybody worked hard and went to church on Sunday. Consequently, she expected her children to do the same thing. Mildred did not fit in socially. She did not shorten her hair, raise her skirt, wear lipstick, or play bridge.

Mildred Brown Martin

Since she did not engage in casual activities or meet the social norms of others, she was something of a misfit—perhaps a woman born "before her time." Although she had gone to business school and had worked before marrying, social mores of the time (and her husband) prohibited her from mixing professionally with the company's business associates. Seemingly, she had minimal stimulating interaction—socially or professionally. Religious and charitable causes became those acceptable venues wherein she could invest her time, her energy and her creativity. At the same time, Roy O. traveled a lot selling lumber.[31] Generally, when he was not on the road making sales calls, he was either at his office on Fenner Street or with his family on Edgewood Drive.

John G. Alley, former long-time pastor of Calvary Baptist Church, Alexandria, where many current Martins attend, observed that most Martin men he knows personally are focused on business, family, and church.[32] Others agreed with that assessment. People of wealth normally exercise care in dealing with other people, never really quite sure who is their friend and who is after their money. But if those early Martins were not accepted locally, it was probably due to their lack of social involvement with

CHAPTER 2 - FOUNDER

local people. In addition, when the Martins first came to Louisiana, they were not wealthy people. They were simply hard-working people who focused on business, family, and church. They were not considered to be part of the local league of those already successful leading lumbermen and other prominent businessmen of the city.

Roy O. could, of course, be domineering. In fact, he was often authoritative to members of his family as well as to his employees. He worked hard; he expected them to work hard. He had a high standard of personal excellence; he expected them to maintain high standards of personal excellence. He brought all three sons into the business at an early age. He expected them to be a part of his business, and he expected his business to continue through them.

As part of his contradiction in character, Roy O. seemed to be a different individual to different people, as especially witnessed by some of his former employees. According to one, he was nice to everyone but employees. Others referred to him as a gentleman. His employee-poet Les Evans wrote of this dichotomy in 1954:

> His drive [was] strong and fierce
> That mighty men oft quake and fall,
> Before his eyes that pierce.
> But many know that 'neath the steel,
> Beats one Big Heart of Gold. [33]

LIFE BY THE BOARD FOOT

Roy O. always dressed nicely. Even around a sawmill he came to work every day dressed in a coat and tie. Until more recent, relaxed times, that dress code was pretty well followed by those who worked in Martin offices.

LAST DAYS

In June 1962, Roy O. moved from the position of president of Martin Industries to chairman of the board. Roy, Jr., succeeded his father as president of Roy O. Martin Lumber Company. While Roy, Jr., operated the Alexandria mill, Ellis ran the mill at Castor. Norman headed the forestry division.

In reporting this major executive change, the *Alexandria Daily Town Talk* noted that

> Martin, Sr., who has been in the lumber business in Alexandria for the past 39 years, built one of the largest lumber mills in Louisiana and a string of related businesses during his tenure as president . . . . Martin gambled by moving to Central Louisiana at a time when other timber experts shied away from the area's future timber supply. Since then he has built a timber empire which includes the Alexandria mill, another mill in Castor, La., retail outlet stores, two residential subdivisions built with Martin products and amassing thousands of acres of forest land in Central Louisiana to insure [sic] wood for his mills.[34]

By the time he reached seventy years of age, Roy O. was slipping mentally and physically. He was treated for arteriosclerosis, commonly known as hardening of the arteries. Today, he likely would have been diagnosed as suffering from Alzheimer's disease. When he started slipping, his health deteriorated rapidly.

Roy O. Martin, Sr.
May 8, 1969

64

CHAPTER 2 - FOUNDER

Still, he went to his office every day. After awhile, the normal routine was that Mildred would call and ask someone from Colfax Creosoting Company in Pineville to come to their Edgewood home to get "the Boss." That employee would take him to the office there for a period of time, then someone from the Alexandria mill would pick him up. He would stay there until noon. Roy, Jr., would take him to lunch and then back home. While he was at the office, he did actual work. He would review reports, sign checks, and generally keep up with, at least a semblance of, his daily office routine.

As his disability progressed, he became more docile. In his last years, Mildred created "busy-ness" that would occupy him for hours: specifically, raking leaves--piles and piles of leaves. Although he had hated yard work during his productive years, during those last debilitating years, he would spend his days piling up leaves from the same kinds of trees that had provided him a good and rewarding life. Though no longer active in the business he had founded, he simply had to be busy at something. Still driven, but with slowing energy, he approached the mundane task put before him with the same determination that he had exhibited fifty years earlier when he purchased his first small sawmill in Alexandria.

Roy O. Martin, Sr., died on February 23, 1973. The founder of the Roy O. Martin Lumber Company and its related businesses that became the Martin Companies of today was eighty-two years old. In an obituary in the February 1973 issue of *The Louisiana Forestry Association Newsletter,* he was described as a "titan of the southern hardwood industry; the man who built the Roy O. Martin Lumber Company from scratch. He never graduated from college, but used an innate sense for business and nerve to become a self-made man in the tradition of John D. Rockefeller and James P. Morgan. He was a charter member of the Louisiana Forestry Association." The obituary also noted that "With the able assistance of three sons; Ellis, Roy Jr., and Norman, Martin constructed a lumber empire reknowed [sic] for efficiency, safety and sound business procedure."[35]

Mildred survived her husband for many years, dying on October 11, 1995, at the age of one hundred three.

The combined legacy of Roy O. and Mildred Martin is notable: eighty-seven direct descendents (as of December 2004) and a successful business. Through astute estate planning, their business was able not only to survive their deaths but also to enlarge and prosper. Roy O. left behind an example of vision, vigor, determination, and business expertise that would continue to characterize the Martin family. Their

LIFE BY THE BOARD FOOT

ongoing commitment to business success, community involvement, churchmanship, responsible citizenship, and exemplary personal lives came from their founder.

Roy O. Martin did more than found a business. He founded a family, and he established a way of life based on the board foot. That family, that business, and that way of life continue past his lifetime.

3.

THE FOUNDATION

. . . I have laid the foundation, and another buildeth thereon. But let every man take heed how he buildeth thereon (1 Cor. 3:10).

When Roy O. Martin bought the Creston Lumber Company mill on Fenner Street from J. M. Peel, he intended to operate the mill as a corporation. However, he bought the mill with his personal funds. At the time of this purchase, the financially strapped Creston mill was not operating.

This mill that would become the foundation for Martin business success had cost $32,000. Terms of the purchase were that Roy O. pay $10,000 cash, $10,000 on or before one year from the time he received title, $10,000 the second year from purchase, and $2,000 the third year. Interest on the outstanding amount was 6%. Roy O. purchased everything on site except the lumber, which was mortgaged. Amazingly, this hard-working entrepreneur eliminated his debt in two years.

Roy O. signed all necessary legal papers on October 30, 1923, and gained possession of the property on November 5, 1923. The Roy O. Martin Lumber Company was then officially organized on November 10 with one thousand shares of stock authorized. At the time of organization, ninety-one shares were issued. Its original stockholders were Roy O. Martin, J. F. Hopkins, Otis A. Felger and Mildred B. Martin.[1] They also became the four original members of the board. Roy O. served as president of the corporation. Felger was vice-president. Treasurer was J. F. Hopkins. Mildred functioned as secretary. The events that resulted in the formation of the Roy O. Martin Lumber Company transpired rather quickly after Roy O. located his mill of promise, an early sign of the future Martin code of "business as usual." Roy O. would make business decisions quickly; he then would move just as quickly to implement those decisions.

LIFE BY THE BOARD FOOT

The mill was not in good shape when Roy O. bought it. Some might have described its condition as deplorable.

Often a mechanic and one or two helpers had to work all night so the mill could run the next day. Those who knew him say that Roy O. did not have much mechanical aptitude. Fortunately, Hopkins did. This sixty-year-old, two-hundred-pound mill operator who had come down from Memphis with Roy O., who had been with Roy O. when he bought the mill, and who was one of his original shareholders, had very little formal education. But Hopkins knew good logs, and he could operate any kind of sawmill. He knew how logs should be cut to get the best grade out of them. A good overseer, he regularly watched log delivery to make sure that the mill received good timber. A good manager, he watched his logging crews carefully to see that they properly scaled all incoming logs. Hopkins could also handle the mill crew well. He was a valued associate to Roy O., complementing him in areas where he was not as strong.[2]

Operating only six weeks in 1923 and, considering costs of incorporation, legal fees, tools, and other start-up costs, the mill showed a loss of only $9,764.19 in 1923. This loss was charged against the profits of 1924, resulting in a net profit of nearly $23,000 in 1924.

CHAPTER 3 – THE FOUNDATION

Early office staff at the Fenner Street mill

During 1924, James McPherson came to Alexandria from Memphis to work with the Roy O. Martin Lumber Company and to purchase some stock in the company. During that first year, he decided that he neither wanted to live in Alexandria nor to continue as a stockholder in the company. The company bought back his stock. Board members also authorized remaining stockholders to purchase all outstanding stock from the $100,000 authorized capitalization of the company. And they declared a ten percent dividend. The first full year of operation showed not only a profit but also a dividend for stockholders. The original stockholders of the company were again, for a while at least, the company's sole stockholders.

EXPANSION

The Meeker Mill

From the very beginning, Roy O. intended to expand and grow his business. He had purposely come to Louisiana to control his family's destiny. And that destiny required that he become a key player in the Bayou State's forest products industry. His Fenner Street sawmill was just a first step toward achieving his vision. Fortunately, the success of that first year of operation at this small manufacturing facility allowed him to take the next step toward achieving his long-term goals.

LIFE BY THE BOARD FOOT

At the January 1925 meeting of the board, company directors adopted a resolution, authorizing their executive officers either to buy or build another sawmill. They felt that another mill would allow them to reduce the cost of manufacturing lumber. Perhaps even more significantly, another mill would increase total production, which in turn could significantly increase profits.

Home Place Land Company and the E. B. Norman Company of Louisville, Kentucky, had a small band mill for sale in Meeker, which is about eighteen miles south of Alexandria. Because of proximity to Alexandria, the Meeker mill seemed to be a good business move. Roy O. put his plan into action.

He arranged a line of credit with the Bank of Commerce and Trust Company in Memphis where he had done business when he worked for Nickey Brothers. The Meeker mill soon became a part of Roy O. Martin Lumber Company.

The company operated the Meeker mill for four months.

Contrary to expectations, operating two mills turned out to be a prohibitively expensive project. Having borrowed money to buy the mill, the company's debt load was heavy. Perhaps more telling, their ratio of quick assets to quick liabilities was out of line. Roy O. asked the Memphis Bank of Commerce and Trust to increase his line of credit, but the bank refused, indicating that the ratio of ready assets to liabilities was too large to warrant an increase.

Fortunately, the company did not have to search far or long for a buyer. Felger had recently sold his interest in a sawmill in Memphis and was looking for a small lumber facility for his two sons to operate. The Meeker mill provided a solution for him and a way out of a bad investment for Roy O. Legal papers were signed transferring ownership. However, the sale made Felger a direct competitor of Roy O. Martin Lumber Company. He necessarily, but agreeably, resigned from Martin's board of directors and sold his stock in the company to the remaining shareholders. With a major reduction of debt due to selling the Meeker mill, the company quickly lowered its credit risk. As a result of their improved credit rating, the Bank of Commerce agreed to grant the previously denied request for an increased line of credit to the Roy O. Martin Lumber Company.

This first of what would be numerous ventures toward expanding the company established a pattern. If a business did not succeed as the Martins thought it should, or if the needs changed that the business originally addressed, it would be sold or eliminated. What emerges as a kind of genetic business

CHAPTER 3 – THE FOUNDATION

acumen allowed Roy O. to sense when he needed to take action. Neither he, nor his sons, or his grandsons become personally attached to any of their businesses to the point that they cannot make the tough decision of eliminating a non-profitable entity. Martins generally know when to cut their losses and get out of an unprofitable business venture or they know how to read economic trends, enabling them to take their profits and get out of what might become an unprofitable venture.

Ellis explained this function of the family business. "Things change. You have to change with them." In a successful business, you must "find out what the needs are, then address them."[3]

In responding to a question about timing in business, Roy, Jr., said, "There are always opportunities, if you know how to look for them."[4] Roy O. looked for an opportunity, saw a need, and addressed both by aggressively expanding his business—or by eliminating those divisions or products that proved unprofitable.

Fenner Street Property

Also early in 1925, the company purchased a lot south of its original property. Giving Roy O. the autonomy he thrived on, his board of directors authorized the purchase of this and other adjoining lots as they became available.

Commercial Lumber Company, an eight-foot band mill, sat on land five blocks south of the Fenner Street mill. The Commercial plant was in receivership, but it also was conveniently located on the Missouri Pacific Railroad. Roy O. assessed the situation as a good business opportunity, musing that "none of them [the Commercial Lumber stockholders] knew much about operating a sawmill, buying logs or selling lumber."[5] The company thus bought the competing mill, which gave them critical access to the railroad. However, because the board did not want any more stockholders in the Roy O. Martin Lumber Company, they formed a new company to operate that mill.

Martin-Wilkie-Hopkins Company

About this time in 1925, W.I. Wilkie came on the scene. Roy O. needed a log buyer for his expanding business. Because the company then owned only two mills and no forest land, they had to purchase all their logs from others who owned property. Having a good timber buyer was critical to survival. Someone recommended Wilkie from Lafayette as the individual who could keep both Martin mills supplied with logs. The on-site interview convinced Roy O. that Wilkie was indeed the person he needed for the job; it convinced Wilkie that a move to Alexandria would be good for him.

And indeed it was. By the end of that year, he had become a partner in the next Martin expansion. This newest company, the Martin-Wilkie-Hopkins Lumber Company, was organized on December 9, 1925. Because Roy O. did not want any more stockholders in Roy O. Martin Lumber Company, he created this new company to operate the former Commercial Lumber Company. Wilkie bought logs for both the Roy O. Martin Lumber Company and the new Martin-Wilkie-Hopkins Company. Stockholders in this jointly owned company were Roy O. Martin, W. I. Wilkie, and J. F. Hopkins. Its officers were Roy O., president; Wilkie, vice-president; Hopkins, secretary-treasurer; and Mildred, director.

Functioning under and financed by the Martin Lumber Company, this #2 mill (as it was called) made a profit each year of its operation. Its profit was at least partly due to Martin Lumber Company advancing money to Martin-Wilkie-Hopkins on each week's cut of logs.

In May 1927 Hopkins resigned from both the Roy O. Martin Lumber Company and the Martin-Wilkie-Hopkins Company. As with stock Otis Felger had owned, the two companies purchased his stock, making it company treasury stock and leaving Wilkie as the only non-Martin stockholder. In July, the name changed to reflect this change in ownership. Martin-Wilkie-Hopkins Company subsequently became Martin-Wilkie Company. The next year the Martin-Wilkie Company consolidated with the Roy O. Martin Lumber Company, since they operated as practically two divisions of the same company. What had been functioning as a #2 mill of the Roy O. Martin Lumber Company became a #2 mill in reality. But its existence was short-lived. The Martin-Wilkie mill burned in 1931. While standing property was insured, the insurance did not cover all losses from the devastating fire. That mill was not rebuilt.

The original Fenner Street mill had been expanded in 1926 with construction of a planer mill, which was used to develop a cypress finish, molding, and trim business. That enterprise fared well for about six months; then the price of cypress lumber plummeted. Roy O. proposed turning the planer mill into a furniture factory. However, because no employees or board members were experienced in the furniture business, other members of the board of directors opposed this plan. He acquiesced to the board and dropped his proposal to begin making furniture.

CHAPTER 3 – THE FOUNDATION

Roy O. Martin Lumber Company of Eunice

Roy O. next partnered with the May Brothers of Memphis to buy the Newell Lumber Company of Eunice, Louisiana. Chartered in Tennessee, this corporation formed in 1926 was called the Roy O. Martin Lumber Company of Eunice; its sawmill was named The Eunice Band Mill Company. Although both Roy O. and Roy O. Martin Lumber Company owned separate stock in the company, the May Brothers were its majority stockholders. As a result, they had controlling interest, which meant they controlled the decisions—a situation Roy O. would not tolerate for long.

Martin's Eunice mill was the only company operation in which logs were transported by water. This was made possible by the Mermentau River, which ran next to the mill. Logs could rather easily be floated down river on barges to the mill.[6]

By contract, most lumber produced by the Eunice Band Mill was sold through the Roy O. Martin Lumber Company. This mill showed a promise of profit. However, because he was not fully in charge, Roy O. could not stay for long with the Eunice Band Mill. Since the May Brothers had controlling interest in the business, he simply could not be happy with the operation. After only a couple of months Roy O. sold his stock--at a loss--to the May Brothers. But he seemed to have learned a valued lesson from that experience. Roy O. later recorded, "My policy ever since has been not to buy any stock in a company that I could not control."[7] He liked to be the one making the major decisions for those enterprises in which he was involved.

The year 1929 was one of continued expansion at the Fenner Street operation.

In February 1929 the company bought the Long Pine Lumber Company site. This twenty-six and one-half acre site was across the railroad track from the original Fenner Street mill. Long Pine mill had closed and subsequently burned. With this purchase, the company gained much-needed land for expansion.

Soon after acquiring this property, the company constructed a railroad spur into it. Alleys were graded and tramlines were built. A loading dock that was sixty-feet wide and four-hundred-feet long was also built, greatly facilitating the loading of lumber onto railroad cars for shipment. A remanufacturing plant, one that turned raw lumber into usable products, was also built on that site. All loading and remanufacturing finally could be done at the same place.

For three years the board of directors had discussed the possibility of constructing dry kilns. In 1929, they decided to follow through with those discussions, building at the Fenner Street site four dry kilns that were twenty-feet wide and seventy-seven-feet long. Each kiln had cooling sheds, automatic controls and other equipment designed for efficient operation. Operators received special training in kiln-drying procedures.

Black Lake Timber Purchase

Roy O. made his first major land purchase in 1929. That was the year the company bought the Black Lake timber block from Southern Advance Bag and Paper Company. This tract comprised 6,560 acres of land along with timber and with timber rights only on an additional 720 acres located in Natchitoches, Bienville, and Red River parishes. For financing, the company floated a bond issue of $150,000, again through the Bank of Commerce and Trust Company of Memphis, Tennessee. These bonds were floated that bleak year when the stock market crashed and plunged the United States into its Great Depression. Succeeding admirably in a horribly difficult economic climate, the four-year-old Martin

CHAPTER 3 – THE FOUNDATION

company paid off its bonds in full at par with interest, even though the third-year payment had to be extended for one year.

What would be a fortuitous purchase, this Black Lake swampland proved significant for two reasons: 1) it heralded Roy O. Martin Lumber Company as a key player in Louisiana's forest products industry, and 2) it yielded, as time would show, heavy revenue from oil-and-gas royalties. Prior to that purchase, the company had generally bought standing timber, but not the land.

This Black Lake land did, however, come with its problems; namely, it had no access for harvesting the timber. A seemingly logical solution was for the company to build its first railroad.

Since most early railroads in Louisiana were built to haul logs and lumber, this was not a unique undertaking. And this first, of what ultimately would be two eighteen-mile-long Martin railroads, was built in 1929 to get logs from the Black Lake swamp area to their Roy Spur near Castor. A second company railroad was built about the same time near Bordelonville to log the Snowden Estate land, a nineteen thousand-acre tract of land belonging to the Snowden Estate in Avoyelles Parish, Louisiana. That agreement called for Martin Lumber Company to cut seven million board feet per year from that property.

Snowden Tract railway,
Bordelonville, Louisiana
1928

LIFE BY THE BOARD FOOT

Lumbering railroads in this era were usually rather rickety affairs. They were not built on properly graded or correctly leveled roadbeds. Rights of way had to be cut. Typically, land was low or swampy. Because crossties used were normally untreated green wood, these wet conditions, compounded by Louisiana's high humidity, were a recipe for certain failure. Over time, these untreated crossties would shrink, expand or buckle, depending on Louisiana's humidity levels. Additionally, bayous and waterways had to be crossed, compounding problems for untreated wood. In both cases for Martin, and especially near Bordelonville, railroad tracks were often underwater for weeks, even months, at a time. This situation not only caused difficulty of access but also caused rapid deterioration of those green crossties on which the rails were laid. The railroad to the Snowden tract of timber had been greatly damaged by flood that year with parts of it under from two to twenty feet of water much of the time. Both railroads had been troublesome and costly: cutting rights of way, making ties, and constructing the actual railroad. In 1929 Roy O. reported to his board of directors that the two railroads had been both expensive to construct and difficult to maintain. In other words, from this newest venture Roy O. realized--and rather quickly--that he was a lumberman, not a railroad tycoon.

THE DEPRESSION YEARS

Roy O. had to have been personally disappointed and professionally anxious regarding this latest financial setback, especially viewing it from the milieu of that era. Some of his feelings of frustration, perhaps even of growing alarm, emerge in his telling comment in his president's report to the board of directors in 1929: Roy O. reported: "In addition to all of this [cost of constructing railroads] the last three months of 1929 witnessed the greatest stock crash in history and our business fell off practically over night, lumber prices went bad, orders were held up and shipments were delayed throughout, and as a result of which we lost money during those three months."[8] Certainly, the stock market crash was an incident outside his control, but this comment shows he personally felt the brunt of its impact on his company.

In spite of this enormous setback, the Roy O. Martin Lumber Company operated continuously throughout the Depression. Unfortunately, they were caught with a large inventory of lumber that was virtually impossible to sell at a profit. For the most part during those years, the sales price of lumber was less than the production cost. The Martin Company had both a debt to several banks and a big bond issue. But Roy O. never missed a payroll – although some were a little late. During this time, his mill was forced

CHAPTER 3 – THE FOUNDATION

to operate under the hourly limitations imposed by the federal government through the National Recovery Administration (NRA). The NRA was a Franklin D. Roosevelt program, which regulated wages, hours, and output of manufacturing facilities. Not only did the company continue to operate, continue to make all its payrolls, continue to pay off its indebtedness, and continue to meet its obligations at full-face value of its bonds, it even continued to expand during those trying years.

Martin reasoning grew out of the logic of survival. Because the company had on hand a supply of oak stock that was suitable for flooring, at the 1930 meeting of the board, Roy O. proposed the addition of a one-unit flooring factory. His board approved the project, but it delayed immediate construction of this newest proposal. When the flooring factory was finally built and began operating in 1935, it faced two insurmountable obstacles: 1) the only outlet for its product was the Arkansas Oak Flooring Company in Alexandria, and 2) the price oak lumber would bring was less than the cost of producing the lumber. Because the flooring factory burned in 1936, it was a short-lived enterprise, operating only one year. It was not rebuilt. Years later the company would build another flooring plant at its Alexandria mill.

In 1932, Gene Glankler, one who had come from Memphis to serve as sales manager with the Roy O. Martin Lumber Company, resigned from his position on the board of directors, selling his stock back to the company. Glankler then bought the Pineville Lumber Company. Roy O. would later buy this Pineville plant from his former employee, a decision motivated in part to bring Glankler back as sales manager, a position he held until his retirement.

Gene Glankler

LIFE BY THE BOARD FOOT

Martin Timber Company

The next major expansion grew out of the aforementioned trouble and expense of building a railroad into the Black Lake swamp. Seeking an easier, more profitable way to get logs from their Black Lake tract to Alexandria, in 1931 Roy O. proposed building a mill in Bienville Parish to process timber from that acreage. The board agreed, voting to build a mill at their Roy Spur near Castor. Their purpose was to reduce the prohibitive freight costs of moving logs from the Black Lake property to their mill in Alexandria, a distance of about one hundred miles. However, the mill was not built until 1933.

In the personal file and scrapbook of Roy O. Martin, Sr., is a letter he sent to all who held bonds to finance the Black Lake purchase and build the Castor mill. Dated January 26, 1933, the letter clearly expresses the company's situation as Roy O. specifically, and convincingly, argues for an "brief respite. . . to readjust" from maturing bonds. Providing a window to the still-depressed economic climate of 1933, the letter also reveals an articulate, introspective, analytical writer who, while empathizing with his bondholders, understands the gambles necessary in developing a successful business. Roy O. may have achieved only a high school education and may have had only a limited business school degree. However, this letter shows him skilled in developing a classical verbal argument. Indeed, the business rhetoric in this letter suggests its writer was a master in the art of persuasion.

CHAPTER 3 – THE FOUNDATION

January 26, 1933

To the Bondholders of the
ROY O. MARTIN LUMBER CO., INC:

As we enter 1933, the fourth year of the most devastating economic upheaval this country has ever seen, we are confronted with the gravest problems that have ever been faced by our government in peace or in war. Upon the quality of statesmanship and the courage with which these issues are met depends the future of our country.

The same is true of our business situation, which is closely dovetailed to our government problems. Successful handling of an organization today requires clear vision and a comprehensive grasp of the factors necessary to economic recovery and stability.

When an individual casts aside fear, when he ceases to yearn for some mythical and magnetic power to draw him from the slough into which we have all fallen, and realizes that by his own efforts and initiative can he be restored to a solvent and self-sustaining member of society - then and only then will he be well on the road to recovery.

Having taken two years to recognize this truth and another year to formulate and establish a policy and plan of procedure, we feel we have the situation in hand. Our individual and immediate need and one of paramount importance is the reduction of overhead. We know now that can be accomplished, but must have your aid in bringing this about.

We are unable at this time to meet our March 1st maturities of our bond issue. For three years we have been paying interest on our bonds and meeting the maturing issues punctually without the aid of this frozen asset - the timber itself. Thus each year we have been compelled to take our cash, our accounts and our lumber and meet timber obligations. This has been a severe drain on our finances. We have now reached a point where it is decidedly unfair to our other creditors to deplete our resources for the benefit of any one class of creditors. Not only this, but it will deprive our company of operating capital. By operating our mill we can overtake the largest portion of our overhead, absorb practically all our losses, continue to function as a going concern and be ready and eager for the recovery which must ultimately come.

We come before our bondholders with a feeling of pride in our past accomplishments. At a time when all securities have depreciated, insome cases to only 5 to 10% of their par value, when almost nothing can be sold for the purchase price of 1929, the holders of the bonds of the Roy O. Martin Lumber Co. Inc. will realize that we have put forth no small effort to maintain the value of our bonds, and we feel these creditors can be congratulated in selecting for investment a bond wherein the interest has been punctually paid, where the security has increased rather than decreased and where the maturing issues have been serially retired.

Page 2:

We now ask that our bonded creditors grant us a brief respite in which to readjust ourselves and that our bonds maturing March 1, 1933, and subsequent maturities be set ahead for a period of eighteen months. All interest will be paid at the regular interest dates, as due. If this is done our business can be maintained, all of our obligations can be discharged and 250 men can be secure in their employment.

We are now taking steps to liquidate the timber covered by this mortgage, consisting of approximately 35,000,000'. With the salvage of our #2 mill at Alexandria, which was destroyed by fire in September of last year, together with the insurance money received, we are now constructing an 8' band mill at Castor, La. This will be a well built, efficient and economical unit, and will cost us complete $20,000.00. There is no other means of liquidating this timber and our bonds cannot be paid except thru converting this timber into money. It is impossible to ship these logs into Alexandria as the cost of so doing exceeds the present market value of logs delivered to our mill there. The freight from Castor to Alexandria is nearly equal to the entire cost of logging, sawmilling, and yarding these logs on the mill site itself. By milling the logs at the timber tract we enhance the recovery approximately 20% as well.

We can log, saw and yard the first six or seven million feet of logs for a price of $7.50 to $8.00 per M', while the freight alone to Alexandria exceeds $6.50 per M'. You can therefore see the futility of any other method of marketing.

We now have some 8,000,000' of timber released from the bond issue and consequently paid for. We have nearly this much more in value tied up in equipment for the railroad which is rapidly depreciating and valueless to us unless put to work. By cutting this timber into lumber we convert it from a deferred to a quick asset, as once this timber is cut into lumber we have started the process of liquidation and will be returning this capital to our business and the orderly liquidation of our obligations. We believe that on the present market this timber will bring us an average of $19.00 to $20.00 per M'. Figuring the cost of conversion from timber into lumber at $8.00 as hereinabove stated, this leaves us $12.00 per M' recovery, less the cost of loading, approximately $1.00 per M'.

With the present condition of general business and the shortage of money, we would be utterly unable to sell this timber to anyone except at 15 to 20% of its value, or from $25,000 to $35,000.

The security behind this mortgage is worth many times the value of the outstanding bonds. Our sawmill, planing mill and dry kilns at Alexandria are in perfect working condition. Our organization is efficient and closely pared. The officers of this company are, and have been, working night and day to the furtherance of your interests and the proper conduct of our business. We have no other or outside interests.

Full cooperation of our bonded creditors is necessary at this time. By extending our maturities eighteen months, we will have an opportunity to complete the mill and put a stock of six to eight million

CHAPTER 3 – THE FOUNDATION

Page 3:

feet of lumber on sticks and a substantial amount on the market, using a part of these funds to retire the serially maturing issues and the remainder to keep the orderly cutting and marketing process in action and liquidating the latter maturities in the same manner.

Only three and one half million feet have been cut from this tract. The mill now under construction will be a guarantee to all the bondholders that the issues can be met without loss to anyone if allowed to proceed in an orderly manner.

Wisdom and safety dictate this policy and we urge your prompt acceptance of same.

Yours very truly,
ROY O. MARTIN LUMBER COMPANY, INC.

By *Roy O. Martin*
President

ROM:S

LIFE BY THE BOARD FOOT

As proposed by Roy O., the Castor mill would be a small, portable (meaning temporary), six-foot mill. He thought he could complete this project for under $20,000. With his board's approval, he began searching for used parts to construct this newest sawmill, the first he would build from the ground up. The plant he ultimately built was an eight-foot band mill. According to Ellis, everything in the mill was bought second-hand. Roy O. bought industrial components wherever he could find them at the best price for which he could bargain. Perhaps the original plan was changed from the projected six-foot mill to an eight-foot mill quite simply because Roy O. found a previously used eight-foot saw at a better price than a six-foot saw. In this instance, availability (rather than "necessity") might have been the "mother of invention." The mill was completed in 1933 at a total cost of $37,000, a figure that Roy O. reported was about $17,000 more than they expected. However, the cost of over-run included an office, a remanufacturing plant, real estate, sawmill equipment, machine shop, and four tenant houses.[9] While this was above the anticipated cost of the mill, it was quite an operation for that expenditure and for that time.

Wilkie transferred from Alexandria to run the mill at Castor.

Castor Sawmill

As indicated in his 1933 letter to bondholders and in other company documents, Roy O. obviously spent much time during the first decade of his company cajoling creditors to give him more time to make payment and persuading lending institutions to extend his line of credit. Often, he received less than friendly responses. At least on one occasion during this period, the Rapides Bank and Trust Company of Alexandria rebuffed his request for extending a note payment. In his Autobiography, Roy O. includes the

CHAPTER 3 – THE FOUNDATION

response he made to J. W. Bolton, then-president of Rapides Bank, who in 1932 requested that Roy O. immediately pay a note of $15,000. This letter outlines what the company had done since 1929 to maintain stability and to reduce indebtedness. Roy O. asked for more time to pay his note. He also expressed optimism that business would increase. The local bank denied his request. When shown a copy of that letter in an interview, Robert Bolton, long-time president of Rapides Bank, indicated that he did not know anything about it since he was a young officer in the bank at the time. When asked if he knew what happened in that matter, he replied, "I expect he paid it."[10] Despite cutbacks, reduced salaries, cashed-in life insurance policies and lumber sold below the cost of producing it, the Roy O. Martin Lumber Company paid that and all other debts during the trying period of the Depression. Those were difficult times for the company as well as for their owners, but they did what they had to do to preserve the family business.

Keith Peterson moved to Alexandria in 1934 to work as an insurance agent. The company for which he worked underwrote some, but certainly not all, of the Martin business. One day, in particular, led to Peterson handling most of the Martin insurance. As the story goes, on this particular day, Roy O. was eating lunch at the Bentley Hotel when he overheard some insurance men at an adjoining table discussing him. What they said was not complimentary. Apparently, they criticized Roy O. for examining myriad and different possibilities when buying insurance, then taking the policy that seemed best to him. As a result, he had coverage from several different companies, a practice that resulted in over-lapping of coverage. Probably hurt or angered, or both, Roy O. used this eavesdropping as a learning experience. Upon returning to his office, he called Peterson and asked for help with his insurance. Martin had what Peterson remembered as "a crate full of insurance policies." He examined the various policies and scheduled them. He then structured all re-issued policies in a way that saved money, saved time, and avoided concurrencies. Peterson later left Alexandria and formed his own company in Shreveport, which specialized in insuring sawmills and lumber businesses. The Keith D. Peterson Company still is the major insurer of today's Martin Companies. Any insurance Peterson cannot carry themselves for the Martins, they outsource to other companies.

When asked if insuring sawmills was not a high-risk business because of the constant danger of personal injury and fire, Peterson smiled and replied that when he started in business all sawmills were of frame construction. It was not a question of *if* they would burn, but *when* they would burn. He cited that the

LIFE BY THE BOARD FOOT

Alexandria mill, the Castor mill, and the flooring plant in Alexandria had all burned, some more than once. In each case, the insurance company paid for the mill. Roy O. never questioned the amount of the settlement for any of the mills.[11]

By 1936 the Roy O. Martin Lumber Company had paid off its bond issue in full. The final installment matured on September 1, 1936. Even though interest payments on the bonds had been deferred in March 1933, the company fully paid all its bonds and all accompanying interest. In addition, bank loans to the Bank of Commerce and Trust Company of Memphis and the Commercial National Bank of Shreveport were also paid. Each of these banks, according to Roy O. in a 1937 report to the board, had placed stress on the company during their time of dire need. As a result, the company was "no longer friendly with them and therefore [we] desired to close our account with both of these banks, which had been done."[12] The company then established a more friendly relationship with American National Bank of Mobile, Alabama, which immediately granted a $40,000 line of credit.

Roy O's background in the lumber business was in hardwoods, which caused him initially to concentrate on those species. The southern lumber industry, however, is considered to be primarily softwood--pine. Walter Kellogg gives an easy definition of the distinction between the two types of wood. Any tree that has a broad leaf is hardwood; a tree that has green needles as its foliage is softwood. "Generally speaking," he writes, "a tree that sheds its leaves in the colder months is a hardwood and a tree that stays green the year round is softwood. The texture or the weight of the wood does not determine its classification as hardwood or softwood."[13] Roy O. Martin Lumber Company cut both types of wood. At times, the mill would operate a twelve-hour shift cutting hardwood, then would cut softwood for the next twelve-hour shift. Most other local mills cut one kind of wood. Adapting to cut both hardwood and softwood shows something about the Martin ingenuity in seizing opportunities and in getting all the value they can from an operation.

SAFETYGAS

Inarguably, Roy O. was a shrewd businessman, but he repeatedly made mistakes in one particular arena—partnering with others. In violation of the promise he had earlier made to himself of not holding stock in businesses that he did not control, in February 1938 Roy O. formed the Safetygas Corporation with George G. DelVallie and James D. Blake, both of Alexandria. The purpose of that business was to buy, sell,

CHAPTER 3 – THE FOUNDATION

transport, deliver, and manufacture liquefied petroleum gas and other fuels. They were also to sell and repair gas appliances, specifically gas heaters, water heaters, space heaters, and light fixtures.

From its beginning, this company did not do well. Roy O. was not pleased with the management and had little confidence in their ability to improve. And, as in previous partnerships, he soon became dissatisfied with that operation. Giving one of the other owners an option to buy his stock, he resigned his position as vice president of Safetygas Corporation in July 1938. Exercising his stock option, Roy O. was out of the liquefied petroleum business in less than six months.[14]

Roy O. was quite the entrepreneur. But he did better in enterprises that were related to what he knew best – the forest products industry and related activities. Also, he was dedicated to controlling all businesses of which he was a part. When those two factors were involved, the corporations he formed generally did well, and he did well with them. Finally learning from his failures, Roy O. stopped entering into partnerships with other people.

That same year, 1938, the company built rent houses adjacent to the site of the #2 mill. These houses were constructed of inferior wood that would have been difficult to sell. Each house was a "shotgun" house of either three or four rooms.

Early rent houses

Three-room houses rented for $2.00 per week or $2.25 if they were papered and painted. Four-room houses rented for $2.50 per week. Forty rent houses were constructed in 1938. Since these houses were built from lumber that would have been waste wood, it was an economical move for the company. By having affordable housing near the work site, construction of these rent houses also served to stabilize Martin's work force. Rental income, meanwhile, helped cash flow during those latter days of the Depression. Later, the company would build, sell, and finance similarly structured houses, creating neighborhoods adjacent to its Fenner Street operation. This introduced many employees to home ownership. The company thus profited from a more stable workforce. And the company also profited from additional income derived from financing the houses.

Wilkie continued to operate the mill at Castor until 1939, the year that mill burned—for the first time. Shortly thereafter, a store, which the mill manager owned adjacent to the mill property, also burned. Disheartened by his professional and personal losses and suffering from ill health, Wilkie resigned his position as director and officer with the company. The Roy O. Martin Lumber Company bought all of Wilkie's stock, thus severing his ties to the business. Ellis was made secretary of the board of directors. Once again, all stockholders and all directors of the board were family members. Then Roy O. sent his newest board member (and oldest son) to Castor to rebuild and operate the Castor mill. Prior to this, the twenty-two-year-old Ellis had managed Pineville Lumber Company, where Glankler was sales manager. Ellis liquidated the groundhog mill in Pineville and headed to his new assignment. Glanker continued to work with the Martin organization, moving his office in sales to the Fenner Street location.

Ellis Spencer Martin
And
Roy Otis Martin, Sr.

CHAPTER 3 – THE FOUNDATION

Since housing was not readily available to rent in the village of Castor, Ellis lived in Ringgold, making a daily thirteen-mile commute to the plant site. The Castor mill was rebuilt. Ellis remembered that, once again, everything that went into the mill was used equipment. As he expressed it, "The boss bought second-hand parts. Everything in it was second hand."[15]

Rebuilt Castor Sawmill
and
New Office

87

LIFE BY THE BOARD FOOT

This was not Ellis' first experience with the Castor mill. He had stayed out of high school for one year to help build the original mill there. During that time he had slept in a ramshackle back office. Because the mill did not have electricity, all nightly illumination the young teenage Martin had at night was an Aladdin lamp. His only reading material was lumber-supply catalogs. One of his major responsibilities then had been to keep the donkey boiler (a straight up-and-down boiler with a smokestack out the top) running. Belts powered by the steam engine ran everything. And he had to cut wood to fire the boiler and keep the mechanism going.

Machine Shop
and
Donkey Boiler
at
Castor Sawmill

Ellis finally had the Castor mill running again after it had burned in 1939. Then both sawmills faced a situation that would dramatically affect their way of doing business. When Japanese planes bombed Pearl Harbor on December 7, 1941, the United States was immediately forced into the war it had been trying to avoid, World War II. In the case of Roy O. Martin Lumber Company, the Depression that had so cramped the nation and so hindered business essentially ended with World War II. Not only were people put back to work, but demand for lumber significantly increased.

Prior to war, but obviously suspecting involvement was imminent, the government had requested sawmills to stockpile lumber. The Castor mill, for instance, was requested to store for the government's future wartime use two million feet of lumber. Each sawmill was assigned a number; all lumber shipped from that mill for government use was stamped with its assigned number. Since there was no civilian construction during those difficult war years, the government was the primary purchaser of lumber. Thus, federal mandates set a price for all lumber produced in the United States.

CHAPTER 3 – THE FOUNDATION

With the outbreak of war, the federal government had a tremendous demand for lumber, needing significantly more than that which had been stockpiled. Military bases and training camps were constructed from wood. Five of these military bases would be located in the immediate area of Alexandria, creating a building frenzy in the local area—and creating a financial boon for both Martin mills. Additionally, ammunition shell boxes were also made of wood. Much military equipment, gunstocks, for instance, was made of wood. As a result, successful manufacturers were seeing their specially marked products shipped to faraway places they never would have imagined possible prior to the conflict. Ellis recalled an African-American man from Lucky, Louisiana, who had once worked at the mill in Castor. While fighting in North Africa, this valiant soldier saw lumber that had the mark of the Castor mill on it – MTC 284.[16] Heroically, this former employee lost both his legs while defending the cause of freedom in that far continent.

Through its lumber, the company even participated, albeit peripherally, in building military landing crafts. Andrew Jackson Higgins of Higgins Industries in New Orleans, Louisiana, had developed a landing craft known as the Land Craft Vehicle Personnel boat (LCVP). Built of wood, this thirty-six-foot landing craft evolved from a rugged, shallow-draft workboat, which Higgins produced in the 1930s for use by trappers and oil companies in the swamps and marshes of south Louisiana. His unique boat could operate in eighteen inches of water, could run across logs and vegetation without fouling its propeller, and could run right up on shore and then extricate itself without damage. These boats found a new calling during the war. They were used extensively on the beaches of Normandy in the D-Day Invasion. World War II general and President of the United States, Dwight D. Eisenhower credited Higgins as the man who won the war for the United States. Eisenhower explained that without those highly maneuverable, shallow-draft landing craft, American soldiers would never have been able to go in over an open beach. Without those boats, the whole strategy of the war would have been changed.

LIFE BY THE BOARD FOOT

Martin supplies lumber for the construction of wooden minesweepers made by Higgins, Incorporated, New Orleans, for the United States Navy. Lumber is also cut for other vessels.

Southern yellow pine was the favored material for these Higgins boats. The head log, or transverse member, was a solid piece of pine located just underneath the hinged-bow ramp. This head log tied the boat's bow together. A solid block of pine was the strongest part of the boat, enabling the watercraft to run at full speed over floating obstacles, sandbars, and onto the beach without damaging its hull. Pine was also used in the forward and aft keels, in the skegs, in the bow posts, in the sternposts, and in the shear-and-chine longitudinals (or spine) of the Higgins boats.[17]

CHAPTER 3 – THE FOUNDATION

Spine of a Higgins Boat

Roy O. Martin Lumber Company provided some of the pine for constructing Higgins boats. Before shipping from the plant, that wood was often cut to specifications for shipbuilders, a step that facilitated the handling of materials.

Manpower in the mills obviously became a serious problem during the war years. Both Roy, Jr., and Norman served in the military. Roy, Jr., was in the Coast Guard; Norman served in the Army. Since the manufacture of lumber was so essential to the war effort, running the Castor mill was an exempt occupation. Thus, Ellis served a critical role at home by managing that now-busy mill. Because most able-bodied men had gone to defend their country, Ellis found that one of his biggest challenges was finding individuals to keep the plant running. Yet, to supply materials for the war effort, he simply had to have a productive work force. As a result, he filled some vacant positions with African-American women whose husbands had gone to war. Chuckling in his remembrance, Ellis recalled that, in order to accommodate these willing women, the company had to send to Chicago to get overalls in special sizes. Although by and large these women were dedicated workers, the plant still needed the strength of male employees. His solution for this problem came from a unique source: a prisoner-of-war camp at Ruston. According to

LIFE BY THE BOARD FOOT

Ellis, this was a win-win situation, giving employment to POWs while providing male workers to the mill. He remembers the Bavarian prisoners as the best workers.

When the war ended and its veterans returned, the company faced another difficult situation. They had to dismiss their female workers who had kept their plants running throughout wartime. The federal government mandated that employers reinstate returning veterans to those jobs they had held prior to the war.

During the war in 1942, Martins had built a small mill at Pleasant Hill, Louisiana. Ellis managed both it and the Castor mill, making the trip at least once a week. Prior to this, the company had been harvesting logs from the Pleasant Hill area, primarily using one logger. This additional small mill provided needed lumber for kilns at the large Alexandria facility. Having a mill closer to the timber supply seemed a logical idea, especially since gasoline and tires for timber trucks were problems during the war. Building a small circle sawmill at Pleasant Hill made sense on paper and in the boardroom. Reality painted a different picture. That mill was a problem from the very beginning, especially its turnover of labor. Fortunately, because it had been specifically set up as a "war baby," this mill was charged off the books when the war ended. It had served its primary purpose. In fact, minutes from the 1947 meeting of the board of directors state, "The President reported the completion of the liquidation of the Pleasant Hill property, with the exception of the ground on which the plant was located. All seemed well pleased that this headache was behind us."[18] When a venture did not work well, Martins historically have been willing to terminate the venture, remove themselves from it and move on. Again, they cut their losses and got out.

THE POST-WAR YEARS

Solvency

As far as finances for Roy O. Martin Lumber Company and for Roy O. Martin personally, World War II brought unexpected, but welcomed, prosperity. In fact, during the desperate latter days of the Depression, the company eliminated its debt. Coming on the heels of the depression, this unwelcome war had found the Martins with a requisite stockpile of lumber, which was available for immediate use for essential military efforts. During the war the Martins continued to produce as much lumber as they could under heavy government restrictions, but they found a ready market for it with the government at set prices.

D. B. Sanders related that, toward the end of Roy O's active involvement with the company, often he and Roy O. would be the only ones working in the office on Saturday morning. Then they would eat

CHAPTER 3 – THE FOUNDATION

lunch together. By that time, Roy O. considered himself wealthy. He would often express to Sanders his sadness at how he had attained his wealth – due to World War II and the profits he and his company made from the war.[19] For the Roy O. Martin Lumber Company, like many other American businesses, World War II not only signaled the end of the Depression, but it also provided the profit necessary to put them on a firm footing for future expansion.

To help meet a growing demand for more lumber, the company made improvements at the Fenner Street mill in Alexandria. By 1947 its interior alleys were concrete. They installed a sprinkler system, which aided in the amount of fire insurance the company could obtain as well as decrease ever-increasing costs of coverage. They also installed another flooring factory in 1948.

At a 1948 director's meeting, the board held a discussion and took action on a matter that Ellis later observed as one of the most important decisions made in their corporate history. They agreed to purposely manage their timberlands. As a result of this forward-thinking decision, they launched what would become an aggressive program of selective cutting, of measured thinning by cutting pulpwood, and of consistently removing defective and undesirable trees. This practice would come to be known as timber stand improvement (TSI). By implementing these then-innovative practices, their sawmill could operate permanently. Roy O. calculated that their normal workweek of fifty-five hours each week would require growth on one hundred thousand acres of land properly managed along with all the pine timber they could buy to keep the mill operating. The next year the board again reiterated the necessity of aggressively buying timberland. They agreed that, with increased competition from paper mills in buying land and smaller-sized timber along with the increased scarcity of available timber, they should go in debt if necessary in order to buy more land. They consequently entered into their later relationship with Banker's Life and Casualty Insurance Company, Des Moines, Iowa, quite specifically for money to buy land. The reason for changing lenders was simple: Banker's Life could lend money for a longer period of time than banks could.

The Castor mill burned again in March 1952. This time the mill was replaced with a six-foot band saw and a five-foot horizontal re-saw. The Castor mill still cut both hardwood and pine timber, although most of it was pine. Much production of its yellow pine was sold through the retail yards the Martin family operated.

LIFE BY THE BOARD FOOT

The Castor mill and all land involved with it were incorporated as Martin Timber Company in 1957. Ellis established a cut-up (or stock-and-dimension) plant at Castor that year of incorporation. Through this dimension plant, short length and shop-type pine lumber could be utilized. This plant provided cut-up stock and wood of specific dimensions to furniture manufacturers, toy makers, and other producers of wood products. Essentially by "cutting to size" pieces their customers ordered, Castor's plant enabled participating manufacturers to save money on both shipping and labor costs. All wood stock was fabricated to meet designated sizes, semi-fabricated or completely machined at Castor, making shipped products ready for use when manufacturers received their orders. Generally, cut-up wood stock was available in both pine and hardwoods.

Some of these original products were spindles for baby beds, bed slats, frame parts for promotional bedroom furniture, bumper rails for pool tables, tent poles, chair arm blanks, and yellow pine moldings. Shortly after the dimension plant began operation, bowling alleys grew in popularity. The demand for materials needed to build bowling alleys increased commensurately. Many carloads of bowling alley bed stock were produced and shipped from Castor's dimension plant. Later, production shifted from predominantly yellow pine to hardwoods. From its hardwoods, Martin Timber produced kitchen cabinet rail and stile parts, clear red oak blanks, clear export blanks, and moldings for bulletin board frames and picture frames. [20]

Both a chipper and a de-barker were installed at the Castor mill. Because International Paper Company (IP) needed chips for their paper mill in Springhill, Louisiana, they offered to install a chipper and a de-barker at Castor. Even more convincing, they offered to finance both machines. Knowing a good deal when it came knocking at his door, Ellis took IP up on their offer. Prior to that, all green material and chips from logs were burned. What had previously been waste material could now be profitably utilized in the paper industry. This chipper and de-barker were paid off in two years. A continuing Martin characteristic is to use every available particle of fiber. "Waste not, want not" is more than a proverbial saying for the Martins; it is a business principle.

Having begun in the Great Depression, the Castor mill operated at a profit during those difficult decades. It had continued to produce lumber during World War II, successfully relying at times on females and prisoners of war to keep production rolling. The mill had also survived a tornado. One hit the mill area on Sunday, February 12, 1950. Clyston Goudeau, paymaster for Martin Timber Company was working at his desk on that Sunday afternoon when the tornado struck at 2:11 p. m. The office building in which he was working caved in around him, but, luckily, he did not receive a scratch.[21] The mill sustained other damage, also.

CHAPTER 3 – THE FOUNDATION

Clyston Goudeau amid damage from 1950 Tornado

But a continuing and frustrating problem for Ellis had been trouble resulting from turnover in the labor force. Seeking to alleviate the headache, he created a plan to build houses for employees of the mill and then to sell them to those desiring home ownership. These company-financed, employee-owned houses successfully stabilized the labor force just as they had at the Alexandria mill several years before when Roy O. had provided low-cost housing for employees there. Home ownership made employees more responsible and also kept them working locally. It was beneficial to both employee and employer.

Providing even more reasonable living accommodations for employees at Castor, Ellis also built rent houses. By the 1960s, about fifty rent houses were available at minimal charge to company workers. Though small in size and basic in design, these structures provided needed housing in a rural area where rental property was virtually non-existent.

After the mid-1960s hardwood was no longer cut in the Castor mill because good quality hardwood logs had become more difficult to find in North Louisiana. From that time, only yellow pine was processed into lumber at the Castor mill.

LIFE BY THE BOARD FOOT

Ellis' second assignment at the Castor mill had been simple: cut out the Black Lake tract and close the mill. He, too, was to "cut out and get out." This time, however, the practice took longer than anyone anticipated. Thirty-five years later, he returned to Alexandria. In those intervening years, he actively contributed to growing the family's business, specifically and significantly by buying timber from surrounding landowners. This practice, along with logging the company's timber, made Castor a profitable operation. In an article in <u>Forests and People,</u> Ed Kerr described it in this way: "Martin [had] called Ellis into the office and told him to build a six-foot band mill, cut the remaining timber and liquidate the holdings. Instead of following these orders, Ellis began to buy timber from nearby residents who wanted to see the mill stay and bought land instead of selling it."[22] Despite increasing involvement in all operations of the Roy O. Martin Lumber Company, Ellis had continued to run Martin Timber Company sawmill at Castor until he moved to Alexandria in 1974 and became president of the Roy O. Martin Lumber Company in 1978.

When asked if his making a success of the Castor mill was an act of defiance, Ellis did not answer directly but said, "I made a profit every blessed year." Rather than follow his father's instructions specifically, Ellis walked in his father's entrepreneurial footsteps in seeing and seizing an opportunity to expand the company.

When Ellis moved from Castor, he left management of Martin Timber Company in the hands of his younger son, Jonathan Ellis Martin (Johnny). Johnny managed the sawmill in Castor until 1981 when he assumed other responsibilities in the family business.

In 1992 Martin Timber Company sold its Castor sawmill to Hunt Forest Products, Inc., of Ruston. The building housing the dimension plant was included in the sale, but not the plant. For three years Martin Dimension leased that space from Hunt. In 1995 the lease was not renewed and the dimension plant closed. Hunt Forest Products closed the remaining Castor mill at the end of 2000. Citing price cutting by competition and falling customer demand, the Hunt company announced in November 2000 that it would close the mill at the end of December of that year. At that time the mill employed eighty-five people with another thirty persons working on logging crews. The Castor sawmill, which was to have been a temporary enterprise, had operated continually from the time Roy O. built it in 1933 until it closed in 2000.[23]

CHAPTER 3 – THE FOUNDATION

Retail Lumber Yards

A lot of pent-up demand for building materials existed with the end of World War II in 1945. Not only were war veterans returning home, marrying, and buying homes but construction that had been stopped during those war years resumed—and resumed at a frenetic pace. Americans were building homes, establishing businesses, and creating a new post-war society.

Martin's company board began to realize a building boom was imminent. To guarantee they were a part of that boom, they knew they had to ensure a steady supply of timber for their mills. If they were to be successful in accomplishing this, they needed someone whose full-time job was to oversee their growing timberlands. Thus, in 1945, Roy O. hired John Munsterman as the first degreed forester in the company's employment. For the next forty years, he was a Martin employee, primarily handling the acquiring of land and the logging of timber in all areas south of Alexandria.

John Munsterman

Whenever possible, in accordance with their policy of aggressively securing a timber base for the future, land was bought. In other cases, long-term surface leases of ninety-nine years were arranged. In these extended leases, the company would buy surface rights but not mineral rights. On other occasions, timber was simply bought off the tract of a landowner.[24] Ten years later D. B. Sanders became a part of the forestry team. He handled the upland areas, pine production basically north of Alexandria, while Munsterman was still responsible for areas south of Alexandria, which were principally hardwoods.

LIFE BY THE BOARD FOOT

D. B. Sanders

When Norman was discharged from the Army in 1946, Roy O. put him in charge of the company's forestry division of the company.

Norman Kittell Martin

CHAPTER 3 – THE FOUNDATION

Land purchases, reforestation, timber stand improvement, and logging were all under his purview during this time. The people were in place, the time was right, and the Roy O. Martin Lumber Company was willing to gamble even more on an almost-certain, post-war building boom.

The company soon recognized an opportunity to profit from two sides of this building frenzy: the wholesale end (as they had been doing as a producer) and the retail end (as they could as a retailer). They then set out to create a retail division. This enterprise was further prompted by a post-war influx of West Coast lumber that had come into Louisiana, lumber that amazingly could be sold cheaper than yellow pine lumber could be produced locally. To remain competitive, Martin mills obviously needed another outlet for their lumber. Retail lumberyards provided this avenue for profit while simultaneously creating an even wider market for all their manufactured goods. According to Ellis, competition drove them into the retail lumber business; the retail lumber business allowed them, in turn, to beat their competitors at their own game.

Howard Lumber Company, established in Natchitoches in May of 1946, was the first Martin retail lumberyard. It was named for Mark Eugene Howard (Mark), Virginia Martin Howard's husband who became its manager.

Mark Eugene Howard

The eldest of Roy O. and Mildred's children, Virginia had married Mark who was a mechanical engineer with a degree from Michigan College of Mines and Technology. For eight years he worked as a staff engineer in the maintenance department of Caterpiller Tractor Company in Peoria, Illinois, before he moved south and worked for his father-in-law. This young couple moved to a "sawmill house" on Stephens Avenue in Natchitoches, remodeled it, and lived there during the eighteen months of their Natchitoches period. After leaving Howard Lumber Company, Mark subsequently became staff engineer for the Roy O. Martin Lumber Company supervising construction. He left that position in 1963 and began his own engineering firm, specializing in sawmill design and construction.

Random estimates of the Martin lumber sold through their retail outlets vary from thirty to fifty percent, according to the one making the estimate. Zack Woodard remembers that for Martin Timber Company, the number was about thirty percent, while for Roy O. Martin Lumber Company the number was less due to its larger hardwood production.[25] Regardless of the actual figure, a significant amount of total lumber produced through their combined sawmills was sold, first wholesale from a Martin mill to the Martin retail outlets, then at retail prices through the retail lumberyards. Not only did they sell their lumber through their retail yards, they also sold a complete line of building materials. In addition, the company developed subdivisions through each retail outlet. In the next thirty years or so, the company would create more than a dozen subdivisions complete with water and sewage, utilities, and paved streets. Martin controlled all materials and construction, from raw materials out of which the lumber was made to finished products on each landscaped subdivision lot. Thus, their ad campaign "From Forest Farms to Cheerful Homes" accurately described their building process.

Two retail centers, Lake Charles and Alexandria, also had commercial contracting departments. Complete building service centers, these locations offered construction loans and arranged permanent financing for builders. Residential home construction departments were also developed in some of the centers. For instance, the Norman Company, which was the home-building division of Howard Lumber Company in Minden, also maintained a satellite operation in Magnolia, Arkansas. Lot sales and land development added to profitability for the retail lumberyards.

Ultimately, the Martins owned thirteen retail lumberyards in three states, although the maximum number they controlled at any time was twelve. Ralph Kees became general manager of the retail division. Weekly, Kees and Chester O'Quin would visit each location, conducting audits. Charles Jeffress, company pilot, often flew them to the various locations.

CHAPTER 3 – THE FOUNDATION

Ralph Kees

Chester O'Quin

Charles Jeffress

Beginning with Howard Lumber Company in Natchitoches, other retail lumberyards were either established or acquired by the Martins:

LIFE BY THE BOARD FOOT

1. Howard Lumber Company in Natchitoches, Louisiana (May 7, 1946)
2. Pointe Coupeé Lumber Company in Lafayette, Louisiana (October 29, 1946)
3. Martin Building Materials in Alexandria, Louisiana (January 1, 1947)
4. Pelican State Lumber Company in Opelousas, Louisiana (October 31, 1951)
5. Lake Charles Lumber Company in Lake Charles, Louisiana (July 31, 1952)
6. Howard Lumber & Supply Company in Minden, Louisiana (March 29, 1956)
7. Howard Building Center in Magnolia, Arkansas (February 2, 1966)
8. Superior Lumber and Supply Company in Monroe, Louisiana (January 31, 1967)
9. Morgan City Lumber Company in Morgan City, Louisiana (November 22, 1972)
10. Lafourche Lumber Company in Thibodeaux, Louisiana (August 6, 1975)
11. Martin Home Center of Sulphur in Sulphur, Louisiana (March 8, 1979)
12. Martin Home Center of Jennings in Jennings, Louisiana (December 12, 1979)
13. Green Lumber Company in Beaumont, Texas (January 4, 1976)

CHAPTER 3 – THE FOUNDATION

LIFE BY THE BOARD FOOT

By 1948, the capitalization of the Roy O. Martin Lumber Company had increased to $1,000,000. The corporation that began in 1923 with $100,000 capitalization had grown to $1,000,000 capitalization in twenty-five years. In May of that year (1948), the ROM board formed the Martin Development Company to operate as a subdivision and real estate arm for the company's building materials. This newest company could buy, sell, exchange or trade all kinds of property, particularly land. By 1950 capitalization for all Martin companies had increased again to $2,000,000. After examining the possibility of changing from a corporation to a partnership, the directors agreed on remaining a corporation. Capitalization increased again in 1955 to $3,000,000. Martin's many enterprises were poised for even greater profit. Their Fenner Street operation covered a space of thirty-seven city blocks near the southern edge of Alexandria's city boundary. This complex was home to their sawmill, planing mill, flooring factory, dry kilns, offices, warehouses and machine shop. Additionally, their scattered lumberyards, which crisscrossed the state, were becoming a competitive force in Louisiana's home-building boom.[26]

As the company grew, their collective business structure necessarily became more complex because of corporate taxation in place. According to Zack Woodard,

> Every new venture we started was set up as a separate corporation due to the corporation tax being assessed at a progressive rate. The tax on profits under $100 million was much lower.... By the 1970s, we had over twenty different corporations. Sometimes Ralph or I and the manager would participate as a shareholder in the new venture. Ellis felt we would take a more serious interest if we had some stake in the deal."[27]

In subsequent years, this practice of awarding stock to faithful, hardworking employees would be phased out as Martins found a more equitable system of recognizing professional merit while, at the same time, keeping company stock in the hands of family members.

In the reorganization of 1973, Roy O. Martin Industries, Inc., was formed. Stock in the retail lumberyards and stock in both the Fenner Street sawmill and the Applewhite sawmill were exchanged for stock in Roy O. Martin Industries, Inc. In the process, Roy O. Martin Industries acquired stock in MHC Properties. The purpose of this complicated merger was to create a corporation without any timberland, in case a future decision was made to take the company public. The reorganization also detailed a cutting agreement between Roy O. Martin Industries and various land corporations.

In 1978, Martin Home Centers, Inc., was formed so as to spin off from Roy O. Martin Industries all assets that were not acquired in the stock swap with Louisiana-Pacific. This, then, was that stock in both Fenner Street and Applewhite mills, which was exchanged for stock in Louisiana-Pacific Corporation. In addition to the LP stock,

CHAPTER 3 – THE FOUNDATION

MHC also owned the retail yards and subdivisions, becoming the operating company for Martin's retail lumberyards and real-estate division. A decade later, when those retail lumberyards would be closed or sold to employees, Martin Home Centers became MHC Properties (MHC). MHC then would become a real-estate holding and development company for the Martin Company.

With the establishment and acquisition of these retail stores, it became apparent that all purchases could--and should--be consolidated. Martins realized another profitable opportunity. By consolidating all purchasing, the company could gain a significant price advantage. This idea led the board to create a centralized purchasing department, which became Martin Distributors, in Alexandria. With Martin Distributors, the company also developed a warehouse and distribution system. These internal developments seemed to place Martins in a good position for continued growth in the retail sector, but winds of economic change forced them in a different direction.

Their retail division had, for a time, been a very profitable operation and a large part of the Martin enterprise. By the 1980s, however, Louisiana's oil industry experienced a major downturn, taking the local booming housing industry down with it. An even greater, more permanent, threat came from large discount building material stores such as Lowe's, Sutherland's, and Home Depot. No longer confined to major cities in distant states, these big-box discounters had invaded Central Louisiana. With competition from them, business declined in Martin's retail operation. Additionally, their retail division was buying more of its lumber from other mills since both Martin sawmills were producing less construction lumber than before. The relationship between their sawmills and their retail yards was not as profitable as it had been. Once again, it was time for Martins to cut potential losses and go in another direction. First, the company closed some of its unprofitable retail lumberyards. On January 1, 1987, Roy O. Martin Lumber Company sold their remaining retail lumberyards and Martin Distributors in a leveraged buy-out to its five managing employees. All that remained in MHC was the real estate and the interest in Martco Partnership. The corporate name was then changed to MHC Properties, Inc.[28]

VERNON PARISH LUMBER COMPANY

and

COLFAX CREOSOTING COMPANY

In 1953 Roy O. Martin Lumber Company bought all stock in Vernon Parish Lumber Company, which was in liquidation. Their main purpose in buying this company was to obtain its 17,000 acres of timberland. Martin had tried to buy this land for six years, but company owners would not sell their land without selling their small physical plant as well.

According to an agreement Martin's company directors made among themselves before purchasing Vernon Parish Lumber Company, they immediately liquidated the manufacturing facility that was part of the newly purchased company, leaving the coveted acreage in the hands of Roy O. Martin Lumber Company. Banker's Life and Casualty Company of Des Moines, Iowa, financed this purchase.

Three years later in 1956, the company found another opportunity to add to their land holdings as well as to embark on a new enterprise: the Colfax Creosoting Company. At that time, Colfax Creosoting was part of the Edenborn Estate. This conglomerate of businesses and large land holdings, along with its founder Edenborn, was a significant player in the industrial growth and development of our nation.

A native of Germany, William Edenborn immigrated to the United States in 1867. In 1870 he invented a machine to make barbed wire. Because he needed a mill to manufacture his wire, he established a plant in St. Louis, Missouri, later building other manufacturing facilities at other locations in other states. His wire mills, operating as American Steel and Wire Company, also made wire for fencing and for telegraph and telephone communications.

CHAPTER 3 – THE FOUNDATION

His company would ultimately be sold to J. P. Morgan, becoming a major component of world-renowned United States Steel Company.

Edenborn came to Louisiana in 1897 to build a railroad connecting Shreveport to New Orleans. By 1907, he had successfully built Louisiana Railway and Navigation Company (L. R. and N.), later extending a line into North Texas to McKinney, Texas, north of Dallas. Edenborn owned a residence in New Orleans, a plantation just outside of Shreveport, and thousands of acres of timberland in Louisiana.[29] At his death, his still-vast manufacturing and real-estate properties were managed by trustees in the Edenborn Estate.

By the mid-1950s these trustees were ready to sell their timberland. However, along with the timberland, they also wanted to sell Colfax Creosoting Company, a fully operating company with almost 15,000 acres of timberland (14,977.44, to be exact), together with a large inventory of creosoted posts, poles, pilings, and lumber as well as all accompanying machinery and equipment. Thirty-three thousand acres of pine timber were also a part of the sale. Both A. J. Hodges, a Shreveport lumberman, and Roy O. were interested in the property. But neither of them, especially Hodges, actually wanted a creosote plant. The final solution was that both Hodges and Martin would buy the acreage, each getting half of the timberland. Out of necessity, then, in July 1956, Roy O. bought the unwanted creosote plant so that he could have the eastern portion of Edenborn timberland.[30] Neither Roy O. nor his board had any experience whatsoever in treating lumber; however, they felt they could not pass up this opportunity of substantially increasing their land base.

As the name would indicate, Colfax Creosoting (now known as Colfax Treating Company) began in Colfax, Louisiana. In 1948 the plant had moved to Pineville where it was located on twenty acres of land leased from the KCS Railroad. The reason for relocating the plant was a better rail connection both for incoming raw poles and outgoing treated poles. The plant had access to six railroads in Pineville; only one railroad had been available in Colfax. At that time, the creosoting plant had one treatment cylinder that treated only with creosote.

Originally, Roy O. managed Colfax Creosoting in addition to his many other daily tasks. He would stop by that facility for a couple of hours each morning before going to the sawmill in Alexandria. As his workload increased significantly, he necessarily sought others qualified to share in the growing responsibilities of his company. One of those was Haywood Nutt who came on as safety engineer in 1959. Another was Maurice Mouton, an in-house attorney who mainly did title work while taking care of other legal matters as they arose.

LIFE BY THE BOARD FOOT

Another administrative change in 1962 was to make Norman manager of Colfax Creosoting Company. When Norman resigned from the company in 1967, Clyde Norton became plant manager, then general manager later that same year.

Shortly after purchasing Colfax Creosoting, the Martins installed another cylinder for the treatment of *pentacholorophenol* – penta. They added a third treatment cylinder in 1968 and a fourth in 1976, increasing treatments from one to four by 2000: creosote, *pentacholorophenol*, borax and CCA (chrome, copper, and arsenic). The computer-operated CCA treatment plant, which was completed in 2000, is a highly modern treating plant.[31] Colfax Treating Company now sits on sixty-eight acres owned by the company.

In 2001, Clyde Norton retired after forty-two years with the company. Norton was originally employed as a forester. His first responsibility with the treatment plant had been procurement of timber.

Clyde Norton

He moved up the ranks to become a vice president of the company, later becoming the first non-Martin family member on the board of directors of a Martin company wholly owned by Martins. Of Norton's move to general manager of the treatment plant Ellis said, "I told him I would fire him if he didn't make money. He made money from the first year. I didn't ever go over there."[32] Surely, he did occasionally visit that facility, but he basically gave Norton freedom to run Colfax Treating profitably.

CHAPTER 3 – THE FOUNDATION

Norton said that they made a deal. He told Ellis, "Look, you let me run it. Give me the authority to do anything I want to do except sell it. If I don't make you more money than you have ever made before, then you can either run me off or put somebody else in charge or put me back in whatever you want me to do."

And Ellis responded by saying, "That's fine with me. That's the kind of deal I like."

Obviously, it was a good deal. Under Norton's leadership, not only did the plant prosper it became a leader in its industry. Carl Johnson, whom Norton hired to work at the plant right out of college, succeeded Norton as general manager of the current Colfax Treating Company.

In recent years environmental issues have played a large part in the treatment division. Under scrutiny by both the federal Environmental Protection Agency (EPA) and the Louisiana Department of Environmental Quality (LDEQ) the company continually seeks to comply with all environmental regulations. Norton was described as "a very sophisticated business man who . . . somehow mastered the art of staying one step ahead of the EPA and the DEQ."[33] Norman's observation was that Norton got in on the ground floor. He cleaned up before contamination became a problem. The plant experienced a $3.5 million upgrade from the late 1980s until 1994 to comply with new rules for air, ground, and water safety. This construction involved removing contaminated soil, concreting all drippage areas, and roofing all production areas where rain run-off could lead to contamination.[34] An in-house inspection team constantly monitors every activity to keep the company well within environmental guidelines.

In regard to environmental matters, Norton stated that his theory was "the quicker you do it, the easier and cheaper you can do it." Colfax Creosoting was the first in its industry to clean up their lagoons, ponds that collect wastewater. They were also the first to install drip pads under their treatment cylinders. In fact, they established the industry standard for drip pads.

In 2003, Colfax Treating took another major step toward reducing any remaining contamination on its grounds. Because the site of their current treating operation had, years before, operated as a railroad repair yard and then as a creosote treating plant, today's environmentally conscious Martins took deliberate steps to rid their property of lingering impurities in the soil. Under the direction of current manager Carl Johnson, workers created twenty-six "bio-piles." These "uniformly sized mounds (typically 30 feet by 80 feet)" are "technically bioremediation mechanisms used to reduce levels of contaminants found in the ground." Each large mound of dirt "could be called an industrial compost pile, not unlike the compost piles many keep at their homes for gardening. When the right conditions are created, naturally occurring microorganisms digest the contaminants. This mostly aerobic process breaks down contaminants (creosote and its sub-components) into carbon dioxide and water. The chemical creosote is biodegradable and actually is the food source for bacteria, given the right conditions."[35] Amazingly, after twelve to fifteen months, when clean-up standards are met, soil from these mounds will be re-used as fill dirt in designated areas at the site.

Originally, most of their poles were cut from company land. By using timber grown on company land, Colfax could realize more from each log used as a treated utility pole than it would bring in lumber. Now most shorter electric and telephone poles, those forty to sixty-five feet long and made from Southern yellow pine, are purchased locally. The company purchases its longer, stouter poles from Washington and Oregon. More than one hundred feet tall and used for transmission lines, these poles are cut from Douglas fir trees.[36] These long poles take up two to three railroad cars and may take as many as four months to make the trip from the West Coast to Pineville. Each pole is individually inspected and graded, an important task since poles come in one hundred ten different classifications. The poles are then drilled, hand trimmed and shaped, branded and tagged to individual company specifications, and kiln dried. Colfax has contracts with seven major utility companies, all having different specifications.

Today, as in earlier years, natural disasters present special challenges for Colfax Treating. When storms hit and poles go down, utility companies call Colfax Treating. Carl Johnson said, "We are their 911 number and fortunately we have always been able to deliver what they need."[37] When Hurricane Andrew hit the Louisiana coast in 1993, Colfax shipped two hundred seventy loads of utility poles to the New Iberia area. When an ice storm splintered poles in Arkansas and the Southwest, the company shipped five thousand four hundred yellow pine poles. During a 1994 ice storm, their crews worked twenty-one consecutive days, around the clock. In 1998 an ice storm hit the Northeast United States and Southeast Canada. Colfax sent one hundred twenty-one loads of forty poles each. Starting loading on a Sunday, they loaded a truck every fifteen minutes until about five thousand poles left for Watertown, New York.[38] Norton's take on that is that in emergency situations, even if they do not have contracts with the utility companies involved, "they are willing to use other people's poles. When the lines are on the ground, you need something to put them on. Our business is built on quality and service. Utilities in the last several years have recognized that as an asset instead of just the cheapest price."[39] Treated utility poles, bulkheads, pilings, bridge timbers, lumber, fence posts, and parking posts are shipped throughout the United States, Canada, Mexico, and overseas. A yard in St. James, Maryland, Utility Supply Company, provides stock inventory for utility companies in

CHAPTER 3 – THE FOUNDATION

that area. In 2001 the plant treated between forty thousand and fifty thousand cubic feet of wood per week. The sales goal was to sell $1.2 million per month. With Norton's retirement, the company created a new management team. In May 2001, the name changed to Colfax Treating Company. It also added a hot-wax treatment to meet requirements of one of its customers. To track its inventory of one hundred ten different pole classifications, Colfax Treating's new management team implemented WILS, the Web Integrated Lumber System to bar code all treated products. Soon after implementing WILS, operators found one pole that had been on the lot fourteen years, not necessarily a record the company notes with pride. All manufacturing divisions in the Martin Companies now use this sales/inventory system.[40]

Even though the Martins rather backed into the Colfax Creosoting Company, it became one of their most profitable enterprises. They had not sought a treatment plant; rather, they had bought it to acquire significant timber acreage. Fortunately, the treating plant introduced new opportunities enabling Martins to utilize some of their own timber and to market specialized forest products in a wider area.

RICHARD'S READY MIX

The Martin Company established Richard's Ready Mix in April 1959 in Alexandria. As Ellis once remarked about the name of a business, "You've got to call it something." Apparently, Richard's Ready Mix was named for Richard Kojis, its manager. The purpose of this concrete plant was to further integrate their home building and subdivision enterprise. A logical fit for their growing retail operation, it provided materials for streets and sidewalks in company-developed subdivisions. Richard's Ready Mix created foundations for homes, patios, driveways, and any other concrete work in the homes Martin built. Located on Industrial Street, it had its own railway spur, which permitted delivery of materials in large quantity by hopper cars. Sand and gravel were stockpiled and moved to the batch plant by a conveyer system. The plant operated by an air and electric system.

This relatively small ready-mix plant not only provided concrete for Martin projects but also for other builders in the Alexandria area. It supplied concrete to England Air Force Base and other government construction projects according to their specifications for concrete. The plant was also qualified to handle large highway building projects.

LIFE BY THE BOARD FOOT

The ready-mix plant profitably served its purpose while Martins were in the home-building business. However, about 1973, several years before the company sold their retail lumberyards, they sold their small concrete business to Frank Treat, Jr., and Edward Kennon from Minden.

In the meantime, the sawmill on Fenner Street in Alexandria continued to grow, slowly becoming a leader in Central Louisiana's lumber industry, slowly making its mark as the foundation for Roy O. Martin Lumber Company. From its solid beginning, by 1960 the company had survived the Great Depression, had become solvent, had unexpectedly profited from World War II, had created a retail division, had purchased a treating company and, most significantly, had acquired significant tracts of land. Roy O. was still at the helm, but the natural winds of change would begin to further layer that company which he had founded almost four decades earlier.

4.

FUNCTION

. . . they grow, yea, they bring forth fruit. . . . (Jeremiah 12:2)

CHANGE IN LEADERSHIP

In early June 1962, Roy O. abruptly told Roy, Jr., to go home and put on a suit. Always attentive to his father's instructions, Roy, Jr., went home and, obediently dressed in a suit and tie, returned to the sawmill. That is the way Roy O. Martin, Jr., replaced his dad as president of Roy O. Martin Lumber Company.[1] Having come to work at the sawmill fulltime immediately following his discharge from the Coast Guard just a few days before Christmas in 1945, Roy, Jr., had become mill superintendent early in 1946 and had worked closely with his father during those intervening sixteen years. Ellis had continued to run the profitable Castor operation while staying keenly abreast of business operations in Alexandria.

Since its inception and until that day in June 1962, Roy O. Martin, Sr., had been president of Roy O. Martin Lumber Company and all of its other related businesses. A plan no doubt concocted by the elder Martin but approved by his company board, Roy O. Martin, Sr., officially resigned as president on June 1, 1962, becoming its first chairman of the board of directors. Roy, Jr., was made company president. Ellis continued as vice-president. Norman became secretary. And Mark Howard, Virginia Martin Howard's husband, became treasurer.

In making the change, Roy O. told his board of directors that he was relinquishing the position of president in order to turn over to other family members more responsibility for guiding and controlling daily affairs of the corporation. In announcing this change in leadership, the <u>Alexandria Daily Town Talk</u> ran a picture of Roy O. and Roy, Jr. (duly attired in suit and tie). The article noted that Roy, Jr., had been associated with the business since 1939. He would "take over the duties as president and continue operating the Alexandria operation."[2] About his promotion, Roy, Jr., commented that whether he was president or not, "Daddy was still the boss."

Roy O. Martin, Sr.
and
Roy O. Martin, Jr.

With Roy, Jr., as president and Roy O. as board chairman, the company continued to progress. The Alexandria sawmill was upgraded and practically rebuilt. Mark Howard did the engineering and Roy, Jr., supervised the construction. They obtained most of this machinery from the West Coast. As innovative, mechanized equipment became more available, the plant would soon become fully automated. Already, the mill had its own generator and supplied its own power, using its hook-up to the Alexandria Utility Department only in emergencies or when crews made repairs to the mill. After a devastating hurricane in 1957, the Alexandria power plant was down for a full week. However, the Martin sawmill continued operating every day, generating its own power and pumping its own water.

CHAPTER 4 – FUNCTION

Damage from 1957 Hurricane

By agreement with the Louisiana Forest Products Corporation, and under the leadership of Roy, Jr., the company began operating a chip mill near Simmesport in 1962. The primary purpose of this mill was to utilize small-growth timber that was not suitable for sawlogs. Roy O. Martin Lumber Company successfully operated the Simmesport mill until 1975 when it had outlived its usefulness.

DURA-WOOD

In the late 1960s, Martins found another opportunity, virtually in its own backyard, to expand their treating operations. National Lumber and Treating Company had built a treating plant on site of a railroad-switching yard on Koppers Street in Alexandria in 1923, coincidentally the same year Roy O. had purchased his Fenner Street mill. Operating with one treating cylinder, National Lumber used coal-tar-based solutions, or creosote, to process railroad crossties, a system they continued until Koppers Company bought their plant in 1944. Koppers made improvements, adding four work tanks and three creosote storage tanks but they, like the previous owners, still treated with only one cylinder. Koppers also began using *pentacholorophenol*-based solutions.

In 1968 Koppers decided to close their plant, which the Martins subsequently bought for $285,000, along with eighty-three acres of land. In this acquisition, Martin eliminated a competitor while enlarging their property and

LIFE BY THE BOARD FOOT

increasing the number of their manufacturing facilities. However, they did not intend to operate this newly acquired facility. Rather, their original idea had been to scrap the plant and develop the property into a subdivision. Moving this plan forward, Norton figured out the scrap value for the plant. Then he and Ellis looked at the purchased acreage to determine a subdivision layout. On advice from their accountants, however, they decided to operate the plant in order to take advantage of depreciation on the high evaluation of the equipment versus the low evaluation of the land.

Under the name of Dura-Wood and under the supervision of Norton, the plant began operations as a component of Martin's treating division along with Colfax Creosoting. With no inventory, no orders and no experience in selling crossties, Norton aggressively called railroads offering to sell them the company's newest product. One day as he opened his mail, Norton found an order from the C and O Railroad for one hundred thousand crossties! Puzzled, because he had had no previous contact with this C and O Railroad, he showed the order to his sales manager and asked if he knew anything about the company and its location. His sales manager replied by saying, "Son, you just sold 100,000 crossties. How many do you have?" He had no crossties. Norton frantically, but successfully, bought enough crossties from small crosstie mills to fill the order. [3] Dura-Wood was up and running.

Dura-Wood treated only crossties. All its crossties were bought exclusively from crosstie mills, requiring a different process and different equipment than that housed at the Martin's Fenner Street mill. Crosstie mills are usually small "groundhog" sawmill operations since bigger mills are not generally equipped to handle the smaller materials used in making these wooden ties that support steel rails in railroads.

Shortly after acquiring the Koppers plant, Dura-Wood began modernizing its equipment. Automatically controlled package-type boilers replaced the antiquated gas boilers. All treatment cylinders were replaced. Dura-Wood became a more modern treatment facility.

When Martins first purchased the Koppers facility, it employed twenty-five people and had annual sales of about $900,000. In 1997 the Dura-Wood operation had grown to sixty-eight employees and sales of $10.5 million. At the time of its sale in 2000, Dura-Wood employed seventy-five persons and had revenue of $16 million. But, once again, time had come for Martins to take their profit and get out of a rapidly changing industry. Southern Pacific, Dura-Wood's primary customer, had recently been sold to Union Pacific. This sale left Dura-Wood with only one customer, Union Pacific Railroad who, as Clyde Norton and Ellis realized, would be in the catbird seat in

CHAPTER 4 – FUNCTION

determining the price for crossties. Realizing they potentially (and probably) would have no control in price-setting their product, Ellis authorized Norton to seek a buyer for the treating facility.

In 2000 the company sold Dura-Wood to RailWorks, a New York company formed by sixteen railroad contractors that are related to railroad companies. Conditions had changed. Railroads had merged, making fewer customers for crossties. Specifications for railroad crossties had also changed, requiring the Martins either to make alterations to outdated equipment in the plant or to purchase expensive new equipment. They felt neither would be good investments. Although Dura-Wood had been a profitable operation, its sale was beneficial to the evolving Martin business strategy of concentrating on the things they grew and produced. They thus realized a substantial profit and exited the business of treating crossties. Again, theirs would be a fortuitous exit. RailWorks Corporation declared bankruptcy in 2001.

NORMAN OIL AND GAS COMPANY

With what was slowly, but methodically, becoming extensive land holdings in the early 1960s, leaders of the Martin companies in that era saw a possibility of oil and gas production on company-owned land. They had already leased some land to others for oil and gas exploration, but they wanted to pursue their own production possibilities. As a result, the board of directors created Norman Oil and Gas Company to develop minerals on Martin land. Obviously, the name for that enterprise came from that of the third son, Norman. A new company required a new name, hence Norman Oil and Gas.

Lewis Wysocki of Shreveport managed this newest Martin division. He successfully sold interest to other developers for several wells and gained participation from some oil companies. Although several wells were drilled, only three resulted in production.

Since it was not a profitable enterprise, the operation was terminated after a few years.

WILMAR PLYWOOD

Southply was a plywood plant set up in Natchitoches in the mid-1960s. Because Southply had no timber supply, it ceased operations after a short time, leaving an abandoned plywood plant for sale. An opportunity came for Martin to enter into what would be another doomed-from-the-start partnership.

LIFE BY THE BOARD FOOT

Willamette Industries, based in Oregon but with a Louisiana presence by that time, and Martin Timber Company formed an ill-fated partnership and purchased the Southply plant. Willamette did not have large timber holdings in Louisiana at that time, but they did have plywood manufacturing and sales knowledge, which the Martins did not. But by now, the Martins did have a ready timber supply in Central Louisiana, which Willamette did not. In their agreement, Martin Timber Company would supply the timber. Willamette would be responsible for operating the plywood plant and selling the plywood. The partnership was formed in 1971, and Wilmar purchased the Southply plywood plant from the Natchitoches Parish Police Jury. This joining of Williamette's skills and Martin's resources seemed logical: certainly a success in the making.

Such would not be true. Indeed, this was not a happy venture for the Martins. Almost immediately, Ellis was dissatisfied with the management of the mill. He indicated that, through this partnership, he learned a lot of what not to do in the plywood business, knowledge that would benefit the company three decades later when they would build their own plywood plant. After two brief, but frustrating, years, Willamette Industries bought out the Martin interest in Wilmar Plywood for a nice profit for the Martins.

MORE LEADERSHIP CHANGES
MORE EXPANSIONS
MORE RESTRUCTURING

Norman resigned his position as secretary of the board of directors in January 1967. In September of that year, he also resigned as manager of Colfax Creosoting Company, a position he had held since 1962. Norman had also directed the forestry division. With these resignations, Norman left the company. Fortunately, for both family and company, Norman left the business without rancor. Although he retained his stock in the company, he neither directly associated with it nor worked in it any longer. Norman explained his actions, "Being the youngest of the three brothers, it seemed best to get out of the company and let them [Ellis and Roy, Jr.] operate it."[4] While never mentioned, obviously all three independent-minded brothers had some disagreements about how the company should be run. Norman took this trait of determinism elsewhere and developed his own successful business interests.

Meanwhile, in the early 1970s, after making a trip to Canada to observe small-log mills, Ellis realized the company needed its own small-log mill to handle logs that would not profitably process

CHAPTER 4 – FUNCTION

through their Fenner Street mill, which was designed for making lumber from larger trees. Thus, in 1972 the Martins built the appropriately named Applewhite Mill on Applewhite Street in Alexandria, conveniently across the railroad track from their original sawmill. Known as a Chip-N-Saw mill, this small-log facility made short boards used in furniture, particularly parts for pool tables manufactured by Sears and Roebuck.

In 1973, in what would be the first of many such moves to streamline operations and improve profitability, the board of directors reorganized the company, creating Roy O. Martin Industries, Inc. The board had, for a time, considered making the company a publicly held corporation. Ellis particularly, along with Zack Woodard, company comptroller, did a monumental amount of work in preparing the company to be listed on Wall Street. However, because of negative economic factors (high inflation/risky business climate), they backed away from public listing. Instead, these two encouraged the board to reorganize the company into Roy O. Martin Industries, Inc. The primary goal for this restructuring was to achieve estate planning for first- and second-generation Martins. In those first years of the 1970s, this became more than a project for Ellis; it became his crusade for both family and company. He doggedly pursued its completion, but he knew he could not achieve his ambitious goal single-handedly.

To succeed in what he saw as the singular goal necessary to guarantee continuance of his family-owned company, Ellis consulted with Ira Marcus. Attorney and estate-planning specialist from Chicago, Illinois, Marcus provided pivotal directions for estate planning, directions that would protect the company in a future and certain event of the demise of any of its primary shareholders. Once the framework of restructuring was outlined, Woodard then spent untold hours explaining to family members, convincing them of the need to act quickly and accomplishing for them a complicated and major reorganization that would allow its implementation. Essentially, the reorganization brought Martin's various business entities together as one corporation.

LIFE BY THE BOARD FOOT

Zack Woodard

During this time of major change, Ellis found himself spending more time in Alexandria than he did in Castor. Woodard had already relocated to Alexandria to work out details of the massive restructuring, which soon manifest itself in overwhelming details. Ellis rather quickly came to realize he, too, needed to be closer to the heartbeat of operations. So, in 1974, Ellis moved from Castor to Alexandria, leaving the Castor mill under the direction of his son, Johnny. This third-generation Martin, who had been with the company only three years, would now manage a mill. Johnny was still in his mid-twenties when he assumed that responsibility.

CHAPTER 4 – FUNCTION

Jonathan Ellis Martin, age 24

MAJOR CHANGES IN MANAGEMENT

The year 1974 was significant because it consolidated management. Prior to this year, the splintered Martin businesses had been managed as separate entities. Henceforth, they would operate as one large corporation. Now that Zack and Ellis both were in Alexandria, they quickly recognized some problems that could rather easily be solved by consolidation. One specifically was that of handling cash accounts. Zack remembers,

> We had a zillion checking accounts all over, and we had to maintain [an] operating balance in each one, so we were constantly transferring and loaning funds from one to the other. We had heard about the zero balance checking accounts at the First National Bank of Chicago. So I worked up a spreadsheet and formulated a plan, and Ellis went with me to see Robert Bolton about Rapides [Bank] doing this for us rather than have to move the accounts to Chicago. [Robert Bolton] didn't know anything about the system and didn't want to do it, but he knew that we were going to do it with him or without him. So we agreed to the plan of consolidating the checking account and investing the balance for one day, and then do this every day. At the time, we got credit for the deposits the day they were made. This gives us the benefit of the deposit float and disbursement float. We continued to modify this and expand it to finally include all checking accounts and to eliminate almost all regular checking accounts. This earned the Company hundreds of

> thousands of dollars in investment income and made cash management much simpler. No one else in the South was doing anything like this at the time. This is now commonly referred to as 'sweep accounts.'[5]

Although this method of financial management may be standard practice today, in 1974 it was highly innovative. Martin fiscal ingenuity, and, yes, Martin aggressiveness, once again had the company on the cutting edge of progress. If Robert Bolton and his local Rapides Bank had not partnered with them in this endeavor, the Martins would have taken their proposal—and their money—to a bank that would have embraced their plan.

Some might say that 1978 was a tumultuous year for the Roy O. Martin Lumber Company. Others might say it was "business as usual" for the Martins. That year, the Fenner Street mill was sold to Louisiana-Pacific. That was the year that Martin Home Centers, operating company for their retail lumberyards, was incorporated to facilitate the exchange of stock with Louisiana-Pacific. It was also the year that Roy, Jr., resigned the presidency of the company.

To say that he resigned is putting it tactfully. Company records show that he offered his resignation. Actually, he was "eased out" of the presidency by action of the board of directors. Ellis is credited with engineering his younger brother's departure from his position as company president. The older brother looked at it strictly as a business decision, not a personal matter at all. Ellis said, "When you are a businessman, you have to do what you have to do."[6] The Martins in general, and Ellis in particular, have an uncanny ability to clearly separate business matters from family matters. According to Ellis, some managerial and operational procedures that Roy, Jr., practiced precipitated the board's decision. According to others, Roy, Jr., had begun to have some health problems that seemed to affect his work. Many now feel that leaving the presidency of the company has prolonged the life of Roy, Jr. Doubtlessly, some sibling rivalry was also involved in what could have been a volatile upset in management. To the credit of Roy, Jr., and his immediate family, any rift that may have occurred initially has seemingly healed with time and with the continued success of the company.

After leaving the presidency, Roy O. Martin, Jr., did not work for the company again. However, like Norman after his departure, he maintained his stock in the company and continued to serve on its board of directors. He still is an emeritus member of the board. During his tenure as president of Roy O. Martin

CHAPTER 4 – FUNCTION

Lumber Company, the net worth of the company had doubled by the time of the reorganization in 1973, which was five years before Roy, Jr., retired.

On September 26, 1978, Ellis Martin became the third president of the Roy O. Martin Lumber Company.

Ellis Spencer Martin

SALE OF THE SAWMILL

Perhaps most significantly in the year that company leadership changed – 1978 – the company sold its Fenner Street sawmill, the mill where it had all begun.

The Alexandria sawmill had been a source of concern for some years. Its physical space was inefficient and limiting, making improvements to the mill difficult, if not impossible. Significantly, the mill was not located near the source of company hardwoods. Freight rates to move logs to the mill from outlying locations were increasing. Adding to this mix of inefficiency, both hardwoods and softwoods (though to a lesser degree) were cut at the mill. Basically, the mill was old and outdated, needing massive remodeling and improvements.

To dismantle the mill and rebuild it at another site seemed to be one solution to the problem. No longer cutting both pine and hardwoods at the same sawmill also was a possibility. Ellis facetiously remarked that what they needed was a good fire. Louisiana-Pacific Corporation (LP) provided another, this time viable, alternative.

LIFE BY THE BOARD FOOT

Louisiana-Pacific wanted to expand its lumber-manufacturing operations. As a result, opportunity once again knocked at the Martin's office door. When representatives from LP approached Ellis about selling their Alexandria mill to LP's larger corporation, he knew he had found a happy solution for correcting growing problems at the Fenner Street complex. That facility, which had provided a solid foundation for the Roy O. Martin Lumber Company, no longer fit the corporation's evolving business plan. Once again, Martins would be able to take their profits and get out of what had become a deteriorating operation.

In July 1978, Roy O. Martin Lumber Company sold to Louisiana-Pacific its original mill on Fenner Street, its Applewhite mill, and adjoining property that had been acquired over the years (except for Martin's office complex on Mill Street). For tax purposes, rather than taking money in exchange for property, the Martin Company accepted common stock in LP. For a necessary period, this stock was restricted. When those restrictions were lifted and they were free to sell that stock, the Martin Company began liquidating their holdings in LP. These stock sales continued for several years until the Martin Company had divested itself of all LP stock in 1989.

MARTCO OSB

Roy O. Martin Lumber Company, Martin Timber Company, and Martin Home Centers (MHC) formed Martco Partnership in 1981. The design for Martco's oriented strand board (OSB) plant at LeMoyen, south of Bunkie, began that same year—an exciting year that would herald tremendous change for the company. Not only would an OSB plant significantly increase employment, it would also manufacture a new product that would yield greater prosperity for its stockholders.

Ellis said that he had looked fifteen years for a way to utilize inferior quality wood and waste wood from their sawmill operations. Thinking he might have solved the dilemma, he had even negotiated with American Forest Products to produce a medium-density fiberboard. However, that effort had failed when Georgia-Pacific bought American Forest Products. Georgia-Pacific showed no interest in continuing those earlier negotiations. Through researching solutions other companies had implemented to solve similar waste-wood problems, Ellis finally found

CHAPTER 4 – FUNCTION

what he was looking for. To implement his plan, however, required two essentials: significant capital and someone to channel that capital into this totally new, totally exciting, and highly ambitious operation.

The fortuitous sale of their Fenner Street mill would provide the significant capital needed. Not only had the sale made Roy O. Martin Lumber Company a significant shareholder in Louisiana-Pacific, it had also given Ellis a seat on the LP board of directors. So that Ellis could make these annual meetings, LP would send a Learjet to Alexandria to transport him to designated meeting places. While at a board meeting in Hayward, Wisconsin, Ellis capitalized on an opportunity to see how LP had dealt with their waste-wood problem. Literally minutes before his departure back to Louisiana, he quickly toured LP's oriented strand board plant, the first of its kind in the United States. There, for the first time, he saw a waferboard, or OSB, panel.

Upon touring the plant, Ellis intuitively knew that this was the product he had been trying to find. This was the product that would make his company more efficient—and significantly more profitable. Hardwood, pulpwood, or pine could be used to make waferboard. The species did not matter. The size of the log did not matter. Upon his return to Alexandria, Ellis was eager to implement his plan. Telling Johnny, who was still in Castor, that his generation would be the one to build and operate such a major investment, he advised this younger son to call his engineering skills into play and make a quick study of the waferboard process. He then sent Johnny on a three-week, whirlwind trip to get a fast course in this exciting new process. Johnny first went to Canada to learn about OSB operations there, to Yugoslavia to view a mill built by a German company, and on to Germany to meet with machine manufacturers.[7]

Johnny would later recall that Ellis had told him to "build a plant that would use the millions of under-utilized small-diameter hardwoods growing in our forests. That is how OSB came to be at Martin. It was a 'new beginning bound by an old tradition.'"[8] And what a beginning it would be. According to Ellis, their OSB venture was a success from the start. Once again, the extraordinary Martin drive (coupled with hard work) and vision (coupled with expertise and more hard work) would yield desired results.

The LP stock the Martins owned had been restricted stock. By this time, the two-year restrictions were lifted. Martin could—and did—sell their LP stock, providing significant capital needed to build the OSB plant. Johnny supervised its planning and construction.

The OSB plant of Martco Partnership (Martco) is located in LeMoyen, Louisiana, on land purchased from Turner Lumber Company. Prior to 1981, Turner Company had cut out and shut down its small mill. John

LIFE BY THE BOARD FOOT

Munsterman found the land and Ellis negotiated the deal for this strategic site, situated near the center of Roy O. Martin hardwood lands. This site seemed made for Martin's OSB venture. Critical for shipping bundles of OSB product, a railroad spur is located on its 220 acres. This complex would soon become the core of Martin's manufacturing operation. It is centrally located 140 miles northwest of New Orleans, near Interstate 49 and close to key ports in the Gulf of Mexico, specifically New Orleans and Mobile.

Construction for the plant began in July 1981; production began in July 1983. Jerry Buckner was the first employee hired by Martco Partnership and would be general manager of the OSB plant until he became a company vice-president.

Johnny Martin with Jerry Buckner (center) and Jim Smilie
(LeMoyen OSB plant 1983)

This first OSB plant to be built in the southern United States marked a pivotal point in the development of the Martin Company. The number of people employed by Martins would increase considerably, essentially doubling within two years. By the very nature of its operation, management assumed a new character. The OSB plant necessarily had to be a managerial operation rather than an entrepreneurial operation. No longer could Martins directly manage it from their corporate office, fifty miles north. It called for more specialized management on site. And Jerry Buckner would be that specialist on site at LeMoyen.

CHAPTER 4 – FUNCTION

Building OSB Press Pit
March 1982

Installing Massive OSB
Press from Sweden
September 1982

LIFE BY THE BOARD FOOT

The Martins made national news in building their OSB plant. An article published in the January 3, 1983, issue of Time magazine heralds their company as one of the first firms in Louisiana to qualify for enterprise zone status under Louisiana's Enterprise Zone Act of 1981.

CHAPTER 4 – FUNCTION

Building the new Martco plant in Louisiana

Creating Jobs

States launch enterprise zones

The biggest thing in LeMoyen, La., used to be Baker's Stop and Shop, the general store that serves as a landmark along Route 71 for this impoverished rural community. With unemployment in St. Landry Parish at 15.3%, the job seekers among LeMoyen's few hundred residents have been lucky to find occasional farm work in the nearby soybean and rice fields. Now a huge $25 million plant is rising in an empty meadow across the road from Baker's. When it opens next April, the Martco plant will churn scraps from southern hardwoods into 130 million sq. ft. of building board per year, providing up to 150 jobs. "We've got about 200 names on file already," says Jonathan Martin, who is supervising construction of the plant. "We must get two or three people in here every day asking when we're going to start hiring."

Martco is one of the first firms to qualify for state assistance under the Louisiana Enterprise Zone Act of 1981, a package of tax-relief measures designed to lure investment to depressed rural and urban areas. Martco and the seven other companies approved so far are expected to generate some 1,200 jobs in exchange for $4 million in state tax breaks over the next five years. Says Governor David Treen: "We think the returns far outstrip what we give up in revenues." Indeed, while Congress has been sitting on President Reagan's federal enterprise zone proposal, made last March, a dozen* states are forging ahead with their own versions.

In some cases, notably in Toledo,

*In addition to Louisiana, they include Connecticut, Florida, Illinois, Kansas, Kentucky, Maryland, Minnesota, Missouri, Ohio, Rhode Island and Virginia.

the state legislation is giving an extra push to experiments that were already successfully under way. City Venture Corp., founded three years ago by Control Data Corp. and other companies in cooperation with the American Lutheran Church and the United Church of Christ, is helping to revive Toledo's rundown Warren-Sherman district, where unemployment is higher than 30%.

The project's centerpiece is an $8 million commercial complex that has acted as a small business incubator for the neighborhood. Companies renting space there were given managerial and technical advice. Area residents, many of whom had never held a full-time job, got free training in the skills they needed and day-care help for working mothers. Additional incentives for new businesses were provided by parking, security and low-cost clerical services for some firms.

As a result, Warren-Sherman is beginning to hum. Twenty companies, doing everything from carpet installation to computer-parts assembly, have set up shop in the district. Some 500 new jobs have been created so far, and 1,500 more are projected by 1987. In October, Ohio designated Warren-Sherman as its first enterprise zone. That promises to reduce state and local taxes for some firms. The next step is a 23-acre industrial park, where Owens-Illinois is now building a plant that will make corrugated boxes.

Some states are creating service jobs by attracting high-tech firms to dilapidated areas. In New Haven, an 80-acre science park is being built near Yale University as part of a larger enterprise zone. A nonprofit, joint effort by Yale, the Olin Corp. and the city, this park offers new companies special access to the university's research and teaching facilities, as well as generous tax abatements. More than a dozen companies have expressed an interest in moving in. Park officials are now busy helping the maintenance, security, restaurant and other support businesses in the zone gear up for their new customers. They expect this district to blossom with up to 300 nonprofessional jobs in the next year, 1,000 by 1988.

In states with no enterprise-zone legislation, some cities are devising their own zones. San Jose, Calif., for instance, has waived taxes and fees that can amount to 4.7% of building costs in order to spur new business and residential construction in a 5-sq.-mi. "central incentive zone" downtown. One result: the Sainte Claire Hilton, product of a $6.5 million renovation, which employs 150 people.

Critics fear that instead of creating new jobs, these zones will simply draw business away from other areas. But in some instances they have attracted companies that could not otherwise have afforded to expand. More important, many workers finding jobs in enterprise zones were formerly dependent on public assistance. Sums up City Venture President George Bardos: "The basic goal is to address unemployment where it is worst." ■

LIFE BY THE BOARD FOOT

Louisiana's willingness to pass its Enterprise Zone Act and Martin's expeditious request to qualify for, and subsequently receive, status under that act did more than provide national notoriety for both the state and the local company. Their joint effort has proved the kind of success President Reagan envisioned when he first proposed federal enterprise zones in March 1982: permanent jobs were created, significantly improving a previously depressed rural area. Of that, Martin takes great pride. And when that first load of logs rolled into the Martco plant, both employer and employees realized their company had entered a new and exciting era of manufacturing.

First load of logs entering Martco OSB plant

Of the facility itself, Martin can also boast that their plant was the first to use Southern hardwoods to manufacture OSB. Some industry naysayers might have initially discounted the untried Martin formula as one doomed to failure. Others certainly questioned their investment. However, Martin would soon prove them wrong with their successful blending of Southern hardwood and softwood wafers into an exceptionally strong and consistent OSB panel. The OSB process takes lower-quality fiber and converts it into structural 4'x8' panels. Incoming logs are heat conditioned, waferized (cut into "wafers" or strands), dried, screened and pressed together, using phenolic resin binders. The heart of the plant is the Dieffenbacher-Schenck forming line and press, where

CHAPTER 4 – FUNCTION

. . . thousands of micro-thin, treated wafers . . . bind together like layers of blankets to become the ultimate OSB. The outer top and bottom, or face layers, are oriented [turned] in the eight-foot direction. The two middle, or core, layers are oriented [turned] in the four-foot direction. Each mat, as it is known, is composed of four layers of strands: top, middle, middle, bottom. This engineering method produces exceptional strength in each panel.

Each mat lies on an oversized 8'x16' screen caul, which produces Martco's superior rough screen-back, non-skid surface when the mat is pressed. After each mat is cut to length and separated by a trim saw, it is loaded into a press pre-loader with fifteen others. Immediately after each press cycle is completed, another set of mats is ready for loading, which allows the forming line to continually operate.

The press is kept at a constant 385-degree temperature. This compression machine uses sixteen million pounds of force to consolidate each mat into an oversized 8'x16' panel. In just over [three] minutes, one press cycle makes more than two thousand square feet of the finest, strongest panels in America. In a year's time that is more than [three hundred fifty] million square feet of OSB, . . . all created with consistent quality control and maintained through the entire process."[9]

OSB Log Yard and Forming Line

OSB Warehouse

131

LIFE BY THE BOARD FOOT

Marketed as TUFF- STRAND®, and available in The GRID®, Martco's OSB panels are used primarily for roof decks and wall sheathing, as well as in utility applications from flooring to shelving.

MARTCO SAWMILL

Construction for a Martco sawmill adjacent to the OSB plant at LeMoyen began in 1983. Actually, plans for a hardwood sawmill at the LeMoyen site had been discussed as early as 1980. However, work on the sawmill was pushed aside when Ellis discovered the wafer process, allowing building of the more-innovative OSB plant to progress quickly.

After a year of construction, Martco sawmill produced its first board in 1984.

This state-of-the-art sawmill utilizes a rich variety of high-quality Louisiana hardwoods. Like all other Martin manufacturing centers, its foresters employ systematic research, planting, thinning and harvesting techniques to ensure a constant, undiminished supply of quality timber while replenishing nature with more than was cut for manufacturing. Martco mills red oak, sap gum, elm, pecan, white oak, cottonwood, sycamore, locust, willow, cypress, and the finest white cabinet ash in America. They were also the first hardwood company to harvest and market large volumes of **SHUGA** BERRY®, Martco's trademarked name for sugar hackberry. This gorgeous wood is exceptional with its uniform white color and beautiful grain.

Hardwoods are brought from Martin's towering forests to Martco's double-band mill, which is a computerized engineering masterpiece among lumber mills. It operates by a carefully designed sequence and interaction among milling, drying, kiln-drying and grading, all steps controlled and monitored with advanced technology. [10]

This Martco facility was the first Southern hardwood mill to install slanted bandmills and computerized carriages and also the first to employ scanning and optimization technology to efficiently process hardwood lumber. The mill currently produces fifty million board feet annually.

CHAPTER 4 – FUNCTION

Martco Sawmill
Right: planer mill
Below: carriage band mill
Bottom right: lumber ready to ship

LIFE BY THE BOARD FOOT

A trade magazine article in 2000 concluded that "the Martco mill may be one of the top two or three most technologically advanced mills in the country. The company does not invest in technology for the sake of technology, however. The technology is used to achieve goals to maximize yield from a limited resource, provide a stable job climate for employees, and supply customers with products that are manufactured to the highest standards of the forest products industry."[11]

While high-tech equipment allows Martin to optimize its processes, more importantly, it allows them to produce more lumber than ever-before possible. This means fewer trees will have to be cut from their forests, leaving more for the future. Thus, through their Martco sawmill, current Martin leadership continues the corporate policies of their founder: "Good forestry practices, sophisticated business and production procedures, and a commitment to economic good health perpetuate a reliable and respected family business."[12]

LeMoyen OSB and Sawmill Complex

CHAPTER 4 – FUNCTION

MARTCO PLYWOOD

The third facility of the trio comprising Martco Partnership is Martco's plywood plant at Chopin, Louisiana. This property, which is located twenty-seven miles south of Natchitoches on the Union Pacific Railroad track near Interstate 49, is adjacent to the Red River Waterway. According to Roy O. Martin III (Roy III), the site is at the epicenter of the company's pine timberland in the Flatwoods area. Also, like the location of its sister facility Martco OSB a decade earlier, the plywood-plant site is in an "economic enterprise zone," which entitled Martco to a ten-year property tax exemption. To qualify for enterprise-zone status, a business must guarantee that at least thirty-five percent of its jobs will go to people who live within the area of the approved zone. Although these economic enterprise zones are created by the State of Louisiana, at that time they had to be approved by police juries in the local parishes, in this case the Natchitoches Parish Police Jury.[13] Before Martins could begin construction of their plywood plant, they had to fulfill all state-mandated requirements and convince the parish's political machinery that their proposed plywood plant would provide much-needed jobs to the locally depressed economy, jobs that would more than offset the waived property taxes.

From inception to production, this plant has set records for even the fast-paced Martins. Martco acquired the site for building in April 1994. By then, engineering/designing for the plant had already begun. Construction at the site began in August 1994. The plant produced its first pressload of plywood on March 8, 1996. Employment of three hundred was predicted at the time of the plant's announcement. Two years later, the plant employed four hundred twenty-eight people and operated twenty-four hours a day, seven days a week. Sixty percent of all new hires at the plant were from low- to moderate-income groups whose income immediately increased more than sixty percent by working at Martco Plywood. Tax-wise, this was a win-win-win venture for Martin, Natchitoches Parish and the State of Louisiana. Through provisions within an economic enterprise zone, Martin may temporarily have paid no property tax, but, in only eight short months, its payroll allowed both the parish and state governments to recoup that exempted amount through sales, payroll, severance and franchise taxes.

LIFE BY THE BOARD FOOT

Martco Plywood
Chopin, Louisiana

This state-of-the-art manufacturing facility uses yellow pine timber for its plywood. More importantly, and the reason for its existence, the plant provides the company with a ready market for its vast pine forests. Fifty percent of the pine timber used at Chopin comes from company land, but timber is also bought from contractors and cut from leased land. The plant uses ninety million board feet of pine timber annually and produces flooring, siding, sheathing, sanded panels, concrete form, and industrial-grade plywood. Industrial uses include parts for upholstered furniture, liners for truck trailers, and frames for bay windows. Since it is near historic Cane River, the plant is a zero-discharge facility, which means it creates no environmental problems. When it was constructed, the Martco Plywood plant was the first new plywood plant built in the South in fourteen years.

Martco's trademark name for its plywood is SmartCore®, which is marketed throughout the United States, especially in areas of the country east of the Rocky Mountains. Martco Plywood produced its first one billion square feet of plywood on March 17, 2000, barely four years from its startup.[14]

CHAPTER 4 – FUNCTION

Lathe

Plugging

Plywood

LIFE BY THE BOARD FOOT

MHC

In 1988 Martin Home Centers was changed to MHC Properties, Inc.

Real estate, obviously, is a very important part of the Martin business. By 2004 the company owned nearly six hundred thousand acres of timberland. But timberland is not the only type of real estate involved. At first, property

CHAPTER 4 – FUNCTION

around the Alexandria mill was developed to provide housing for employees. An area was developed; houses were built with lumber from the original sawmill; those houses were then sold to employees and financed by the company. This development was known as the Roy O. Martin Subdivision.

With growth of Martin's retail lumberyards, subdivision development began in numerous areas near company-owned lumberyards. Management pursued significant subdivision development in these areas. Lots were sold to contractors who bought their materials from the lumberyards. In some cases, Martin lumberyards also had construction teams that built and sold houses. The slogan of "From Tree to Key" was accurate. Martin Park in Alexandria, Martin Park in Natchitoches, and Martin Park in Lafayette are examples of subdivisions developed by the Martins.

Until December 2003 when it was merged into Roy O. Martin Lumber Company, MHC Properties handled both commercial and residential properties throughout Louisiana. The fifteen-year impact of MHC Properties is certainly notable. Business Park in Alexandria on which the ROMEX World Trade Center is located in one of its commercial developments. Several Central Louisiana subdivisions developed by MHC Properties are still thriving: Cooley Crossing near Alexandria Golf and Country Club, Oak Shadows near Kincaid Lake at Alexandria and Fox Chase and Forest Park, both in Pineville. Acadiana Place, The Glade, Hunter's Ridge and Brunswick are all Lafayette subdivisions. Jennings also has a Martin Park.

The Martins not only buy land to increase their timber holdings, but they also sell land. When Roy O. first sold houses to employees near the Alexandria mill, his purpose was to encourage home ownership. Ellis had that same purpose in mind when he built and sold houses to mill employees at Castor. Encouragement of home ownership of a different type is still pursued through the retail sale of properties in company-developed subdivisions.

ROMEX World Trade Company

Continuing to expand its markets, the Martin group created its ROMEX World Trade Company, L. L. C., in January 2000. Martin board members established ROMEX World Trade as the sales and marketing agent for Roy O. Martin Lumber Company and Martco Partnership. Sales groups for hardwood lumber, oriented strand board (OSB), softwood plywood, and residual products (chips, peeler cores, landscape timbers, 2"x2" stickers, and fuel) were consolidated. The traffic group and administrative support also became a part of this new company.

LIFE BY THE BOARD FOOT

ROMEX is responsible for sales and marketing of all company products. It also operates an import/export company, allowing Martin to bring products from Asia, Latin America, and Europe to Martin customers and to North American markets. Also, it enables ROMEX to export non-company products as well as company-manufactured products to other markets throughout the world.[15]

This fairly recent formation of ROMEX did not indicate that the company was just beginning to export lumber. To the contrary, lumber for export had been sold almost from the beginning. As early as 1928 Roy O. made a lumber sales trip to Mexico. And in 1959, Roy O. Martin Lumber Company shipped about 250,000 board feet (250 mbf) of lumber to Cuba. Interestingly, this was the last American-produced lumber shipped to Cuba before the United States severed free-market trade agreements with Fidel Castro.[16]

Headquartered in one office building since October 31, 2001, all Martin companies now function efficiently in a modern building, their ROMEX World Trade Center. Composed of two wings with an open courtyard separating the two, the west wing houses the executive, forestry and land, and construction management departments on the second floor. Human resources, training facilities, break room, and computer department are all on the first floor. The east wing houses accounting and storage upstairs with sales, library, and boardroom downstairs. With this new office structure, sales and accounting work for all the Martin facilities are finally centralized under one roof.[17]

ROMEX World Trade Center

CHAPTER 4 – FUNCTION

CRITICAL REORGANIZATIONS

Martin Companies have undergone three major reorganizations during their lifetime of eighty-plus years.

The first reorganization occurred in 1973 as a result of estate planning, first for Roy O. and then for the five second-generation Martin children. Ownership of all operating companies was put into five personal family holding companies: Howard Associates, Inc.; Ellis Investments, Inc.; Arbor, Inc.; Southwood Development Company, Inc.; and Somerset, Ltd. Initially, the company planned to go public under the name of Roy O. Martin Industries, Inc. For various reasons, the stock offering was never made even though a prospectus had already been printed. The reorganized, still closely held, company became Roy O. Martin Industries, Inc.

The second major reorganization occurred on January 1, 2000. Because federal tax laws had changed, some benefits from the 1973 reorganization had diminished. Additionally, in late 1990 the State of Louisiana provided franchise-tax relief to entities organized as limited liability companies (LLC). Significantly for Martin's privately held company, LLC status also provided owners a shield from tort and creditor liability while giving operating officers more flexibility than that afforded to corporations. Working with Pete Marwick of KPMG, Roy III restructured Martin companies into these limited-liability formats to take advantage of newly available tax breaks:

- Roy O. Martin Lumber Company, Inc., was liquidated after transferring tax-free all its assets to Roy O. Martin Lumber Company, Limited Partnership, which is controlled by Roy O. Martin Lumber Company, L. L. C. This company is owned and controlled by ROML, L. L. C.

- MHC Properties, Inc., was liquidated after transferring tax-free all of its assets to MHC Properties, L. L. C., which is owned and controlled by MHC Holding Company, L. L. C.

- Martin Timber Company, Inc., was liquidated after transferring tax-free all its assets to Martin Timber Company, L. L. C., owned and controlled by MTC Holding Company, L. L. C.

- ROMEX World Trade Company, L. L. C., was formed.

- Martco Partnership was composed of the Roy O. Martin Lumber Company, L. L. C., Martin Timber Company, L. L. C., and MHC Properties, L. L. C.

In an email explaining this complex reorganization, Roy III writes in third person:

> Shareholders saw no difference in ownership but enjoyed the tax savings that the new, more complicated structure provided. This very expensive transaction was completed on December 29, 1999, around 11 p.m. Central Standard Time. Ellis Martin always said that Roy O. Martin III would be the end of Roy O. Martin Lumber Company, Inc.

LIFE BY THE BOARD FOOT

> He was right. After 77 years of operation, Roy O. Martin Lumber Company, Inc., liquidated. When the news was printed in the Alexandria legal recorder, many panicked vendors called the office thinking we had just declared bankruptcy. Roy III had fun with a few of them, but finally explained this was merely a re-organization and our notable Dunn and Bradstreet 5A1 rating was still good. This was just a new company for the new millennium. The cost of this transaction was large but the investment was recovered in three months and secured perpetual tax savings for the future.
>
> Jonathan Martin joked that Roy III created a new company every week. As usual, he exaggerated. New companies were created [in 1999] at a mere one per month. None of this could have been accomplished without a connected and cooperative family dedicated to preserving the Company for all time.[18]

Maybe Johnny was not joking, after all. Obviously, Roy III was not finished restructuring the Martin organization. His next intricate plan would dissolve several existing companies, create other new companies and even reunite some that had previously been separated.

This latest and third major reorganization of Roy O. Martin Lumber Company occurred December 31, 2003, in what Roy III calls the "Mother of all Mergers." Even for him, this was a corporate coup, made possible in part from the stock market and OSB market both rebounding from "three years of malaise." Because Martin's

> corporate structure looked like a city map of Houston, management decided to finally simplify [it]. In addition, the election of Subchapter S tax status for the five personal holding companies provided another opportunity. In 2003, the three companies comprising the Roy O. Martin Lumber Company, and the two companies comprising MHC properties were merged to form one company. The two pieces of Martin Timber Company were reunited through another merger. All preferred stock of the companies was redeemed or converted to common stock. This simplified the corporate structure tremendously. In addition, individuals who owned ROM stock individually formed a new company: Martin Companies, LLC ROM. The personal holding companies were merged with the new company to form one family holding company that can be taxed as a Subchapter S corporation. This new company has 72 shareholders. And, because the Bush tax plan reduced long-term capital gains rates to 15%, shareholders can enjoy lower total taxation of Company earnings. Each entity, Martco, Martin Timber Company, Roy O. Martin Lumber Company, and Martin Companies can file one tax return.[19]

One particular word reverberates in the text of each Martin restructuring plan: "tax." Securing legal tax savings at various levels, corporate and personal, has prompted each of the company's three major reorganizations: 1973, 1999 and 2003. Martins expect to pay their fair share to subsidize both state and federal governments. After all, they pride themselves on being good corporate and individual citizens in their communities. However, monies being taxed three, sometimes four times, before reaching stockholders does not make good business sense in a capitalist economy. In fact, redundant taxation often forces companies to cease operations when they can no longer justify their existence. Determined that his company would not be one of those statistics, now or in the future, Roy III simply took advantage of changing tax laws and a growing economy to implement a complex plan that will benefit both company and stockholders.

CHAPTER 4 – FUNCTION

Intelligence, focus, vision, frugality—those traits that defined the character of Roy O. Martin, Sr., and then shaped the corporate culture of his organization—are alive and well in today's Martin Companies. Those genetic traits may have even mutated to a more excellent power. However, no family member would discount the talent, dedication and commitment of their founder.

Indisputably, the foundation of all Martin family business success was that original Roy O. Martin Lumber Company and its groundhog sawmill on Fenner Street in Alexandria. However, the function of the company has gone far beyond that as it continually renews its entrepreneurial spirit, forming additional companies and creating new enterprises. By the end of the twentieth century and more than eighty years of business life, successors to Roy O. Martin have participated in more businesses than one even as visionary as Roy O. could possibly have imagined when he stumbled upon that decrepit little mill in Alexandria, Louisiana, in 1923. Growing and expanding the vision of their founder, Martins continue to operate from the fundamentals Roy O. taught his sons (Ellis, Roy, Jr., and Norman) who taught their sons (Johnny and Roy III) who are now guiding the next, that is the fourth, generation toward continued success in the lumber business—having become an indisputable leader in their industry.

Life By the Board Foot: 5

Fundamentals

. . . we will go to this or that city . . . carry on business and make money . . . (James 4:13, NIV).

"From shirtsleeves to shirtsleeves in three generations" is a business aphorism. It may be true that in many, if not most, family businesses, the founder begins in humble circumstances and achieves substantial wealth, but, by the third generation, the business has deteriorated to the point that its principals are again in dire straits. This aphorism, however, is not true for the Roy O. Martin family.

The Martin Companies in 2004 are in the third generation of family leadership. Roy O. was the first president of the Roy O. Martin Lumber Company. He was followed by Roy, Jr., then by Ellis who became chairman of the board of directors on April 4, 1994. At that date Jonathan E. Martin, Ellis' son became president and CEO. In December 2004, he became chairman and CEO serving alongside Roy O. Martin III who is currently company president and CFO. Not only is the business still prospering, it is expanding. And it is still family owned.

LIFE BY THE BOARD FOOT

What explains this success of the Martin family companies? Do Martins follow certain fundamentals in their business life that ensure progress? Indeed, they do. That business philosophy and those professional principles have been rather consistent throughout their history as a company. These specific fundamentals serve to explain their success and their continued progress.

THE FAMILY BUSINESS SYNDROME

Fewer than one in three family concerns survive into a second generation; fewer than one in ten make it to the third generation asserts Paul Karofsky, executive director of Northeastern University's Center for Family Business.[1] That the Martin Companies have moved into this third generation puts them in a minority situation, but it also is a testimony of their family and business solidarity.

Some emerging problems of a family business are obvious. Succeeding family members may not have the same interests as their founding members. Others may not be willing to work as hard as their founders. Founders or older, more experienced, family members in the business may have trouble letting go of their grip or may fear losing their authority. Differences in vision for what their business can do or for what it can become often create major problems. One writer observed, "Lots of family companies struggle just to succeed. The struggle places tons of pressure on the family unit, within which there's always plenty of emotional inventory anyway. But growth is a huge problem, too, and managing it presents family firms with rosier but no less complex issues."[2] Naturally, the problem of succession in leadership is a major problem: who will succeed whom in business leadership? Add to that the problem of legal succession at the death of the founder. Without proper estate planning, the entire business could be lost to taxes and estate succession.

David Bork, family-business consultant, developed ten keys to success in family business. He identifies them as

- shared values,
- shared power,
- traditions,
- willingness to learn and grow,
- activities to maintain their relationships,

CHAPTER 5 - FUNDAMENTALS

- genuine caring,
- mutual respect,
- assisting and supporting one another,
- privacy, and
- well-defined interpersonal boundaries.[3]

According to Bork, successors of a family-owned company must embrace and exercise these operating precepts if they hope to exist.

The Martins have successfully utilized most of these keys. Not only does Martin leadership today share **similar values**, they specify them in their vision statement: Respect, Integrity, Commitment, Honesty, Excellence and Stewardship. Forming the acronym RICHES, these values have become something of a mantra among Martin's leadership, reminding them of the ways they are to react and respond to daily occurrences in the Martin workplace.

Although it may not have been true for previous generations, the current Martin leadership successfully **shares power**. Johnny as chairman and CEO and Roy III as president and CFO not only share responsibility and recognition with each other, they willingly—and purposefully—delegate responsibility to their managerial team, providing opportunities for growth and advancement within the company. In December 2003, long-time employee Scott Poole, already vice president of land and timber, was named chief operating officer (COO), the first non-Martin to hold this position. Having worked in the company for seventeen years, Scott proved his ability and showed his commitment to the Martin vision. First as forester, then as forest manager, and finally as COO, Scott is one of the current Martin team who will move today's Martin Companies from entrepreneurial to managerial status.

Certainly Martin as a company and Martins as a family have **traditions**. One is represented by the grand piano in the foyer of their ROMEX headquarters. Graciously donated by Virginia Martin Howard, this piano most notably reflects the musical heritage of Mildred while it perpetuates an important Martin tradition. Since music touches the soul and calms the human spirit, this piano in the Martin workplace typifies the contradictions that, in many ways, define this successful company.

Willingness to learn and grow is not just encouraged, it is practiced, almost with a vengeance, by both Johnny and Roy III. Johnny continually searches for ways to work smarter, operate more efficiently, and develop more innovatively. Roy III aggressively stays abreast of (some say ahead of) ways that are more fiscally prudent, hence more financially successful, than yesterday. They also require this willingness to learn and grow from those managers and employees who look to advance within the Martin family of companies.

Both the Martin companies and the Martin family engage in **activities to maintain their relationships**. Annually, each division hosts a family day for its employees and their families. This casual "fun day" provides relationship-building activities for employees and management, away from stress of the workplace. Of course, the primary activity that maintains relationships among the now nearly one hundred Martin family members is their annual shareholder meetings. More than business meetings, these yearly gatherings are family reunions, which, in an important way, remind them of the heritage that is theirs.

Genuine caring seems to be a trait inherent to Martins. Showing beneficence to their community and practicing stewardship in their churches are simply ways of life for most of them, done without prodding or without expecting recognition. Naturally, then, this trait of caring is an intrinsic part of their "taking care of business." One obvious example is their staff of chaplains. These spiritual ambassadors maintain a presence at each facility, providing an arm of personal ministry while daily addressing individual needs of company employees.

Not only do Johnny and Roy III jointly share responsibilities as CEO and president, respectively, they show **mutual respect** for each other. Recognizing the talents of the other and giving each the latitude and authority to use those talents to move the company toward even greater success, they work together as a team. And this energetic, creative, talented Martin duo **assists and supports each other** professionally for the company and personally for the family. All the while, they respect the **privacy** of the other. One does not have to micromanage the affairs of the other, intruding into the other's private domain. Rather, they have succeeded in creating **well-defined interpersonal boundaries**, allowing each to use his business acumen and professional ability to their greatest good for both company and family.

CONTROL

After his experience with the Roy O. Martin Lumber Company of Eunice, Roy O. stated in his autobiography that he did not want to own stock in any company he could not control. That attitude (perhaps in the DNA) has filtered down into the rest of the family. While family members have investment

CHAPTER 5 - FUNDAMENTALS

portfolios that include other stocks, their major investment is in the Martin Companies. And they control those companies.

In April 1944, the board looked into liquidating their company in order to change from a corporation to a partnership. Ellis was appointed liquidator. Reasons for this proposed operational change had to do with federal taxes. The years 1936-1939 provided the base years for figuring excess profit taxes during World War II. Those were not good years for the forest products industry. Taxes were heavy. Timber had become more difficult to procure. During the war years, labor had also been a problem, a big and expensive problem. Searching for a solution to their tax problem, Ellis worked on the liquidation process for six or eight weeks. Then the board called off plans to liquidate. After that abrupt shift in direction, the company received additional tax advice, providing them an alternate solution. Consequently, and fortunately for successors, in July 1944 Ellis resigned as liquidator; the board rescinded its action.

Three decades later, during the 1973 reorganization, the company board again faced a tax problem, this one the growing estate-tax burden facing company shareholders. As a means of solving this problem, the board considered making Roy O. Martin Lumber Company a publicly held corporation. All necessary work had been done on the proposal; the prospectus had even been printed. The stock market, however, took a bad turn downward in 1973, and the step toward public ownership was never taken.[4] Making the company a publicly held business would have increased available cash, but it possibly (and probably) would have taken control of the business from family hands. Keeping the company a privately held business was in line with Roy O's earlier desire: "I preferred to have a company that was wholly owned by family."[5] Attorney Charles S. (Charlie) Weems III of Alexandria's law firm Gold, Weems, Bruser, Sues and Rundell has worked with the Martins since the early 1970s. He stated that in retrospect they made the right decision in not going public.[6] To remain a privately held business was a conscious decision.

While still holding ownership and control, the Martins have also well utilized non-family members in key company positions. Some of these invaluable non-family employees in the Martin companies have long tenures of four decades or so and have risen to major executive positions. Descendents of Roy O. Martin comprise a big family, but only four third-generation Martins work for the company: Johnny, Roy III, Mary Martin Fowler, and Carole Martin Baxter. In 2004 the company employed only three fourth-generation Martins: Spencer Martin, Nicole Robbins Harris, and Natalie Martin Monroe. Ellis said, "I told them [Johnny and Roy III] that . . . they would have to hire people from the outside. [They] have done a good job in hiring good people. They are doing a wonderful job."[7] Consciously employing professional managers, today's family members at the helm of the company are employing non-family members to handle key areas of responsibility. Martins have successfully and profitably found a way to share responsibility between family and non-family members while maintaining control of their business.

FOCUS

As earlier indicated, Roy O. was a focused individual. He concentrated on developing his company and did not give much time or energy to other matters. That trait continues through his descendents. John G. Alley observed that Martin men he knows are focused on business, family, and church.[8] Accountant Paul C. Hood agreed with that evaluation.[9]

This focus on business enables these professional Martin men--and women--to make a distinction between business decisions and personal decisions. No sentimentality is involved. Weems observed that, to the Martins, business is business; they do not let personal feelings get in the way. The decision to sell the Fenner Street mill, even though it was the cornerstone of the family business and had been in the family for more than fifty years at the time of its sale, was a business decision. Ellis declared that the decision to move Roy, Jr., out of the company presidency was strictly a business decision, not personal at all. He said, "When you are a businessman, you have to do what you have to do. . . . I had to do it."[10] Similarly, when Johnny was building the OSB plant at LeMoyen, he told his pastor that he had a budget for the construction of the plant. And if he did not come in under or on the budget, Ellis would fire him. His pastor protested, "Not your own father." Johnny's reply was, "He ought to."[11]

Because they are centered on professional productivity and generally do not mix their business affairs with personal affairs, members of the family have, certainly for the most part, successfully worked together. Norman reported that when Roy O. was no longer able to function in the business, the three second-generation brothers divided professional responsibilities. Ellis was in Castor. Roy, Jr., ran the sawmill in Alexandria. And Norman managed Colfax Creosoting. Norman left the business in 1967. He said that since he was the youngest brother, he thought it was best for him to get out of the company and let

CHAPTER 5 - FUNDAMENTALS

the older brothers operate it.[12] Ultimately thereafter until a new manager was hired, Ellis, as president of the company, necessarily was responsible for Colfax Creosoting.

The present Martin leadership of Johnny and Roy III work well together in tandem. One individual close to the company said it is amazing to him that they work so well together. He noted that they have a line of command and follow it. Weems observed that Johnny and Roy III complement each other.

Johnny and Roy III make a good team, working together for their personal gratification and for the collective benefit of their fellow stockholders. Each respects the talents of the other. Johnny's talents lie in production and management; Roy III's proficiency is in finance. Each knows his limitations; each is aware of the other's strengths. Indeed, each complements the other, both giving the other space and authority to perform his particular expertise.

With their focus on business, Martins are able to set goals and then methodically reach them. Paul Hood summarized the secret of their success as setting specific goals then working hard and tirelessly to achieve those goals. Succeeding Martin leadership seemingly have understood and grasped the vision of their founder; so far, each generation has worked to make the vision of their father and grandfather their current reality. Weems stated that Roy O. was brilliant in overall strategy. Hood quoted one of the original partners in his accounting firm who advised him never to underestimate Roy O. His opinion was that, until his incapacitation, Roy O. knew exactly what he was doing all the time. Weems also added that in leadership Ellis had a clear vision that allowed him not to get bound up in details. Ellis' explanation of that was, "Find out what the needs are. Then address them."

This seemingly innate focus of most Martins subsequently led to hard work. Indeed, they are hard workers. Keith Peterson, long-time insurance agent for the Martins, said of Roy O., "He just worked. That's all he ever did: work. He worked eighteen hours every day." Later in the interview he added, "He was busy all the time. He didn't spend time trying to get into social life. He was more interested in building the business than in socializing."[13] That work ethic has been passed on to the successors in the Martin Companies. Martins work hard, and they expect those who work with them to work hard as well. When employees perform according to the Martin standard, they are then well rewarded.

LIFE BY THE BOARD FOOT

LAND

Accountant Paul Hood spoke of the "all-powerful land." He explained the expression by saying, "I see the land as the basic foundation of the whole business. Land, rather than the Alexandria sawmill, is the foundation for their success."[14] Ellis also identified their decision to purchase land to secure a solid, perpetual timber base as one of the significant keys to the company's comfortable fiscal status today.

Martins consciously and aggressively began acquiring land after World War II. They realized that a consistent supply of timber was necessary for their business to become a permanent operation. To procure timber methodically and regularly, however, they needed an employee whose job description specifically included that purpose. John Munsterman was that employee. Joining the company in 1945, he was Martin's first degreed forester. And purchasing land was one of his responsibilities. It quickly became his major responsibility. A year after he was hired, in 1946, the board of directors authorized their foresters to invest $500,000 in timberlands. As rapidly as they could, these timber scouts were to buy land at reasonable prices. Several years later, at the 1949 board meeting, Ellis pointed out some serious competition the company faced from paper mills that were buying timberland and barren land for prices in excess of what their sawmills were paying for land. Available land had become harder to find. Prices had quickly escalated. However, as a result of their commitment to preserve their future, they agreed to go in debt if necessary to acquire more land. Ellis observed that if there is no timber, there is no business. He said that during World War II, at least twenty-five sawmills had operated within thirty miles of the Castor mill. By the end of the 1940s, timber was being wiped out in all directions. He told his father they had to get land. That is when they aggressively began buying timberland.

In those earlier days of land acquisition, Munsterman primarily worked with hardwoods from Alexandria south. About ten years after Munsterman was hired, D. B. Sanders came to work with the company. This new forester principally worked north of Alexandria with pine timberland. At times, of course, pinelands would lie south of Alexandria and hardwoods could be found to the north. They then would each work in the other's territory. At other times, they would work together on bigger projects.

So the Martins began aggressively to locate and purchase land. At times purchases would be in twenty- or forty-acre pieces. At other times, tracts would be thousands of acres. The largest single land purchase, to date, is seventy thousand acres the company bought from Texaco Oil Company in 1989.

CHAPTER 5 - FUNDAMENTALS

Purchased from VanPly, a plywood company that was a wholly owned subsidiary of Texaco, this "Texaco land" (as it is known in company circles) had been previously a part of Hillyer-Deutsch-Edwards Lumber Company near Oakdale, Louisiana. By 2004 the Martin Companies owned about six hundred thousand acres of land in twenty-eight Louisiana parishes, with almost one hundred thousand acres being purchased from Louisiana-Pacific in two separate negotiations in 2002 and 2003.

Buying land on the open market, usually by competitive bids, they have methodically acquired significant land because they were willing to pay for it. Consequently, Martin has become not just "a player" but "the key player" in Louisiana's lumber industry in terms of manufacturing and acreage owned. "Just as with the board-foot-by-board foot, acres-by-acres do add up." [15]

Raccourci Island in the Mississippi River is an interesting tract within the Martins timberland base. This island is about eleven thousand acres in size. Of this total acreage, Martins control nine thousand eight hundred fifty-five acres, actually owning seven thousand two hundred acres. Martins bought their first tract on this island in 1956. Like most of their land purchases, this region of timber was bought in smaller parcels, often forty or eighty acres at a time. The remainder is on a ninety-nine-year lease begun in 1951. Logs cut from this site are carried off the island over a wing levee that connects the island to the mainland.

Not only do the Martins buy land, they also effectively manage their land. In that all-important 1948 annual meeting, their board of directors made a conscious decision not only to purchase more acreage but also to aggressively manage their timberland. Due to a unanimous desire to make their operation permanent, they began selective cutting of their timber. Defective and crooked trees were toppled and discarded. Heavy stands of pine were thinned by cutting pulpwood. Their forestry team practiced timber stand improvement (TSI) by removing undesirable trees and shrubs from the property. And they bought every piece of property they could find and finance. Roy O. once estimated that it took one hundred thousand acres of land to give enough growth to supply the mill for a fifty-five-hour workweek. Owning the land on which the timber is produced and properly managing that land ensures the company of a continual supply of timber. Therefore, it could stay in business for the foreseeable future.

Norman asserted that they were one of the first in Louisiana to practice timber stand improvement. When introduced to TSI, board members and forestry personnel immediately saw its potential and quickly began implementing--and improving--existing TSI techniques. Using a technique of girdling invasive trees

LIFE BY THE BOARD FOOT

they had learned from an experiment station in Crossett, Arkansas, a crew worked on improving all stands of marketable timber on company land.[16] Today, intensive site preparation, chemical control of exotic and invasive plants, site fertilization, controlled burning and intermediate stand thinnings are other techniques Martin uses in improving their timber stands. One of the most critical Best Management Practices (BMPs) as developed by the Louisiana Forestry Association, and practiced by Martin, is the protection of Streamside Management Zones (SMZs). SMZs are areas adjacent to bodies of waters. They include

CHAPTER 5 - FUNDAMENTALS

streams, lakes, rivers, bayous, and canals. The soil type, slope, vegetative cover, and stream character of each body of water determines the width of a zone. A substantial portion of timber within these zones is not cut. Replicating those sheltering canopies provided by great virgin forests of a previous century, the resulting cover produces shade, maintains water temperature, reduces sediment deposition, and protects wildlife habitat. Martin voluntarily implements SMZs to help improve water quality while improving the overall natural environment.[17] Certainly, since 1985 the company has become more aggressive in land management of this type.[18]

Reforestation is an integral part of land management. It takes the wood from a one-hundred-foot tree (about .75 cords) to keep the average American supplied for a year with newspapers, books, magazines, tissue paper, housing, furniture, desks, fences, grocery bags, boxes, and numerous other wood products. Americans consume two hundred forty million trees annually. Eight times as many trees are planted as are consumed. Fortunately, for consumers and for the Martins, timber is a renewable resource.

Although Quentin Hardtner of Louisiana Longleaf Lumber Company at Urania is considered one of Louisiana's pioneers of reforestation, Martin started reforestation early. That earlier (now archaic) cut-out-and-get-out philosophy of lumbermen no longer applies. Today, through selective cutting of mature timber followed by scientific reforesting of the land, a sawmill can operate in the same area for an unlimited period of time. Norman said that much of the land they bought was cutover land. They would replant it. As he said, "We were looking out for the future."

Hardwood areas are generally reforested by natural regeneration, which occurs through seeding from standing trees or by trees sprouting from the root systems or stumps of harvested trees. Some natural regeneration occurs from softwoods (pine), but most pine reforestation is from planting seedlings. Artificial regeneration involves harvesting a stand of trees, preparing the site or burning the area then planting the seedlings at a spacing that will help ensure survival and growth.[19]

Quite simply, reforestation means replacing an acre of cut timber with an acre of planted trees. In Louisiana, trees are planted from December through March, with most planting done in January and February. Crews prepare selected sites by cutting and removing any remaining timber. They then clear the land, piling, bedding and burning as is necessary. Finally, seedlings are planted. In 1999, for example, the three pine districts of the Martin Companies planted 7.5 million loblolly pines and 700,000 slash pines covering 14,700 acres. Reforestation ensures a constant timber supply for the future.[20] These are truly tree farms, with careful cultivation yielding bountiful crops.

One of Martin's more interesting reforestation projects involved planting cottonwood trees in the Atchafalaya River Basin. Cottonwood is a fast-growing tree. In twelve years a cottonwood tree can grow to be a three-log tree with a fourteen-inch diameter at the stump. In their project, Martin foresters planted twenty-inch cuttings of cottonwood, some coming from Louisiana and others from Tennessee. With three plantations of cottonwood, the results were mixed. Those planted from Louisiana switches in the right soil types on the riverbank did well. Other plantings did not fare so well. Martins once again cut their losses and got out of a bad business decision. They accepted this experimental venture as a lesson learned.

Along with land acquisition and land management, any valuation of Martin's land has to take into consideration the multi-use potential of that land.

The first and most obvious use of Martin land, of course, is the growth of timber for their production of lumber and other wood-related products. A primary reason for the company to begin

CHAPTER 5 - FUNDAMENTALS

purchasing land was to ensure a continuing source of timber. Competition for available land increased with other lumber companies buying land, with paper mills and plywood mills buying land, and with land being lost to urbanization. A 2001 study by the U. S. Forest Service found that, by 2020, urban sprawl could reduce forests in the South by twelve million acres. According to this study, about six percent of the region's forests are likely to be lost.[21] With this competition for timber-producing land, acquisition of land that would produce timber to ensure permanency of the business became essential.

According to Ellis, an unexpected benefit of land ownership was the land as a hedge against inflation. The value of the land continues to rise. Land that was cutover when bought and reforested becomes much more valuable as inflation sends land prices up.

Martin land has also produced revenue through mineral leases, especially through oil-and-gas leases. In cases where production has occurred, revenue increased considerably. Along with sub-surface leases for oil and gas, some company-owned land has also had surface leases for lignite coal. In one case, a leasing company paid $1,000,000 for a lignite coal lease then later learned that a stream running through the tract was protected by the Scenic River Law. Not even a test hole could be drilled. The Martin Company received the negotiated lease money, but no lignite coal was ever mined. In another lease, lignite coal was successfully mined from company land in DeSoto Parish.

Gravel has been sold off company land in Rapides, Natchitoches and Red River parishes.

Hunting leases, especially recently, have become a source of rather significant revenue for much of Martin-owned land. Beginning in the 1950s, hunting rights to some selected land were leased to hunting clubs. In fact, Roy O. Martin Lumber Company signed its first hunting lease in 1958. Not until twenty years later, however, did the Martin Company begin aggressively leasing land for hunting. They then realized these leases could be another tool for managing their land as well as yielding an additional source of income from that same land. In 1996 nearly 750 hunting and campsite leases were in effect throughout the company.[22] In 2004 all land south of Alexandria and most, if not all, north of Alexandria is currently leased to hunting clubs. Today, the number of hunting leases is 1,132, representing a 95% lease rate for Martin properties.

LIFE BY THE BOARD FOOT

CHAPTER 5 - FUNDAMENTALS

These numerous hunting leases are profitable to the company in ways other than the revenue derived from them. Individual hunting clubs post the land. By terms of lease agreements, hunting clubs protect Martin land from dumping and defacing the property, from intrusion by trespassers, from unauthorized cutting of timber, and from fire. Diligent hunters report infestation of insects like the Southern pine beetle, lightning or storm damage, flooding, beaver damages, and encroachment by adjacent landowners. As serious in their responsibility toward the environment as they are about bagging their targets, hunting clubs police their members' activities on the lease and require adherence to both state and federal wildlife and hunting regulations, which makes hunting on leased property safer than hunting on un-leased property. The Louisiana Department of Wildlife even issues alligator hunting permits for some Martin-owned land.

Who gets the leases to hunt on Martin land is determined by bid. According to one long-time observer of the company, the bid process has created some hard feelings against the company recently in some areas where people who had hunted on the land for years were shut out. But the bidding process is fair since it is open bidding for hunting rights. Although preference is given to local clubs, leases generally go to the highest bidders. Also, by this process Martin company stockholders get the biggest return on their investment. Because of its current acreage, a staff of foresters could not possibly patrol all Martin-owned land. Through effective use of hunting leases, others patrol and protect land for the Martins – and they pay the Martins to let them do it!

Not only are hunting leases profitable for the Martins, they reflect the company's collective consciousness toward preserving and maintaining the natural environment, which includes both the land and the native flora and fauna on that land. On much Martin-owned property, the topography is reminiscent of those lush, vibrant forests of a bygone era. Undergrowth is healthy, and streams are crystal clear—reflecting, in part, Louisiana's proud slogan: "Sportsman's Paradise."

Martin land contains numerous scenic spots. Company foresters are encouraged to locate and, then working with holders of leases, carefully preserve these pristine areas for future generations.

LIFE BY THE BOARD FOOT

Streamside Vegetation

Natural Waterfall

CHAPTER 5 - FUNDAMENTALS

Raccourci Point

Effective conservation of wildlife is positively correlated to the practice of leasing land to hunting clubs. Hunting clubs desire land on which they can hunt, but without game on that land, the best of leases would be meaningless. Beginning in 2001, the company offered three-year to five-year, long-term hunting leases to various hunting clubs. In order to have a long-term lease on Martin land, however, hunting clubs now are required to join the Quality Deer Management (QDM) program administered by the Quality Deer Management Association (QDMA). Hunting clubs joining the QDMA receive a reduction in their annual lease fees. In September 2001, eighty-two percent of the hunting clubs and eighty-eight percent of Martin acreage were in this program. Today, ninety-eight percent of all Martin property is enrolled in the Quality Deer Management Program.

The Quality Deer Management Association is a national non-profit organization dedicated to the preservation of white-tailed deer through proper herd management.[23] Martin is proud to be a part of this rapidly growing, environmentally conscious organization.

The company is also involved in efforts to increase the black bear population in the upper Atchafalaya River Basin. Louisiana's Black Bear Conservation Committee (BBCC) encourages education and landowner cooperation to promote the recovery of black bears in that area. From 2000 – 2005 the BBCC proposes to release female black bears and their cubs at specific sites in the Atchafalaya River Basin area. Since the Martin Company owns considerable land near the release sites, they have a vested interest in this ongoing preservation project. The company has supported the BBCC financially while providing use of their land for studying the black bear.[24]

Forester Don Gremillion
with two
Louisiana Black Bear Cubs
found on
ROM's "Hackney Tract"

(on the east side of the
Atchafalaya River
in
Pointe Coupeé Parish
southwest of
Raccourci Island)

Martin foresters annually meet with Greenwing chapters of Ducks Unlimited to encourage them in conservation practices and to teach them about forestry. Company foresters generally spend a day with the youngsters, aged five to fifteen, of the Bayou Chapter Greenwings of Ducks Unlimited, sharing information about forestry and the environment, boating safety, and wildlife law.[25] Educating future generations about environmental stewardship is another way Martins seek to preserve the "all-powerful land."

Certainly, some land is bought for the specific purpose of selling it later. For example, land for subdivisions, obviously, was bought for real-estate purposes. In those early days after timber was cut from the Black Lake tract, part of that cutover land was sold for farms. Roy O. later regretted they had sold that property. To have retained that land would have increased their holdings in that area. As their vision for the

CHAPTER 5 - FUNDAMENTALS

business evolved, so evolved their philosophy regarding forestland. Early in their operations, they abandoned the "cut out and get out" practice, finding more responsible and more creative ways to preserve their investment. Today, land is sometimes traded with other lumber companies or other landowners to consolidate holdings. In many cases, swamplands and lakes have been traded for good timberland, thus improving company forests. In some cases, parcels of land have been expropriated. The Red River Waterway, for instance, took Martin land in Avoyelles, Rapides, and Natchitoches parishes. The federal government also claimed land in Rapides Parish for a military bombing range. Fortunately, though, such expropriations have been infrequent.

Land truly is important, if not all-important, to the Martins. Revenue is derived from their land in several ways. While a constant and consistent supply of timber is guaranteed, their land sometimes produces champion-sized trees that Martin does not cut. For instance, the Louisiana state champion sycamore tree, a tree 162-feet high with a circumference of 22 feet 11 inches and a limb spread of 105, once stood on Martin land in the Atchafalaya River Basin.[26] The Louisiana state champion cypress tree once found on Martin land was equally impressive. Unfortunately, both huge trees succumbed to natural decay.

Louisiana State Champion Cypress Tree

LIFE BY THE BOARD FOOT

Today, the state champion loblolly pine can be found on Martin property. To encircle its girth requires three adult men, as the photo indicates.

A trade journal notes that with the Martins "starting at such a late date [to buy their timberland] meant very few large tracts were still available. Thus, ROM holdings have taken the shape of whatever has come on the market over the years. The company's patchwork timber holdings dot the map from the northernmost parish all the way down the Red River and into the Atchafalaya Basin in parcels ranging from twenty acres to several thousand. Species range is as varied as the patchwork itself. Hardwoods cover about 150,000 acres, primarily in the Basin, and the remaining 450,000 acres are a mix of pine and hardwood stands. Pine plantations have been planted in roughly sixty percent of these sites. These numbers are fluid, of course, as Martin's forest management team pursues an active acquisitions and land exchange program."[27]

CHAPTER 5 - FUNDAMENTALS

Map of Louisiana with ROM Acreage Highlighted

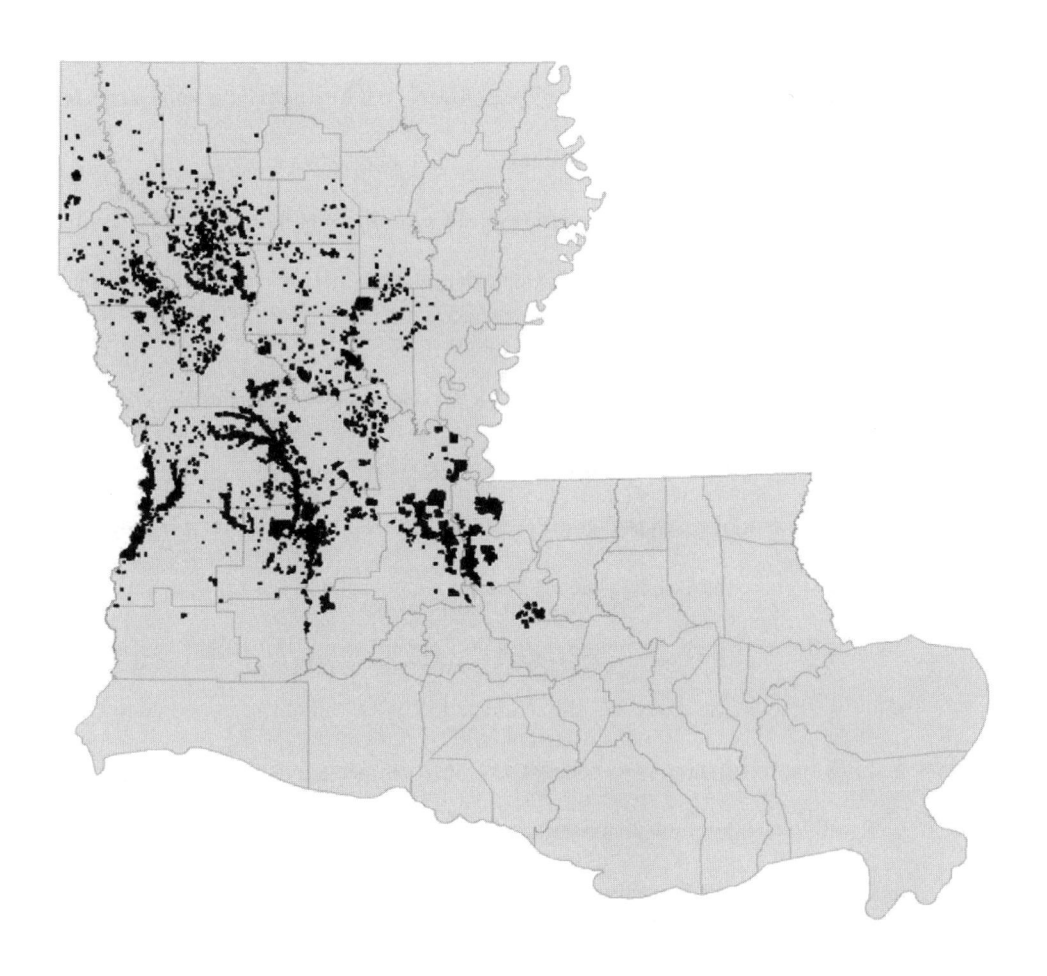

LIFE BY THE BOARD FOOT

LONG-TERM, LOYAL EMPLOYEES

In any analysis of Martin success, the contribution of long-term, loyal employees emerges as a significant factor. Several key players in Martin organization worked for the company for four decades and longer. One family member said that the company could not have succeeded without them. Roy O. undoubtedly appreciated his valuable employees, but he might have sometimes had a quirky (perhaps eccentric) way of showing his gratitude.

A case in point is an action toward Gene Glankler who first worked with Roy O. at Nickey Brothers in Memphis. He came to Alexandria shortly after Roy O. bought the Fenner Street sawmill to be sales manager. In the 1930s he left the company to buy a small sawmill himself in Pineville. Needing this valuable employee in his organization, Roy O. later bought that mill in order to get Glankler back as sales manager. All was well for a while. Then one day Roy O. drove into the parking lot and spotted a new Cadillac automobile. Asking whose Cadillac that was, he found that it belonged to Glankler. He ordered Glankler to take the Cadillac back to Southern Chevrolet in Alexandria where he had bought the car. An unusual demand, perhaps, but it typifies the concern Roy O. had about the appearance of ostentation. Quite frankly, although he drove a Cadillac himself, Roy O. did not want people to know his employees were making that much money—a concept easy to grasp for one having grown up under a stout Puritan work ethic. Glankler must have understood Roy O's reasoning because he remained with the Martin group until he retired. His retirement gift was a new Cadillac.[28]

Roy O. hired Ralph Kees shortly after he graduated from Louisiana College. Kees stayed with the company, working at several positions throughout his tenure with the Martins. He oversaw the retail division at the time of his retirement.

John Munsterman was hired in 1945 as the first forester in the company. He worked until 1985.

Chester O'Quin went to work for the Martins when he graduated from Northwestern State University of Louisiana with an accounting degree. Forty-two years later he retired from the company.

Clyde Norton started work as a forester in Oakdale. When Norman left the company to pursue other interests, Norton became manager of operations at Colfax Creosoting, then later its general manager.

CHAPTER 5 - FUNDAMENTALS

When he retired after forty-two years with the company, he was vice president of the treating division and a member of the board of directors.

Zack Woodard went to work for Ellis in Castor in 1959. He quickly became Ellis' right-hand man. Woodard became semi-retired in 1993 after working thirty-four years with the company, after implementing critical financial planning and serving as a vice president and member of the board of directors. To his credit, much of the financial and estate planning and numerous fiscal policies were the result of his expertise, dedication and hard work. During his semi-retirement, he remained in almost-constant contact with the office through telephone, fax and email. Having fully assimilated into the Martin culture of hard work, he was not ready to relinquish all his responsibilities until 1998 when he entered full retirement.

Not all long-term employees have been executives. One hourly employee came down from Memphis to Alexandria with Roy O. He operated the derrick machine and worked until his death in the mid-1940s.

Like the Martins, many of their long-term employees, especially their executives, are focused on business, family, and church. They are family-oriented people who are actively involved in church life, but who are also committed to their business responsibilities. When asked if those qualities were considered when hiring people, Ellis responded by saying, "That's the kind of people you want working for you. You don't want people with bad reputations." Norton agreed that, historically, Martins hire people who reflect their own values.

These long-term employees are cited as an illustrative list, not an exhaustive list. In 2003 employee records showed that two hundred eleven employees had ten years or more in tenure with Martin Companies. Roy III observed, "Loyalty cannot be bought. It must be 'cultivated' over time from a group of employees who believe in the purpose and core values of the Company." [29]

WORK ENVIRONMENT

This work environment contributed not only to the tenure of long-term employees but also to the overall health of the companies. Historically, Martin companies have provided employee benefits that make

LIFE BY THE BOARD FOOT

long tenure with the company not only a personally profitable experience but also an enjoyable one. As one faithful employee said, "I liked it there or I wouldn't have stayed."

An early employee benefit was the gift of a turkey at Thanksgiving and a ham at Christmas. Since these Thanksgiving turkeys were sometimes live, presentation parties could get quite raucous.

Jim Hendrix
distributing live turkeys
to
Martin Employees
(circa 1928)

When the federal Social Security program was adopted, quite obviously Social Security for those covered under it became a company benefit.

Roy O. believed very strongly in personal savings—for himself and for his employees. He saw the advantage of having a profit sharing plan that would entice and hold good employees. Apparently, he carefully researched various options for creating a plan for his company. His extensive notes can be found in the cover pages and margins of his personal copy of Franklin J. Lunding's Sharing a Business: The Case Study of a Tested Management Philosophy, published in 1952. With ideas from this text and certainly other sources, Roy O. inaugurated the company's profit sharing plan in 1956. Not many other companies had retirement or profit sharing plans at that time. Initially, theirs was more like a savings plan. An employee contributed at least one percent of his wages with a maximum contribution of ten percent. Out of its profits, the company then matched the employee's contribution up to a maximum of $200 per year. In 1976 the plan was amended to make it a true profit sharing plan. Under it, an employee could contribute a maximum of ten percent of his wages; the combined companies contributed a percentage of their profits.

CHAPTER 5 - FUNDAMENTALS

Initially, these retirement funds were invested in first mortgages from homes built and financed through company retail lumberyards. With a change in the federal Internal Revenue Service regulations, the investment fund was invested in stocks, bonds, and mutual funds. With this change, the company's contribution to an employee's profit sharing plan has often been the fifteen percent maximum allowed by law.[30] Today, the Roy O. Martin Profit Sharing Plan, also referred to as the Retirement Plan, is a significant employee benefit. Martins are proud to note that, to date, two loyal employees have retired with more than one million dollars in their retirement accounts.

Health insurance is another important employee benefit. The health and welfare of employees involves not only their health and well-being, but also their days at work, their productivity, and their safety. In the early 1970s with assistance from employee-benefit consultants, the company drafted a plan for comprehensive health benefits based on an 80/20% scale. Employees with ninety days or more of service were automatically covered with the company paying the premium. With a dramatic increase in costs of medical care, on April 1, 1980, the company went to a program of self-insurance. This health insurance plan, the Employee's Benefits Trust (EBT), is self-funded and self-administered by the company, resulting in considerable financial savings to both employee and employer. Benefits have significantly improved over its years of operation to now include zero-deductible options for both employees and dependents, pre-tax deductions for employee portions of the required premiums, flexible medical spending accounts, a prescription drug plan and PPO arrangements with area hospitals and physicians. The company continues to pay premiums for their employees, with employees paying one-half the premium for their dependents.

Key company personnel have a long-term disability program, which provides a continuation of income in case of disability. Short-term disability insurance is provided for other employees. The company pays both long-term and short-term disability premiums. The company also provides life insurance and accidental dismemberment insurance for employees, providing them an opportunity to purchase additional supplemental insurance.

Additional employee benefits include scholarship opportunities for children of employees. The Martin Foundation initially funded scholarships at three area colleges: Louisiana College in Pineville, Northwestern State University in Natchitoches, and Louisiana State University at Alexandria. Today, that list has grown to nine colleges and universities statewide where Martins provide scholarships to deserving students:

>Louisiana State University at Baton Rouge
>Louisiana State University at Alexandria
>Louisiana State University at Eunice
>Northwestern State University at Natchitoches
>Southeastern Louisiana University at Hammond
>University of Louisiana at Monroe
>University of Louisiana at Lafayette
>Louisiana Tech University at Ruston
>Louisiana College at Pineville

Children of Martin employees have priority for these scholarships. In addition, the Martin company is a sponsor of the U. S. Chamber of Commerce's "ConSern - Loans for Education" program. This program offers competitive interest rates, extended payback times, and other unique features not found with conventional bank loans or other financing arrangements. That program is available to all Martin employees.[31]

In the fall of 2000, the company began a program of scholarships for employees. This program provides tuition and money for books for approved employees who take college courses.

Adult literacy programs and GED preparation courses are also available to benefit company workers. Additionally, continuing education and training programs in various areas throughout the company keep employees prepared for the work they do while making them eligible for advancement.

MARTIN CARES began in October 1997. Contracting with Marketplace Ministries, Inc., to provide another important employee benefit, Roy O. Martin Lumber Company inaugurated a chaplaincy program for all Martin employees.

Marketplace Ministries is a Christian-based, non-denominational, unobtrusive organization that hires carefully screened local chaplains to cover the company's workforce. These chaplains are dedicated to

CHAPTER 5 - FUNDAMENTALS

providing lifestyle mentoring and pastoral counseling for complex issues. Their program of ministry recognizes and operates within the premise that an indisputable correlation exists between one's environment at home and his satisfaction at work. Inefficient and ineffective job performance, workplace tension, and employee dissatisfaction often reflect personal or spiritual struggles, struggles that can lessen through intervention of trained chaplains. And training for chaplains in the MARTIN CARES program is specific, preparing them to carry out numerous, sometimes demanding, responsibilities. Serving the Martin family of workers, these chaplains are willing

- to be on-call twenty-four hours a day, three hundred sixty-five days a year for crisis intervention or emergencies;
- to make worksite visits as well as hospital, home, or jail visits, when appropriate;
- to provide individual as well as family pastoral care for issues including, but not limited to, marriage, divorce and remarriage, serious illness, death and dying, and child-rearing;
- to assist with funeral arrangements and, if asked, conducting the service, as well as following up with pastoral grief care;
- to assist with wedding arrangements and, if asked, officiating at weddings, as well as counseling for premarital planning;
- to address gambling addictions, alcohol/drug abuse addictions, depression and financial matters.

Martin's chaplaincy program with its fourteen chaplains adds a spiritual dimension to employee benefits, rounding out the previously established physical and financial benefits provided by the company. [32]

As a part of the company's safety program, in early 2001, Martin added its first occupational nurse. They added another one in 2003. Believing that employees must stay healthy in order to work safely, these nurses develop and implement health programs and safety activities. Registered nurses, these medical professionals have had previous experience with workmen's compensation case management. They partner with physicians in determining when employees should return to work and what tasks they should be assigned. Martin's occupational nurses also participate in educating employees on these and other basic and specific health issues:

- providing brochures and literature dealing with a broad range of health items and answering questions employees might have;
- directing a Health and Wellness program for employees, a long-range company goal that will help employees maintain a healthier lifestyle;
- offering CPR training for employees;
- aiding in hearing conservation; and
- administering annual flu vaccinations.

Both nurses consider themselves employee advocates, helping employees to understand health issues that relate to working safely.[33]

In order to communicate effectively with employees, Martin began its first company newsletter, *Martco News*, in July 1993. By the second issue, and as a result of an employee contest, the name was changed to *The Sawdust Gazette*. With volume four in January 1996, it became *ROM Today*. First published monthly, then bi-monthly, it ultimately became a quarterly publication. The name change indicated the growth of the company and the growth in distributorship. With the addition of Martco Plywood at Chopin, the company had increased from six hundred to about one thousand employees. Markets had also increased. The focus of this new publication then was to reveal the current Roy O. Martin organization and showcase its products to the company's many employees, vendors, customers, and stockholders. The newsletter thus became a valuable public-relations tool. It is under the editorial direction of Maggie Martin, wife of company CEO and chairman Johnny. Having a Ph.D. in English from LSU, Maggie and her staff also produce the *Employee Focus,* a quarterly publication designed primarily for Martin company employees.

CHAPTER 5 - FUNDAMENTALS

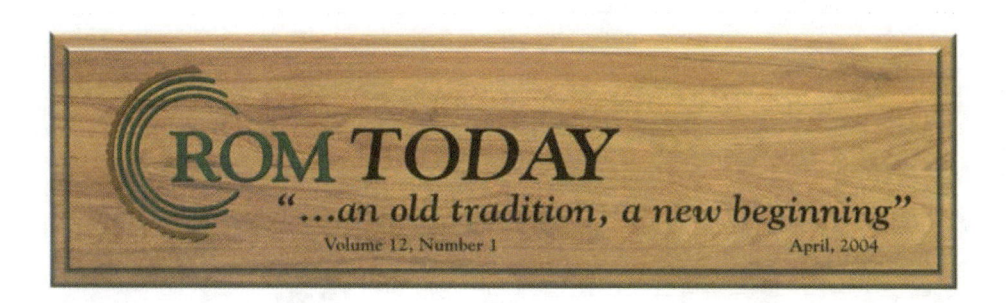

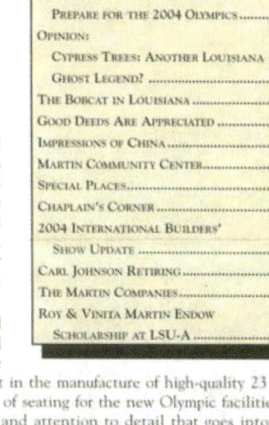

LIFE BY THE BOARD FOOT

EMPLOYEE FOCUS
A supplement to ROM TODAY

Volume 3
Issue 1
March 2004

MARTCO ★ STAR ★ PERFORMERS

Martco OSB

Matthew Marchand (B-shift Assistant Press Operator): As the assistant press operator, you have to learn all the different aspects of running the press, what the different controls do and the different operations it takes to run the press. I started in November 1992 working in the waferizer and then worked in the infeed and then back to the waferizer then to assistant press operator. I have been the assistant press operator for two years. I enjoy learning different things. It is my responsibility to jog the press if something stops, check the spreaders to watch the flow of material for the line. If the press operator sees something wrong, he will send me to check it out to see what's not right. We have good teamwork on the shift. It is important to make sure everything stays running with the least amount of downtime.

Andrew Porche (B-shift Supervisor): Matthew is a very good worker. For him to make the transition from flaker operator to assistant press operator in less than a year tells you he is smart and grasps things easily. When someone is on vacation, he runs the press. He can run it as good as the regular operators. Matthew is a big asset to our shift. He knows the sawline, the blenders and the press. It is very helpful to have an assistant press operator who knows all that.

Martco Plywood

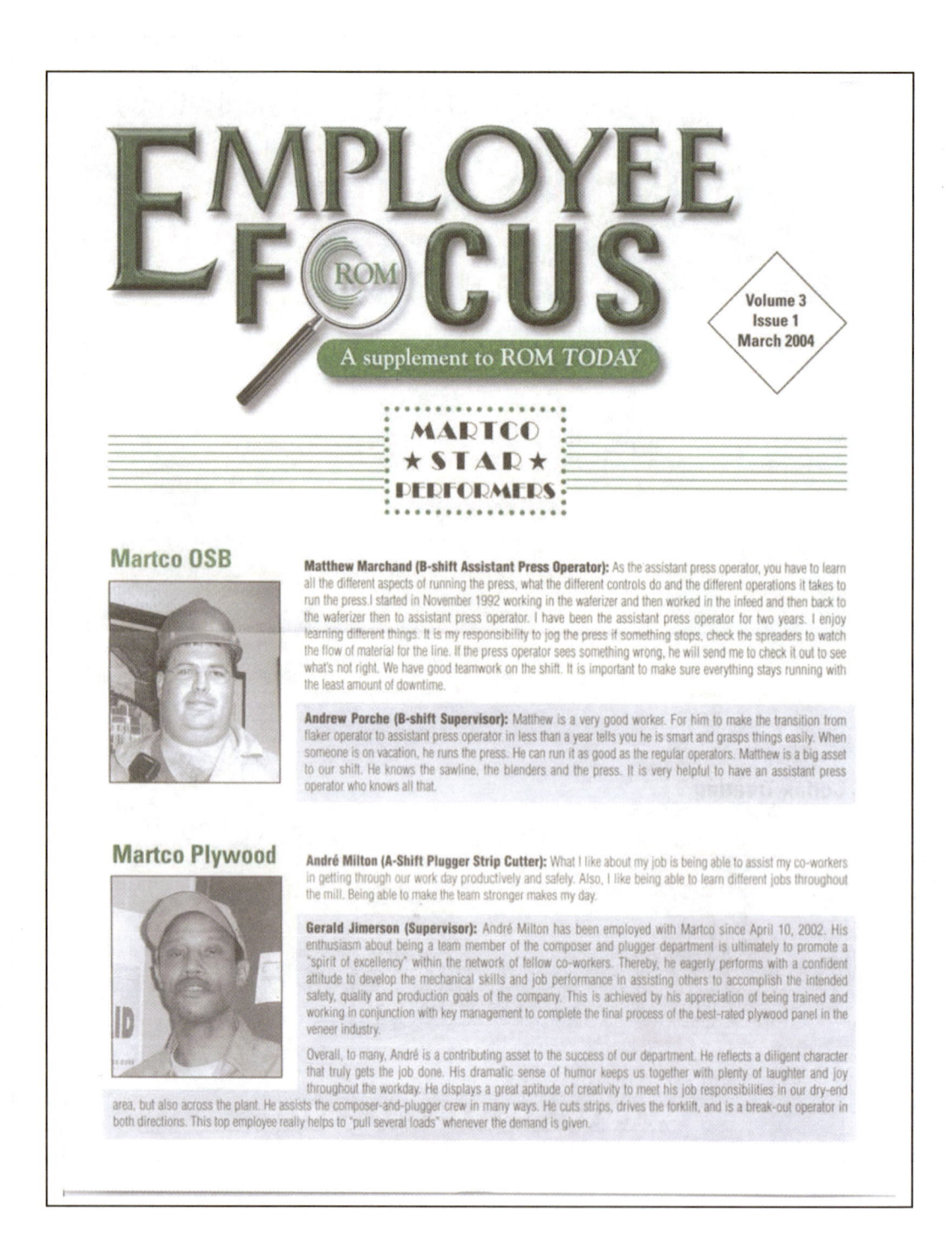

André Milton (A-Shift Plugger Strip Cutter): What I like about my job is being able to assist my co-workers in getting through our work day productively and safely. Also, I like being able to learn different jobs throughout the mill. Being able to make the team stronger makes my day.

Gerald Jimerson (Supervisor): André Milton has been employed with Martco since April 10, 2002. His enthusiasm about being a team member of the composer and plugger department is ultimately to promote a "spirit of excellency" within the network of fellow co-workers. Thereby, he eagerly performs with a confident attitude to develop the mechanical skills and job performance in assisting others to accomplish the intended safety, quality and production goals of the company. This is achieved by his appreciation of being trained and working in conjunction with key management to complete the final process of the best-rated plywood panel in the veneer industry.

Overall, to many, André is a contributing asset to the success of our department. He reflects a diligent character that truly gets the job done. His dramatic sense of humor keeps us together with plenty of laughter and joy throughout the workday. He displays a great aptitude of creativity to meet his job responsibilities in our dry-end area, but also across the plant. He assists the composer-and-plugger crew in many ways. He cuts strips, drives the forklift, and is a break-out operator in both directions. This top employee really helps to "pull several loads" whenever the demand is given.

An article in the February 1, 1994, issue of *The Sawdust Gazette* gives ten good reasons to work at Martco. These reasons, reflecting in part the Martin culture and work environment, are still applicable today:

CHAPTER 5 - FUNDAMENTALS

- Stability – A secure and stable supply of timber, a steady demand for our products.

- Compensation – One of the largest employers with an annual payroll in excess of $10 million.

- Benefits – Retirement Plan, medical coverage, life insurance, indemnity, paid holidays, vacation, and more.

- Safety and Health – comprehensive safety program including training, awards - a SMOKE-FREE WORKPLACE.

- Future – Martco provides long-range growth potential employment.

- Production Bonus – Monthly bonus program that provides a significant bonus only when scheduled production is achieved.

- A Company that Cares – A partnership of Roy O. Martin Lumber Co., owner involvement in day-to-day activities.

- On-the-Move Growth – Steady improvements, renovations to maintain a state-of-the-art manufacturing facility.

- Quality Products - Our OSB waferboard and hardwood lumber is of the highest quality produced anywhere. A source of pride is evident throughout Martco's operations.

- Decisions and Answers – Martco operates with a minimum of red tape. Questions can be answered quickly; decisions are made without complex, lengthy delays.[34]

These ten reasons could doubtlessly still be repeated at all Martin worksites. All worksites, for instance, are smoke free. The Promotion Opportunity Program (POP) could be added to that list. This program, initiated in 2001, emphasizes promotion from within the company. All employees now have regular opportunities for promotion, creating real possibilities for bettering their personal and professional lives.

Numerous people have worked for the Martins. Several who now have their own businesses in the forest products or building materials industries got their first experience with a Martin company. One long-time Martin employee estimated that at one time, before Alexandria began to grow and expand, probably as many as twenty-five percent of the people in Alexandria either worked for the Martins or had worked for the Martins. Others agreed with that assessment, although Ellis thought it was too high.

LIFE BY THE BOARD FOOT

Martins have successfully created a work environment that encourages long-term employment. One interviewee quoted Roy O. as saying, "If you take my paycheck, you owe me loyalty." And for the most part he had, and the present company continues to have, loyalty from employees. That is seen in the number of long-time, loyal employees of the Martin Company.

MANAGEMENT STYLE

Accountant Paul Hood observed that there is a right way to do things, a wrong way, and a Martin way. Indeed, a Martin management style has emerged over the years. A number of components combine to compose the Martin management style.

Responsibility/Accountability. Roy O. began the process of giving an individual specific responsibility for carrying out tasks and then making that person accountable for achieving them. Chester O'Quin said that Roy O. could not be called a hands-on manager. He had people working for him who could handle various critical responsibilities. He added that Roy O. "assigned you a job to do and expected you to do it."[35]

Roy O.'s formal training was in bookkeeping. Roy Jr., stated that the fastidious Roy O. never made a bookkeeping error. When asked if Roy O. looked over his shoulder as a bookkeeper, O'Quin replied that he did not, but that he always knew what was going on. Not only in bookkeeping, but also in salesmanship where he likewise had experience, Roy O. allowed his employees the necessary freedom to carry out their jobs. One of his salesmen who was also a lumber inspector is Richard Landry. When asked the same question about Roy O. looking over his shoulder as a lumber salesman, he responded the same way: "No."[36]

So even though he had experience in various areas of the business, Roy O. would give his employees with specific responsibility the latitude to exercise that delegated responsibility. They would have the requisite authority to go along with their designated duties. But he would also hold them accountable for correctly and effectively completing their assigned jobs. Landry thought that Roy O. had the knack for picking the right person for the right job. Zack Woodard said that he never knew of either Roy O. or Ellis going behind someone's back to get done what that person had the responsibility to do.[37]

CHAPTER 5 - FUNDAMENTALS

Roy O. always wore a suit and tie to work. If at all possible, he did not get his hands dirty in the production of lumber or in the maintenance of his sawmill. Other people had that responsibility – and he expected them to carry it out.

That same component of giving people responsibility and making them accountable for it continues in the company. Ellis was more involved in day-to-day operations than was Roy O. In fact, he would purposefully be in the mill every day. While in Castor, from his office he could see the smokestacks at the mill. If no smoke came out of those smokestacks, indicating the plant was not running, he would, as quickly as possible, go to the mill to find out why.

Seizing the Opportunity. Perhaps it is related to the vision that Roy O. had, but the management of the company has also been marked by their willingness to seize an opportunity. Roy O. was characterized as a person always in a hurry. Time was an enemy to him. He made business decisions rather quickly. Fortunately, they were usually good business decisions.

Martins did not particularly want Colfax Creosoting when they bought available acreage from the Edenborn Estate. But to get the land they wanted, they necessarily had to take the creosoting plant.

LIFE BY THE BOARD FOOT

Consequently, they seized an opportunity that opened a door to another opportunity. And that opportunity, an initially unwanted creosoting plant and its resulting treating division, became an extremely profitable entity for the company.

Entry into the retail lumberyards was primarily to sell Martin lumber in the face of competing, less expensive lumber from the West Coast. The company thus seized its opportunity to open retail yards. Ultimately Martin had thirteen yards in three states, although twelve were they most they operated at any one time. From that venture came the development of subdivisions and the construction of homes and buildings. All of these were profitable enterprises. They came about because Martins saw an opportunity and seized it. This pattern treads its way through Martin's winding road to success, emerging once again in a way that would propel the company in a different, even more profitable, direction.

Ellis indicated that he had looked for fifteen years for something to do with hardwood pulpwood and other trees that could not be utilized for lumber. When he discovered oriented strand board at that Louisiana Pacific board meeting in 1979, he lost no time in pursuing it as his next profitable venture. The company already owned land with a rail spur at LeMoyen. They also needed to have a sawmill closer to their hardwood lumber supply. Thus, an OSB mill was built at LeMoyen. A hardwood sawmill, which utilized lumber-quality hardwood logs and moved the waste trimmed off those logs next door to the OSB mill, followed soon thereafter. Through Martco Partnership operations at LeMoyen, Martin seized the combined opportunity of having a sawmill close to the source of timber and of utilizing material that otherwise would be wasted.

Roy, Jr. said, "Everything's changing all day long. . . . There are always opportunities if you know where to look for them."[38] Historically, Martins have known where to look for opportunities and have been quick to grab hold of them when they came.

The Courage to Cut Losses. Along with their attribute of seizing an opportunity, Martins also demonstrate the courage to cut. They are willing to cease any operation if it is no longer viable or profitable. A distinct visionary aspect of the Martin management style also comes into play with this attribute.

When the flooring mill at Alexandria burned, Ellis argued against rebuilding. His observation was that carpeting was becoming very big in home construction. People were using carpet rather than hardwood

CHAPTER 5 - FUNDAMENTALS

flooring on their floors. After some discussion, board members agreed to his recommendation. Within a relatively brief period of time following that decision, thirty or forty flooring mills went out of business.[39]

When discount or large-volume building-supply stores like Lowe's and Home Depot came into the market area of local retail lumberyards, Martin faced another big decision. Recognizing the major competition those businesses would bring, they divested themselves of their retail lumberyards. Originally, those lumberyards had done a thriving business. They had been a meaningful part of the Martin business story. But when the time came to move beyond retail operations, the presiding Martins had the courage to cut that operation.

Many crossties were sold through Dura-Wood. But railroads went to nine-foot crossties rather than eight-foot crossties. This presented a problem for Martin. To cut two crossties out of a log required an eighteen-foot log instead of a sixteen-foot log, which is the more traditionally accepted length in hardwood lumber markets. Dura-Wood could have made that adjustment and continued in business, as it had made other adjustments, for example, in the environmental protection area. But when the opportunity to sell Dura-Wood to RailWorks came about, this profitable part of the treating division was not retained, but sold. Conditions changed; Martins saw the effects the change would have on them; thus, they cut the Dura-Wood plant from their operation.

Often, almost always, it is easier to start an enterprise than it is to stop an enterprise. With the Martins, sentimentality plays no part in making business decisions. When an opportunity came to sell the Fenner Street sawmill in Alexandria, which was the foundation of their business, they sold it with no hesitation. That sale was a wise business decision because it led to other business developments that were not only very profitable but ones that have become the heart of their present business activity.

The courage to cut and to move on is a definite component of the Martin management style. That component is a major factor in their business success.

Innovation. Quite consistently, Martins have been innovative in their business practices as well as in their business activities. The mills they operate through the Martco Partnership are frequently described as state of the art. They are. They are state of the art because the company is willing to make the innovations necessary to keep them that way. An article in *Forests and People*, official publication of the Louisiana Forestry Association, describes the plants at Chopin and LeMoyen as "highly sophisticated."[40]

LIFE BY THE BOARD FOOT

Commenting on the Martin's continual practice of updating its machinery, a trade journal reports in 2002:

> While each of the individual enterprises might be managed as a separate company, the overall goals - in terms of technology and product quality – are common to each . . . . One important hallmark of the Martco plants is extensive investment in the most modern equipment possible . . . Each plant features state–of-the-art technology, and it is continuously upgraded as newer and more advanced technology becomes available.

The article then quotes Johnny as saying,

> Martco chooses to operate at a level that most other sawmills cannot afford, but with the success of our customers at stake, we cannot afford not to. We take great pride in our product so that our customers can be proud to buy, sell, or use Roy O. Martin's lumber.[41]

An earlier trade journal reporting a previous up-grade explains why innovation is such an important part of the Martin management style. This 1989 article states, "Overall, management has achieved a 40% production gain from a 20% increase in capital investment."[42] Innovation is profitable. By maintaining state-of-the-art equipment, Martin Companies not only operate more efficiently but they also operate more profitably. But state-of-the-art equipment is not the only factor involved. Training and maintaining a loyal employee base to operate the best available equipment is also critical to this process.

The company practices innovation not only in technology but also in company organization. The re-organization that occurred in 1999 is a case in point. Certainly, the company benefited from the re-organization from a tax standpoint, but it also benefited from increased efficiency of operation. The same is true for the 2003 reorganization. Both made Martin a leaner, meaner (more profitable) organization.

Moving into the ROMEX World Trade Center brought together the sales force of all Martin enterprises in another innovative move. While still organized as separate companies so each enterprise can account for its own activities, this centralization of workforce produced efficiency of operation.

Innovation moves in more than one area in the Martin Company. But it is a vital part of the management style that has brought about company success.

Analysis. In mentioning such factors as seizing the opportunity, having courage to cut, and incorporating innovative principles, one must not gain the impression that decisions are hastily made or entered into without thorough analysis.

This analysis might be the more informal method of Roy O. calling Ellis before he made a decision or asking Ellis to look at a tract of land with him before he bought it or, later, of Ellis asking Clyde

CHAPTER 5 - FUNDAMENTALS

Norton, "What do you think?" when Norton made a proposal to him. Or another analysis could be the more formal method of employing management consultant firms. But the company constantly analyzes its methods and operations and seeks advice and guidance from the expertise of others.

Pete Marwick of KPMG, the major national accounting firm, guided the 2000 re-organization.

Beginning October 2000, Perforex, a management consulting firm specializing in forest product mills, worked with Martco to improve profitability. Their work was in both the Chopin and LeMoyen facilities as well as in forestry and sales. The perceived outcome is that, "With these tools acquired through Perforex, Martco will seek to become a more profitable company for our employees and a better provider of hardwood products for our customers around the world."[43]

Making a critical decision or determining a crucial direction proceeds through both the informal and formal methods of analysis, through meetings between company officers and management, and through conversations about the proposed procedure or product. Through intensive analysis of what has been done and what works, company management makes more informed decisions and creates more purposeful work.

As a result of this analysis, in 2000 the company senior management team known as SALT (Strategic Action Leadership Team) identified "Key Result Areas" to implement throughout the company. The key result areas for that year included employee development, profit improvement, forestry management, new technology, and new business. This team then set specific objectives for each of those particular areas, breaking down stated objectives into smaller, more manageable parts and assigning them to various departments and specific people for execution. By assigning specific and measurable objectives, senior management gets a fairly accurate picture of whether each person does his/her job effectively. Employee contributions are more easily recognized and rewarded when objectives can be measured and accountability can be assigned.[44]

This process of analysis is ongoing. In every area of company life, analysis is a component of Martin's management style.

Profit Motive. In a unique way, a discernible profit motive runs throughout the company organization. Not only company leaders and stockholders but also employees are aware of the company's profitability. An article in *ROM Today* describes this sentiment: "And while the company must measure its long-term success by profitability, we can all contribute to the journey by doing our jobs a little better everyday. By working together and focusing the necessary attention on achieving the objectives that support the Key Result Areas, we can all share in the rewards of a successful company."[45]

Clyde Norton related that his salesmen at Colfax Creosoting, and earlier Dura-Wood, gauged their success by how much they made from their sales, not by how much they sold. He said that they judged sales by how much they made off the sales, not by the volume of the sales. Martins look to the bottom line, not to misleading numbers.

This kind of thinking permeates the company, as salespersons and other key employees focus on potential profit rather than the hours put in or the volume of business. The company profit-sharing plan, which originally was based on actual profits of the company, may have something to do with this mindset. It serves to heighten an awareness of profits on the part of employees. The company's bonus-incentive plan for production doubtlessly contributes to it. But actually, it is just a part of the Martin company culture. And that pervading company culture encourages personnel to think of the company's profits.

These are some of the basic components of the Martin management style. They are not necessarily confined to any one of the five Martins who has headed up the company through three generations. Rather, they run through company management in a unique, inherent thread of management style. As the company has progressed, a managerial rather than an entrepreneurial style of doing business has developed.

ESTATE PLANNING

All three sons of Roy O. Martin, Sr., agree on one matter: the company continues in business because of estate planning. They even use almost the same words: "The company is here today because of estate planning."

Estate planning is critical for family-owned businesses. Nearly seventy percent of family-owned businesses are either liquidated or sold after the founders retire. Only ten percent of family-owned businesses make it through the third generation. The CEOs of family-owned businesses typically serve six times longer than those in publicly held businesses. Estate taxes are due upon the death of the founder. Heirs who are not interested in the business may need to be bought out. Even though estate planning is critical for family-owned businesses, according to one survey, only about fifty-one percent of businesses

CHAPTER 5 - FUNDAMENTALS

had a strategic business plan and, of those, only twelve percent had written plans.[46] Today's Martin Companies have both.

Ellis led the family into estate planning. In the 1960s he saw that Tremont Lumber Company at New Rochelle had sold after the principal's death.

Tremont Lumber Company
New Rochelle, Louisiana

Abandoned
Tremont Lumber Company

LIFE BY THE BOARD FOOT

He thought of other companies that failed, often due to estate taxes, when the founder died. Ellis thus became determined to create a fiscal plan that would save his family's company from a similar fate.

"None of us could afford to die," he said. For a number of years Martin siblings had bought life insurance to use to pay estate taxes. But the company's assets had increased, therefore prohibitively increasing insurance premiums. As the age of the family increased and their health commensurately decreased, they knew that life insurance was not the answer.

According to Ellis, Ira Marcus from Chicago "just showed up" at Castor one day. Likely, it was not as coincidental as that because one does not just "show up" or "pass through" Castor, Louisiana. It has to be a point of destination in rural Bienville Parish. Marcus' visit actually came about through Ellis' association with Armac Industries, Incorporated, then a customer of Martin Timber Company. Ellis, in his search to solve his family's estate-tax problem, had learned that Marcus, a Chicago attorney, had effectively resolved the same problem for Armac. In devising a plan to take Armac public, Marcus had secured sufficient cash for its owner to mitigate his estate problem.

Other attorneys had recognized Martin's estate problem, but they could not provide a solution. Working closely with Zack Woodard, Marcus devised an estate plan for the Martin family. Since Roy O. was in his seventies, the plan would begin with him and Mildred. Although these first-generation Martins had regularly given company stock to their children and grandchildren, they still had substantial company holdings at that time. A joint-and-survivor annuity was worked out for them in exchange for their stock. When Roy O. died in 1973 and Mildred died at one hundred three in 1995, neither of them had an estate-tax liability.

Commonly known in the family as "the 1973 reorganization," the ensuing estate plan for the five children of Roy O. and Mildred involved a major reorganization of the Martin Companies. Ownership of all operating companies was put into five personal holding companies, one for each of the Martin children (Virginia, Ellis, Roy, Jr., Norman and Esther). Five separate partnerships (VMH, ESM, ROM, NKM and JEF) were created for the purpose of exchanging shares in ROM Lumber Company for a joint-and-survivor annuity to Roy O. and Mildred Martin. For the most part, ownership of these partnerships skipped to the third generation, partially solving the estate problems of second-generation siblings. Additionally,

CHAPTER 5 - FUNDAMENTALS

insurance trusts were formed at the same time. These insurance trusts, which still exist in 2004, were co-owned on a split-dollar arrangement by ROM Lumber Company and Martin Timber Company. The purpose of these insurance trusts was to fund estate taxes, when necessary.

All of this complex restructuring was part of Ira Marcus' plan to take the company public. Because the market cratered, the Martins wisely abandoned the idea of public ownership. Instead, they retained their company's existing corporate under the name of Roy O. Martin Industries, Inc.

Because of its scope, this plan was inordinately complicated, taking more than two years to complete. Its primary purpose was to provide a means of reducing the estates of both Martin founders and their five children. Simultaneously, it separated all operating companies from any problems with paying estate taxes when one of its major shareholders, either Roy O. and Mildred or one of their five children, died. Its purpose was accomplished. Woodard agreed with the Martin sons when he said: "This re-organization and estate plan was most likely the most significant thing that was done to preserve the continuity of the Martin Companies."[47]

Roy III continued the preservation process in 1999 with restructuring the company into limited liability companies and again in 2003 with implementing his "Mother of all Mergers." So far, fruits from some of his labor have been evident. "The year 1999 proved to be the most profitable in company history. Each facility reported a good-to-great profit, and the company's investment portfolio soared, just before the stock market crash of 2000."[48] As for the 2003 merger of companies, which greatly simplifies corporate structure, the verdict is still out. "The road to our present structure has been a long, confusing process. Our cooperative efforts have produced the most tax-efficient organization in our history. Time will tell if we anticipated all of the issues, but right now, we will reap the benefits."[49] If Martin history repeats itself, this latest reorganization, like others before it, will prove to benefit company stockholders. If not, then one can be certain these current Martins in charge will look for—and will find—a solution that will enable them to cut their potential losses and get out of a fiscally imprudent corporate structure.

LIFE BY THE BOARD FOOT

THE ROM FORMULA FOR SUCCESS

In the company's seventy-fifth anniversary year, board member Walter Jacobs Smith wrote an article in the company newsletter, astutely and succinctly describing the Martin formula for success. Titling his article "The ROM Formula for Success," Smith begins by writing,

> It is rare indeed in today's business world of acquisitions, mergers, and leveraged buy-outs to find a company that has endured for 75 years. It is even rarer to find one that is privately owned. Rarer still is one that continues to grow and prosper like the Roy O. Martin Lumber Company. This growth and prosperity results from the long-term vision set out by its founder Roy O. Martin, Sr. His recipe for success was really rather simple, and it still works today in any business – hard work, sacrifice, and knowledge of your product and business.

Smith further states:

> Publicly held companies are more concerned with short-term profits because management can and will be terminated if favorable profits aren't always forthcoming. Labor and needed improvements can be sacrificed to cut expenses to boost profits. Because our company is privately held, ROM management can look more to the long-term, knowing that growth and profits will ultimately come if they care for their employees and continue with the founder's recipe for success.[50]

Smith was on to something. Roy O. succeeded in the company because of his hard work, his personal sacrifice, his knowledge of the product, and his knowledge of business. He worked hard at it, and it succeeded. His successors have worked hard at it, have fine-tuned the same formula for success, and have both succeeded and expanded. The fundamentals that Roy O. established have been consistently followed. And they provide the fundamentals of the business. These fundamentals help to explain the Martin Companies and their continued success.

Roy, Jr., expressed it. When asked if he could give the characteristics of his father that would explain his business success, his first response was, "The good Lord smiled on him."[51] The Martin family would agree: God has blessed them.

Quite obviously, God did not bless them without their vision, their focus, and their hard work. But they would agree that God has blessed their efforts—both collectively as a business and individually as family members. Indeed, Martins themselves include the blessing of God among the fundamentals of their life and work.

Life By the Board Foot: 6

FAMILY

Love not sleep, lest thou come to poverty; open thine eyes, and thou shalt be satisfied with bread (Proverbs 20:13).

Many mornings Roy O. awakened his children by quoting a verse of scripture: "Love not sleep, lest thou come to poverty; open thine eyes, and thou shalt be satisfied with bread (Proverbs 20:13)." In so doing, he accomplished at least three personal goals. He called his children from sleep to start the day; he accustomed them to hearing scripture passages, thus making them more familiar with the Bible; and he conditioned them to think that each day was a workday and that one's work would be rewarded.

All five children of Roy O. and Mildred accomplished those three goals. Not only did they accomplish them, they have carried each out in ways that would have made their parents proud. Viewing their lives retrospectively, all these second-generation Martins reflect energy and eagerness to get on with tasks at hand. All are church members and have generally shown an active life of faith. To say they were willing to work may be an understatement. Most have tended to be overachievers. Their work has brought them the satisfaction of a job well done, but their endeavors have also brought them success and financial security.

As a footnote to this recollection, Zack Woodard writes that he remembers a variation of this scripture, which circulated the office. Although he did not personally hear Roy O. saying it, he recalls Ralph Kees and Chester O'Quin reciting what they remembered as Roy O.'s favorite slogan: "Early to bed, early to rise, work like hell and economize." Perhaps Roy O. tempered the language of his apparently well-known slogan, citing instead the biblical verse when he awakened his children.

Each member of the family has been involved in the business in some way. Although the two daughters were not actively involved in company employment, in past years, they both had considerable stock in the company. Yet all have also made their individual and unique contributions. For each of them, life has been by the board foot.

THE FAMILY BUSINESS

Roy O. wanted the company to be a privately held, family business. Even though he and his board of directors looked at the possibility of carrying the company public, they retained it as a closely held corporation. Early on, Roy O. gave stock in the company to his children and later to his grandchildren. He also deeded some company land to both his children and grandchildren.

His purpose was not only to share what he developed with his family, but also to involve his children, especially his sons, and later his grandsons, directly in the business. Giving them some personal ownership in land would, he believed, give them a vested interest in the company. In 1961 Roy O. wrote,

> Inasmuch as I preferred to have a company that was wholly owned by the family and as my sons had shown an interest in our company, I felt that a substantial interest in their own name would insure [sic] there not ever being any question as to what they would do when they became 20-24 years old. It worked out beautifully as all three of our sons are now in the business and control all of our companies.

Roy O. expressed pleasure in that decision as he went on,

> This indicates that it was the right move to make and was successful in every way. There are good relations among all of the three boys. They cooperate in managing the properties held by the two girls.[1]

A letter found in family archives provides evidence of his deliberate generational plan to involve future Martins in the business. Eight-year-old David, older son of Ellis, writes thanking his grandfather for the "land you gave us."

CHAPTER 6 - FAMILY

July 26, 1950

Dear Grandma and Grandpa,

Bonnie, Susan and I want to thank you for the land you gave us. Next time I come to Alex, I want you to take me out to see it. I am feeling fine now. Jonathan is growing so much. He talks a lot. I help take care of him and he likes to climb in my bed every morning. Have a nice time at the cottage.

Love,
David

LIFE BY THE BOARD FOOT

All three sons of Roy O. became involved in the business at early ages.

Seated: Norman and Ellis
Standing: Roy, Jr.

Each of them worked at the Fenner Street mill in summers when they were in high school. Ellis even dropped out of high school for a year to help build the mill at Castor. Although all had some college education, about two years each, none of them graduated. When their college careers were interrupted in order to work (as in the case for Ellis) or for military service (as in the case for Roy, Jr., and Norman), they did not return to complete a degree. Roy O. has been quoted as saying that they could learn more from him than from school. Each son was given heavy responsibilities when still quite young. Of that, Roy, Jr., said that Roy O. gave them the responsibilities to see if they could handle them.[2] Apparently, each handled those assigned tasks well, rising to sometimes-difficult occasions when circumstances demanded.

The family still runs the business. Its two top positions today are held by third-generation Martin men: Johnny, chairman and CEO, and Roy III, president and CFO. Now with a limited number of Martins

CHAPTER 6 - FAMILY

actively participating in the business, the company is moving toward one being run by professional managers. As it has evolved, today's corporation is a skillfully managed business. But for the foreseeable future, a Martin will be at its helm.

The Martin Company is still privately held. Like their founder, Martins of today prefer to own and control those businesses in which they are involved. Their business **is** their family. Consequently, annual gatherings more closely resemble social reunions than stodgy corporate meetings. Generally, more than half of the nearly one hundred Martin stockholders, and many with their spouses, travel from throughout the nation—from California to Washington, D.C., from Michigan to Texas, and numerous states between-- to reconnect with relatives having a common bond: the Roy O. Martin Lumber Company.

To better understand both the success and the distinctive elements of the Martin business, a look at the Martin family is helpful.

MILDRED BROWN MARTIN

Roy O. and Mildred Brown Martin met at business school in South Bend, Indiana. Following his return from teaching at a business school in Beaumont, Texas, they renewed their acquaintance when Roy O. saw her at a church service in South Bend. He took her to lunch. They spent the afternoon together. And their courtship began. According to a daughter, she must have resisted marriage to Roy O. at first. But he was persistent. Mildred's mother apparently encouraged her daughter's marriage to Roy O., telling Mildred, "This young man, Roy, is gonna amount to something. He's gonna make a name for himself."[3] That observation turned out to be prophetic: Roy O. Martin amounted to something, and he made a name for himself, one that is emblazoned on products, advertisements and stationery that travel to various destinations worldwide.

LIFE BY THE BOARD FOOT

Their marriage occurred in the Brown's family home in Hartford, Michigan, on October 8, 1914. Mildred was twenty-two years of age at the time; Roy O. was twenty-four.

Business was always an important part of their marriage – even on their honeymoon. At the time of their nuptials, Roy O. worked for Nickey Brothers of Memphis, running their sales office in Rockford, Illinois. Following their long-awaited wedding and reception, the young couple went to Chicago by train for what was supposed to have been their honeymoon. However, upon checking into their hotel, Roy O. received a telegram concerning a problem with a carload of lumber in Kankakee, Illinois. Consequently, what was to have been a romantic honeymoon turned into a business trip—at least for Roy O. Presumably, believing his bride could wait, but the lumber could not, on the morning after their wedding, the groom left his bride in the hotel and traveled to Kankakee to deal with the pressing problem. The next day he made sales calls in Chicago then left for Rockford that evening where he rejoined his new wife. This established a precedent for succeeding generations. Martin men still mix business with any trip. Vacations frequently include contacts with customers.

In Rockford the newlyweds rented both a small apartment and a one-room office. When Roy O. was away on selling trips, Mildred handled the office, and, by all accounts, handled it quite professionally.

After moving to Alexandria and forming the Roy O. Martin Lumber Company, Mildred did not have a great deal to do with the business. The reason was simple: Roy O. did not like women around the office or at the mill.[4] She was, however, a stockholder in the company from the time of its incorporation (with one share of stock initially). Apparently, Roy O. wanted her to own stock and to be involved in the company, but not too involved. Mildred served on the company's board of directors from the beginning and became secretary of its board in 1925. The corporate minute book shows that she participated in discussions and often made motions that resulted in company decisions. From all indications, at least during those first years in Alexandria, she tried to assume a relatively active role in her husband's business. However, with three young children and another son and daughter born to the family within three years after relocating to Louisiana, personal responsibilities conflicted with her professional aspirations. Naturally, she had demanding home responsibilities, which precluded much participation in company

CHAPTER 6 - FAMILY

business. Too, by all indications, Roy O. fully embraced the early twentieth-century familial premise that a "woman's place was in the home."

In family Studebaker Mildred with Roy, Jr., and Ellis (standing)

After living in Alexandria for a few years, the family moved to Pineville where they lived in what was then a twenty-acre forest on Edgewood Drive. Originally, this property had been a retreat or a camp with only a small three-room house on it. More than one Martin child said that the move was for Mildred's health, but none of them knew what the health condition was or how it was affected by their move to Pineville. Since Pineville, with an abundance of trees, is a higher elevation than Alexandria, it is also a cooler, more pleasant place in the summertime, especially before the advent of air conditioning. That may have been the health consideration. Necessarily, the existing small cottage was enlarged to accommodate a family of seven. The expansive Edgewood property allowed the five children to have their own farm, of sorts; chickens, cows, horses, and even goats roamed their Pineville place. At one time, both a cow barn and horse barn stood on the property. As a result, the Martin siblings certainly were entertained in ways they could not have been at their Alexandria home on Marye Street where lots were small and houses were juxtaposed together.

LIFE BY THE BOARD FOOT

Artist rendering of tree house on Edgewood Drive

In other ways, though, they worked harder than perhaps they would have in their previous home. Each of the five children had chores and regular responsibilities. One daughter felt that because her mother grew up on a farm she never got the farm and country living out of her system. Others remember Mildred saying that her children could learn more from playful squirrels than from their neighbors in Alexandria. Whatever the reasons that prompted the move, according to those who knew her well, Mildred never seemed comfortable in the Alexandria social set and seemed content to avoid contact with other lumber families in the area.

Esther indicated that part of the reason might have been due to Mildred's frustration that she was not allowed to be an active participant in the business. Apparently, the couple was often at odds concerning the role a "dutiful wife" should play. Roy O. once bought her a black velvet dress and a nice necklace. He

CHAPTER 6 - FAMILY

wanted her to be decorative. She, as evidenced by her practical tastes, did not want to be decorative; she wanted to be on an even footing with Roy O. in the business. Esther also said that many of them thought that if Roy O. had given her a lumberyard to run, it may have saved a lot of other stuff from happening.[5] We can only guess at what this "other stuff" might have been. However, she apparently felt herself capable of active business involvement. In this time before women's liberation, those who knew her well surmise she felt stifled by her lack of professional opportunity.

Since Mildred was also a strong-willed, high-energy, active person, she necessarily found other ways to channel her energy and work out her frustration. One of her most ambitious (and most successful) projects was the founding of a public library in Pineville, a testament to her commitment to her community. The Martin Library celebrated its fiftieth anniversary in 2000.

Mildred Brown Martin

Most, if not all, Martins are musical people. Not only do they appreciate music, they also participate musically. Today, many are accomplished instrumentalists; others are professional vocalists. And Mildred fostered that musical background in all her children and as many grandchildren as she could influence. When Martin children turned four, Mildred would start their musical training by teaching them to identify middle "C" on the keyboard. Music was an integral part of her life, and she was determined to make it integral to the lives of her children and grandchildren. This personal love of and passionate appreciation for music provided an avenue for many of her community contributions.

After she and Roy O. moved their family to Pineville, some of their children, the youngest ones, attended Pineville Elementary School. Finding that the local public school did not teach instrumental music, Mildred began her campaign to remedy that situation. Typical of a Martin on a mission, the results were immediate. In the 1930s she hired a music teacher and personally paid his salary. She also helped organize a summer band, arranging for Werlein's Music Company of New Orleans to come to Pineville and set up a program of renting band instruments to Rapides Parish students. She ran the music program herself for about two years before the Rapides Parish School Board agreed that music indeed had a place in elementary schools.[6] This would be the same battle that Virginia Slaughter Martin, Ellis' first wife, fought fifty years later.

Just as Mildred had seen the need for public school music, she also saw the need for a park for African-Americans. By this time, their company had built housing adjacent to their original mill for employees, creating a neighborhood abutting the industrial site. Mildred realized this newly created neighborhood had no parks or recreation areas. She was burdened that children in the area had no safe place to play.

Her idea for a neighborhood park near the Fenner Street mill coincided with events brought about by World War II. A great influx of military personnel in the area (five military bases in Alexandria/Pineville) brought even greater numbers of African-Americans to Central Louisiana. Apparently, word had spread to Alexandria's African-American community leaders that Mildred wanted to build a park for local children of color. Desiring to ease the relocation burden for these military families in and around Alexandria, this group approached Mildred with their problem. Obviously, she had already proved her mettle as one woman who could get things done in her community.

In those days of segregation of races, the only park for African-Americans in Louisiana was in New Orleans. Sadly, people of color were not permitted in other public parks. Assuming the mantle of helping the underprivileged, she headed up a campaign to raise funds to buy park property for Alexandria's rapidly growing numbers of children of this race. Apparently, hers was not a formal committee; rather, she saw a need, and, not unlike her husband, she took the initiative in meeting it. With help from local banks

CHAPTER 6 - FAMILY

and other community leaders, like Louis Wellan, she made appointments and presented her appeal. Mildred successfully raised all necessary money for the park. With that money, her informal committee bought eighty acres in Alexandria. Broadway Street was cut through the property. Not only did these interested and involved citizens buy necessary land and dedicate it to the city for a park, their efforts opened the way for two schools to be built on the designated property – Peabody Junior High and Peabody High School. Both of these, prior to integration of all public schools, were originally intended for African-American young people.

The project for which Mildred is most remembered, however, is Camp MilMar. She personally owned eighty acres of land in Pineville fronting Highway 165. Ellis Drive ran through her property. Representing her independence, these eighty acres were hers to develop and manage as she saw fit. Apparently, she wanted to use this property to show Roy O. and her community that she, too, could succeed.

One of her first endeavors with the eighty acres was a children's day camp, established about the time she dug a lake on the property. She built a bath house and pavilion on the Ellis Drive side so area children and Martin grandchildren could participate in usual camp activities: swimming, boating and archery. This project lasted two or three summers.

Her real dream, however, was to establish a music camp on her eighty acres that would be similar to Interlocken in Michigan. But, as Roy, Jr., pointed out, in Michigan in the summertime the temperature is forty degrees in the morning while in Louisiana it is one hundred ten degrees at noon. Nevertheless, she began constructing a campus for overnight campers, one, however, that would not rival Interlocken. Mildred's ambitious music camp did not fare very well, lasting only about two years.

For one thing, its architecture was not really attractive, reflecting her practical, utilitarian tastes. One family member stated that her idea of construction was to hire a carpenter and tell him to build a building. Ellis said that whenever she wanted to build something, she would call him and he would send her a load of lumber. She bought all furnishings for the camp herself. Those with a more discriminating eye could see they were not always the most comfortable or the most attractive furnishings; instead, they were simply the ones most readily available—sometimes pieces that were found in someone's attic or storeroom.

LIFE BY THE BOARD FOOT

Cost was apparently the primary, if not the only, factor in her selection of furnishings; bottom line, she wanted to get them as cheaply as possible.

Another problem with the music camp was that Mildred could not let go of her control. Family members and friends remember her as a domineering person. She was not good at hiring people, then letting them carry out their program of duties. When she found trash on the property left by a teacher carelessly dropping a cigarette butt or by a child just as carelessly discarding a candy wrapper, not only would she pick it up herself but she would also complain about it, endlessly complain about it. Unable to delegate responsibility, she tried, unsuccessfully, to micro-manage the whole operation.

Some think that she began the camp because she was jealous of growing recognition and accolades that Roy O. received due to his business success. Perhaps she simply wanted to do something to make her mark and raise the cultural level of Central Louisiana. Certainly, Roy O. was not in accord with her dream for the property. He thought it ought to be made into a subdivision and sold as lots. In fact, one portion on the Pineville side was developed residentially. Ellis Drive runs through the front hill of the property, just off Military Highway in Pineville.

After the failure of Camp MilMar as a music camp, Mildred tried various other ways to utilize its property and buildings. She prepared for a kindergarten; but it did not materialize. At one time she envisioned a home for unwed mothers. Daughter Virginia opined that she was the last person to run something like that; she would be preaching to them all the time.[7] Mildred was not one to refrain from commenting, especially regarding morality.

A nursing home followed next on the Camp MilMar property. That lasted for about two years, also. The major problem with her retirement facility resulted from necessary licensing and state regulations mandated for nursing homes. Mildred also tried to micro-manage this worthwhile endeavor, but she was not careful about consulting state regulations. Basically, her ideas did not comply with those of the State. Naturally, the State won, and Mildred was once again out of business.

Ultimately, her beloved eighty-acre property was divided. A few years before she died, in June 1988, she donated equitable portions to each of her five children. Subsequent to that, the five siblings gave the southern portion of the total acreage to the Boy Scouts and the northern portion to the Girl Scouts, roughly valued at a $270,000 donation to each group.

CHAPTER 6 - FAMILY

First United Methodist Church of Pineville is now located on the Camp MilMar property. Norman related that he learned the First United Methodist Church in Pineville was interested in relocating from their site on Main Street right at the entrance of Louisiana College. This congregation of Methodists was interested in some property Norman owned. He offered to give his property in question to the church with the condition that Louisiana College would have the right of first refusal on the church site when they sold it. Necessary legal papers were signed. Doing their due diligence before building a new facility, these Methodist leaders had someone evaluate the sites they were considering for relocation. They learned the site Norman had given them was not as feasible as the portion of Camp MilMar the Boy Scouts owned. So the church sold the property Norman gave them and bought the Camp MilMar site from the Boy Scouts, building a new Pineville First United Methodist Church on that location. In 2003, the church bought the adjacent land owned by the Girl Scouts. Norman observed, "So they sold the site that I gave them. They bought the MilMar site and built a church there. The Boy Scouts got some money out of it, too. The Boy Scouts were happy. They were out of debt for the first time. The Girl Scouts are happy. The church is happy. My wife and I are happy that the church is happy. That was a win/win deal. It is one of the nicest turn of events I have seen."[8]

Mildred's Camp MilMar property went through quite an odyssey. The final disposition of property brought a happy conclusion to her saga. Her dream of enriching the spiritual and cultural climate of the community is also realized in the continuing ministry of the Methodist Church of Pineville, which now owns the entire eighty acres.

Another spiritually driven project of which Mildred was a part was Miracle Camp near Ringgold. N. A. Woychuck who was then pastor of the Cumberland Presbyterian Church in Shreveport formed the Bible Memory Association (BMA) in Shreveport in the early 1940s. This aggressive bible-learning program involved the memorization of biblical scriptures. Through a five-year cycle, young people would memorize from two hundred to two hundred fifty scripture verses a year in a ten-week or twelve-week period annually within that five-year cycle. Each week its participants received an award, usually a book and a Bible at the end of the first year, as well as a week of camp in the summer. After utilizing a rented camp for its first few years, the BMA established Miracle Camp at what was known locally as Parker's Pond on Highway 7 just north of Ringgold. Because Mildred was interested in the work of the Bible

LIFE BY THE BOARD FOOT

Memory Association, she became involved in the purchase and development of Miracle Camp. Through her many years of commitment, she gave a good deal of money to the project.

Mildred outlived Roy O. by more than twenty years. She died on October 11, 1995, at the age of one hundred three.

VIRGINIA MARTIN HOWARD

Mildred Virginia Martin, daughter and first child of Roy O. and Mildred Martin, was born on May 27, 1916, in Memphis.

Roy O.
with
Ellis and Virginia
Overton Park, Memphis

CHAPTER 6 - FAMILY

Mildred Virginia
with
Ellis
Memphis, Tennessee
(circa 1921)

When the family moved from Memphis to Alexandria to incorporate their new company, Virginia was seven years old. As evidenced by old photos, apparently Mildred tried to make their Alexandria home and city lot a healthy playground for her growing family. An early "playmate" for her children was Spike, the pet goat.

Virginia and Ellis
with
Spike
Marye Street
Alexandria, Louisiana

The small yard, however, provided insufficient room for the Martin children to play and grow—at least in the manner Mildred deemed fit. The move to Pineville would provide desired acreage for Mildred, but it caused adjustments for her children.

201

LIFE BY THE BOARD FOOT

During this era, Pineville did not have a secondary school. Necessarily, then, all Pineville students went across the Red River to Alexandria to finish their studies at Bolton High School. Virginia graduated from Bolton at the age of sixteen and enrolled in college, first at Stephens College. Unfortunately, her college career was interrupted—several times. After one semester at Stephens, she attended Louisiana College. Then she enrolled at Oberlin Conservatory of Music for a brief time. Virginia indicated that her mother did not understand credit hours and course prerequisites. Because her college career had been disrupted for various reasons, she had lost numerous hours. Another setback to completing her education resulted from an unwanted hiatus. Her parents kept her out of college for a time to help at home. This oldest Martin sibling finally graduated from Louisiana State University six years after she had finished high school. Determined, however, to continue her musical studies, in 1951 Virginia earned a master's degree in music from LSU after also studying at Julliard.

Virginia Martin

As the eldest child, Virginia had much responsibility at home. She would often baby-sit the younger children. Since she was a serious person, she tried to make them behave, correcting them in what she thought was a motherly fashion. Naturally, because she is only one year older than Ellis and only five years older than Roy, Jr., friction would often develop between her and especially those two brothers. Not only did she have to baby-sit, she also shopped for the family. When she was just fourteen years old, Mildred took her to the grocery store and taught her how to buy groceries. By the time she got her driver's

CHAPTER 6 - FAMILY

license at fifteen, she would drive to the grocery store and do all the family's shopping. At sixteen, she was cooking three meals a day for seven people. She did the family ironing, which she remembers taking three and one-half hours twice a week. At times, Virginia felt that she was an unpaid maid.[9] Having begun music lessons when she was four, Virginia continued the family's interest in music while assuming the Martin propensity for hard work.

Virginia married Mark Eugene Howard of Benton Harbor, Michigan, on October 5, 1940.

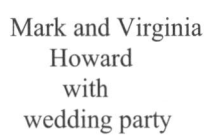

Mark and Virginia
Howard
with
wedding party

When the couple married, Mark held a mechanical engineering degree from Michigan's College of Mining and Technology. Their son Mark Eugene Howard II (Gene) is a retired electrical engineer living with his wife Irma in Austin, Texas.

Mark was working for Caterpillar Company in Peoria, Illinois, when he and Virginia moved to Louisiana for him to work with the Martin Company. He managed the company's first retail yard in Natchitoches; in fact, it was named for him – Howard Lumber Company. Mark and Virginia moved what she described as a sawmill house to Natchitoches where it was reassembled. This small frame house was constructed of unfinished wood and divided into two parts. The Howards lived in these humble accommodations for about eighteen months.

While a good engineer, Mark was not a good retail manager. After leaving Natchitoches, the Howards moved to Pineville while Mark worked as an engineer at the Alexandria sawmill, planning and supervising construction. He left the company in 1963 and formed his own sawmill-engineering firm. Mark Howard died suddenly and unexpectedly in 1979 from a heart attack while planting a blueberry bush at their Pineville home.

Virginia has not personally played an active part in the business. She said her father never wanted women around the mill. When Mark died, she asked for his seat on the board of directors, but that request was denied. She has, however, shared in joint ownership of company stock and land with other siblings.

Virginia Howard has also maintained her unique interests. She has taught music as an adjunct professor at Louisiana College, has given piano concerts on occasion, and has played with a symphony orchestra for benefit performances at least twice. She has a personal foundation - VMH Foundation. She also is a life member of the board of directors of both the Moravian Music Foundation and the Stearns Foundation of the University of Michigan. In 2004 Virginia Martin Howard continues to live in her home in Pineville.

ELLIS SPENCER MARTIN

Seventeen months after Virginia's birth, Ellis Spencer Martin was born on October 14, 1917, in Memphis.

Roy O. and Ellis
(circa 1918)

CHAPTER 6 - FAMILY

He had just entered the first grade when the family made their move to Louisiana. Ellis graduated from high school at Bolton High School, Alexandria.

The college career of this eldest son began auspiciously. One day after Ellis returned home from a lumber-selling trip, Roy O. told him not to unpack his bags. Without telling him where they were headed, he put Ellis in the car, drove him to Baton Rouge, and enrolled him in Louisiana State University. Ellis stayed at LSU for two years until calculus "did him in." When he came home from LSU, he told Roy O. that he could do whatever he wanted to with him, but he was not going back to school. The first thing Roy O. did was to send Ellis to Michigan to pick apples. Perhaps the agricultural interlude was intended to help Ellis appreciate school more, or perhaps it was to make him more willing to work in the sawmill. Whatever the purpose, he returned home to work with the company, where he continues in 2004 after almost seventy years.

This was the environment where he felt most comfortable; this was the environment for which he seemed destined; this was the environment in which he had literally grown up. The oldest son of "the boss" (the name Ellis uses when referring to his dad), he remembers his father carrying him in his arms around the mill, telling him about projects and explaining business procedures to him. This may be the reason that several interviewees feel that Ellis inherited more of his father's business sense than the other two brothers did, although both of them have done very well in business themselves. Neither of the other sons remembers accompanying their father like that. He began working in the sawmill in summers as a high school student, even laying out of high school one year to help build the mill at Castor.

Several years later when he was tapped to return to Castor, Ellis was running the small sawmill in Pineville that Roy O. had bought from Gene Glankler. Still a young man, Ellis was only twenty-two years old when Roy O. sent him to north Louisiana to rebuild that "temporary" mill, to cut out the timber on the Black Lake tract, and then to close the satellite operation.

LIFE BY THE BOARD FOOT

Ellis Spencer Martin
and
Roy O. Martin, Sr.

Since there was no place to live in Castor, he lived in Ringgold, about twelve miles away, renting a room from Marvin Hill and his wife. For the six months or so that he lived with the Hills, Ellis forged a close relationship with Marvin, whom he affectionately called "Pop." Indeed, in many ways, he respected this older gentleman much the same way he respected his own father, often seeking his advice. One such instance provided Ellis words that would become a cornerstone of his professional philosophy.

As the story goes, an individual had come to the Castor office, offering Ellis fifty cents per acre to lease part of the Black Lake property for oil and gas exploration. Having no prior experience with mineral leasing, Ellis did not know if this was a fair price. He asked Pop Hill for advice.

Pop responded, "How much did you pay for the oil and gas rights on that land when you [the company] bought it?"

Ellis replied, "Nothing."

Pop then countered, "Ellis, it's hard to go broke making a profit." The revised slogan, "You can't go broke making money" continues to reverberate through Martin's corporate offices today.

Ellis would work at Castor and live in Ringgold for the next thirty-five years, extending by a bit the mandate his father had given him—cut out the timber and return to Alexandria.

Ellis met Virginia Ruth Slaughter ("Ginny," to Ellis) through his mother Mildred. She arranged for her eldest son to come to one of her regular Sunday-afternoon musical soirees where she had invited the young Louisiana College student Virginia to sing. The set-up worked. Ellis married Virginia Ruth

CHAPTER 6 - FAMILY

Slaughter of Arcadia, Wisconsin, on July 29, 1941. Another mid-westerner transplanted in the South, Virginia had come to Louisiana—presumably only temporarily-- with her father who was an army officer serving in the Alexandria area.

Virginia Ruth Slaughter
and
Ellis Spencer Martin

At the time of their marriage, Ellis was twenty-three and Virginia was eighteen. Ellis and Virginia had five children: David Spencer, Bonnie Lou, Susan Annette, Jonathan Ellis (Johnny), and Mary Virginia. The two boys have each had association with the company. David left the employ of the company. Currently, Johnny is chairman and CEO. Youngest daughter, Mary Fowler, is corporate internal auditor.

The Martins were good neighbors, according to Mr. and Mrs. Cob Cook, who lived next-door to them in Ringgold. In fact, the two families were fast friends. After Cook was discharged from active military service following World War II, Ellis insisted that he work in the sawmill at Castor. Cook started as a shipping clerk and worked in several positions until he retired thirty-three years later.

While in Ringgold, Ellis and Virginia were active members of First Baptist Church. Ellis taught Sunday school and was a deacon. Virginia led music as a volunteer all their years of membership there. One year, Ellis' Sunday school class wanted to give him a Christmas gift, but they were not sure what the gift should be. After all, Ellis had no hobbies. Work, family and church—in that order—occupied his time. Mrs. Cook suggested that he could use a new suit. He had only one suit, which he would wear on Sunday, have cleaned during the week, and wear again the next Sunday. (Obviously, unlike his dad, he did not wear suits to work at Castor.) To determine his suit size without his being measured, his class members laid out his existing suit on the floor, measured it with string, and carried the results to the department store in Shreveport. Ellis was proud of his new suit – which fit perfectly.[10]

Virginia continued her active involvement with music after she and Ellis moved to Alexandria in 1974. For several years she taught music at Lincoln Road School in Alexandria, a predominantly African-American school. Although vocal music was her talent, she is credited with beginning the string music program in Rapides Parish public schools. Ellis, also, has an interest in music. He plays a musical saw.

Virginia apparently suddenly developed heart trouble at sixty-seven. She had open-heart surgery in Houston, Texas, and came through the surgery well. Unfortunately, she died two hours later on September 5, 1990. According to John Alley who conducted her funeral service, Virginia was the glue that held the Ellis Martin family together.

Ellis remarried in February 2000. He and Martha Avodna Walker, known as Moppie, continue to live in Ellis' Pineville home.

Even though Ellis had a tougher edge to him than either Roy, Jr., or Norman, according to most observers, he also had a softer side. As a neighbor, he often mischievously tossed pinecones from his yard into the Cook's yard in Ringgold. When he saw that employees or friends needed something, he would frequently provide it without claiming credit for his sensitive generosity, just seeing that it was done through the company commissary. He always saw that children of his mill employees had shoes for school. He still annually funds scholarships at a theological seminary in the Philippine Islands. Attending a high school musical in support of one of his granddaughters prompted another time of seeing (or feeling) a need, then acting to correct that need. He painfully endured the production, literally and physically, because of worn-out auditorium seats. Shortly thereafter he gifted Alexandria Senior High School with new seating for their auditorium.

In his business dealings, Ellis was nothing if not resolute. Attorney Charlie Weems told of a time in the early 1970s when he first became associated with the Martin enterprise that Ellis was involved in

CHAPTER 6 - FAMILY

negotiating an oil-lease deal. This occurred shortly after Ellis moved to Alexandria from Ringgold. When the oil industry was developing the Tuscaloosa Sands formation through the Atchafalaya River basin and eastward, W. A. Moncrief, a noted Texas oilman, came to Alexandria to negotiate an oil-lease deal with Ellis on Martin company land. Negotiations went well except for one point, not even a major point, on which they could not agree. Neither Ellis nor Moncrief would budge on that particular issue. Finally, Ellis called Weems aside and asked if they were right on that point. The young Weems replied that he thought they were. They went back to the conference table. When that point came up again and Moncrief would not relent from his position, then Ellis stood up and said, "This discussion is over" and walked out, leaving literally millions of dollars on the table.[11]

Perhaps, because he worked with him so closely for so many years, Zack Woodard knows Ellis better than anyone. He recalls, "I spent so many years accompanying him on business trips to negotiate deals I can say he was the best negotiator, [at least] until he got up in years, that I have ever seen. For example, the labor union at Castor, after years negotiating with him, decided to drop out at that location. He also negotiated the union contract at Alexandria. . . . He had a way of putting the other party on the defensive almost from the outset."[12]

Without doubt, Ellis' business acumen and leadership brought the company far beyond where Roy O. left it. Ellis acted on principle. As with the oil negotiation, once he decided on the right way to do something, he did not deviate. Weems described him as visionary, unswerving, and focused on specific goals for the company. He had a clear vision that allowed him to get any task done without getting bound up in distracting details. He was a risk taker. Like his dad, he, too, would give responsibility to a person to do a job, then hold him accountable for it. Weems described what Ellis stated: if a person could not do a job, he should not have it. Under Ellis' leadership, the company became performance oriented. Ellis has said that he does not care who does the job, as long as it is done. He had a toughness that allowed him to lead the company. Ellis, too, had the ability to make the right business decision. As Weems observed, whether it was happenstance, God's grace, or keen business instincts, he usually made the right decisions. And the company has profited from them.

Ellis had great admiration and affection for his father. He wrote, "I give credit to my father for instilling his methods and for taking time to explain and guide me in the lumber manufacturing and selling process. From an early age, he explained everything to me and guided me in the whole business. No child had better training and in return I loved him and tried to succeed in all that he gave me to do. . . . We talked a lot and were as close as father and son could be."[13]

      The following letter that Ellis wrote to his dad in 1944 provides a rather clear glimpse into their father-son relationship. At the time of this writing while Ellis was operating Martin Timber Company in Castor, he and his dad most probably interacted, at least on a daily basis, as perhaps any other employer to manager, manager to employer. Certainly, they disagreed about some company issues. And, obviously they exchanged occasional terse words asserting their professional opinions to the other, as evidenced by Ellis' admission of being "sorta hot like the other night." However, their overriding connection was father to son. Not only did Ellis recognize his dad as a positive role model, professionally and personally, he used this letter to voice his appreciation for all Roy O. had done for him and for the entire Martin family.

CHAPTER 6 - FAMILY

ROY O. MARTIN LUMBER COMPANY
INCORPORATED

Manufacturers of Hardwood and Yellow Pine Lumber

CASTOR, LA.

April 22nd, 1944

Dear Roy O.:

Monday is your birthday I think and I hope that this gets to you on that day.

I wanted to take time to remind my "Pop" that I love him and think the world of him and I didn't want him to pass away before I told him so.

There are times that I get sorta hot like the other night. I really meant nothing by it, you see I had just talked to a fellow that was backing out of this POW camp and I was mad at him before you called.

What I am today and all that I have is the result of your teaching, your generosity toward your children and the fact that you love them all and for myself, I think this is all that any father can do for his children. I hope that I am as good to David as you were to me.

I also appreciate my Mother more than she thinks and for not spending more time at home you will have to forgive as things are just too muddled up now to leave one's mind in the clear.

The Martins' are a pretty lucky bunch of people; not much sickness, no deaths as yet, lots of future and a pretty lucky past. What else could one want out of this world except a closer relationship between the children and parents? Maybe we can work on this next.

Take more time out Roy O., be assured and confident that we are all behind you and if it comes to the worst we will be happy that we are united.

All my love,

WE OPERATE OUR OWN MODERN
DRY KILNS :-: PLANING MILL :-: TIMBER SIZER
BAND MILLS AT ALEXANDRIA AND CASTOR, LA.

LIFE BY THE BOARD FOOT

Ellis' method of training his sons in the business was similar to that of Roy O.'s method with him. Ellis put a desk for David, then later for Johnny, in his Castor office and had them observe everything he did.

Other than what his father taught him, Ellis said that he had no training in his method of management. He said, "I didn't know how to do any of this stuff." But, in his words, he did what had to be done. And, obviously, he did it well.

When the company celebrated Ellis' eightieth birthday, Scott Poole, current COO, shared some thoughts about their leader:

> Mr. Ellis, as I know him, has always provided his employees with a solid example to follow. Like clockwork, his schedule and attendance to matters are both astonishing and confirming. You can't help but see our company in the walking-talking form of his gentleman. His attire and habits aren't hard to recognize.
> Mr. Ellis has sported those same old khakis long enough for him to see and create major changes in the timber industry. . . .
> Mr. Ellis, affectionately referred to as The Boss, has driven that same blue Oldsmobile (in progressively newer models) while regulations from local police juries and guidelines from the Environmental Protection Agency have created major changes in the cost and production of raw materials for our manufacturing facilities. . . .
> He has donned that standard equipment, his old tin hard hat, while our product line has evolved from pine lumber at a peckerwood mill to high-density hardwood OSB panels and SmartCore plywood manufactured at some of the most innovative and technologically advanced facilities in this country. . . .
> He has continued to wear those same old leather boots from a time when this company had no land base for timber supply until today, when we can draw from over 500,000 acres to meet the needs of our customers.
> No matter how our company has changed and will continue to change, some things simply won't. Some things are not supposed to change because, if they did, we would lose sight of what is important, of what got us here in the first place. . . .[14]

CHAPTER 6 - FAMILY

Ellis in khakis and boots

In 2004 at eighty-six years of age, Ellis goes to work every day, although he can no longer spend long days touring the woods he loves so well. Not only does he maintain office hours, he also visits the Martco mills at LeMoyen and Chopin on a regular schedule each week. He was never actively involved in civic affairs. His routine involved work, home, and church. In fact, for someone who headed an organization of the size and strength of the Martin enterprises, he is not well known in the Alexandria/Pineville area. Ellis said that he learned business procedures from Roy O. Not only did Ellis learn business procedures from his father, he also learned focus and drive.

LIFE BY THE BOARD FOOT

ROY OTIS MARTIN, JR.

Roy, Jr., was born in Memphis on June 3, 1921.

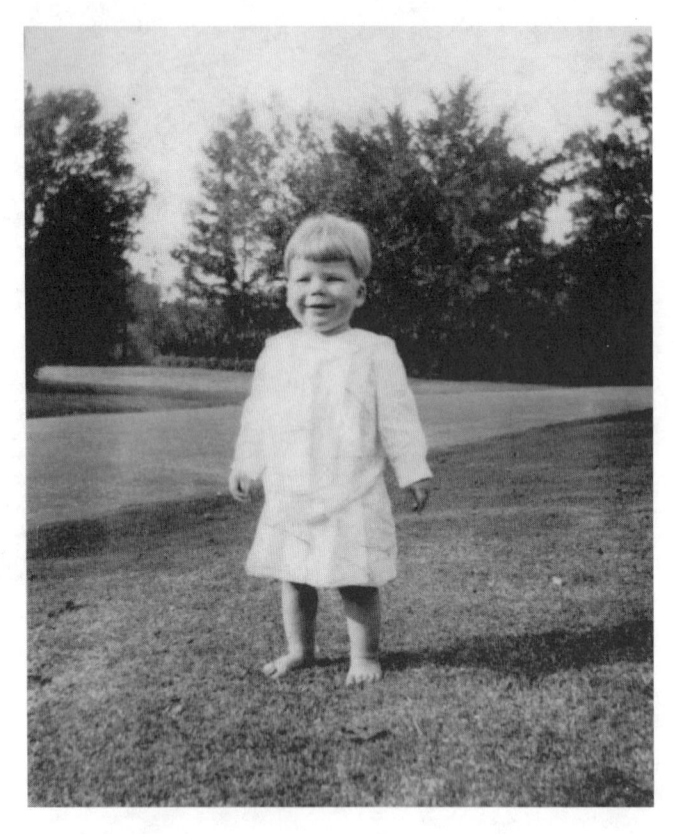

Roy Otis Martin, Jr.

He graduated from Bolton High School and enrolled at LSU, where he spent two years studying mechanical engineering. Then for nine months, he worked as a welder in New Orleans shipyards, gaining experience he intended to take back to his dad's sawmill. That job ended precipitously with World War II. With some of his friends Roy, Jr., joined the United States Coast Guard, all thinking they would spend their war years in New Orleans, out of harm's way. Instead, he spent those tumultuous war years in the North Atlantic on an air-sea rescue, weather ship.

On October 8, 1942, Roy, Jr., married Barbara Lee Morros (Bobbie) of Bunkie whom he met at LSU.

CHAPTER 6 - FAMILY

Roy, Jr. & Bobbie

They had four children: Barbara Marilyn, Joyce Anne, Mildred Carole, and Roy Otis III. When their four children were in school, Bobbie was very involved with all their activities, serving as room mother for many years. Carole recalled that her mother's after-school Halloween parties at their home on Georges' Lane were legendary, still fondly remembered by those childhood friends who were fortunate enough to be included in the festivities. Later, after her children had left home, Bobbie assumed responsibilities of Arbor, Inc., learning to perform accounting duties on the computer. She continued to maintain the Arbor books, even after she was diagnosed with cancer. Bobbie died in May 1993 after a valiant fight.

Two of the four third-generation Martins working for the company are children of Roy, Jr., and Bobbie: Roy III (president and CFO) and Carole Martin Baxter (accountant for Roy O. Martin Lumber Company, L.L.C., Martin Timber Company, L.L.C, and the concentration account).

Roy, Jr., and Vinita Grace Strackeljohn Johnson were married in October 1994.

Like older brother Ellis, Roy, Jr., began working at the mill in summers and on vacations when he was in high school. He remembers as a child hiding in the back seat of the car when Roy O. came home for

LIFE BY THE BOARD FOOT

lunch and then going with him to the mill. He would reveal himself only after they got to Fenner Street. Not wanting to spend unproductive time returning him across the Red River to Edgewood Drive, Roy O. would allow Roy, Jr., to spend the afternoon hanging around the mill, "getting in the way" he said.

When Roy, Jr., was twelve years old, he recalls traveling with his father and Wilkie to Memphis.

Roy, Jr.
(circa 1932)

The time was 1933 during the Depression when the Memphis Bank of Commerce wanted to call in the Martin's loan. One can only imagine the reaction Roy O. had to their suggestion to liquidate his company's stock of lumber and close his business in order to repay this advance. Certainly times were tough, but Roy O. already knew his business was sound. With that trip Roy, Jr., saw some of the grim realities of the business world. He also saw, he said, how hardhearted bankers could be.

Right after he came out of the Coast Guard just before Christmas 1945, Roy, Jr., like his older brother before him, went to work with the company.

CHAPTER 6 - FAMILY

Left to right: Roy O., Bobbie, Roy, Jr., Virginia, Esther, Ellis and Mildred

That January, only a short month on the job, Roy O. made his second son plant superintendent. With that promotion, the yard foreman quit, declaring that he was not going to take orders from a kid. Running a family business sometimes causes negative repercussions such as this. Integrating family members into positions of responsibility while affirming existing employees is often difficult, sometimes impossible.

In June 1962, with Ellis still running the Castor operation, Roy, Jr., became president of Roy O. Martin Lumber Company. Roy O. maintained his position as chairman of the board of directors while continuing an active role in operations. As Roy, Jr., expressed it, "No matter what your title, Daddy was still the boss." During his presidency, the physical condition of the mill was improved considerably. Alleys and walkways were concreted. New machinery was installed and upgraded. In fact, the mill was practically rebuilt. In most cases, Mark Howard did the engineering and Roy, Jr., oversaw the construction. While Roy O. was not adept at mechanical matters, Roy, Jr., was, thanks to his studies in mechanical engineering. He would often get greasy working on machines in and around the plant.

LIFE BY THE BOARD FOOT

Roy, Jr.
at
Roy O. Martin Lumber Company

Roy, Jr., continued as president of the company until 1978 when the mill was sold to Louisiana-Pacific. Both he and Ellis refer to his departure from the position as his being fired. The question usually comes up as to how Ellis could fire Roy, Jr., when they, as well as other family members, were stockholders and directors of the company. The normal answer to that question is, "You have to know the Martins." Following this departure from his role as company president, Roy, Jr., no longer worked for the company. He still retained his company stock, however, and his seat on the board of directors. He continues to serve as an emeritus board member for today's Martin Companies.

Roy, Jr.'s personality is different from either Ellis' or Norman's personality. He is generally considered more out-going and generous. Charles Jeffress related that when he would fly Roy, Jr., somewhere in the company airplane, Roy, Jr., would always give him money beforehand to cover any expenses. His temperament and social skills also allowed him to take more public positions than did Ellis. Following his father's service on the board of directors of Rapides Bank and Trust Company, Roy, Jr., served for many years on that bank board. He has been an active member of the Lion's Club in Alexandria. The Salvation Army has benefited from his forty-five years of service on that board.

CHAPTER 6 - FAMILY

Both Roy, Jr., and Vinita received Distinguished Service Awards from LSU at Alexandria due to each funding an endowed professorship at the school.[15] He also provides scholarships to Interlocken, a music camp attended by his girls. Of that beneficence he said, "When there is talent, it needs development."[16] His way of aiding in the development of talent was by funding scholarships.

Other Martin siblings are Baptist in religious faith. However, the original Roy O. Martin family had attended First United Methodist Church in Alexandria when they moved to Alexandria. After relocating to Pineville, the family began attending First Baptist Church in Pineville. As an adult, with a family of his own, Roy, Jr., returned to the Methodist church. He has a picture of a cornerstone at the former site of the Alexandria First United Methodist Church of three Roy O. Martins. The picture includes Roy O., Roy, Jr., and Roy III as a little boy. Roy O.'s name is on the cornerstone due to his financial help toward constructing the building. Today, Roy, Jr., and Vinita are actively involved in First United Methodist Church of Alexandria.

Roy, Jr., and Vinita continue to live in Alexandria. He keeps himself busy with his community activities, with his Arbor Company, and with his continued involvement in board activities of the Martin Companies.

NORMAN KITTELL MARTIN

The third Martin son, Norman, was born in Alexandria on August 29, 1926, the first of the two Martin children who would be born in Louisiana.

Norman Kittell Martin
(about age 10)

LIFE BY THE BOARD FOOT

Graduating from Bolton High School, he departed from his older brothers' example and attended Louisiana Tech. After eighteen months at Tech, he went into the Army.

Norman married Lorraine Dorothy Bentley on December 2, 1950. Norman and Lorraine have seven children: Patti Ann, Norman Kittell, Jr., Brenda Lorraine, twins Lisa Annette and Linda Louise, Robert Keith, and Julia Marie.

Lorraine Dorothy Bentley
and
Norman Kittell Martin

Like his male siblings, Norman began work with the company at an early age. During a summer break in high school, he worked in the planing mill. In fact, he credits his loss of high-frequency hearing to that summer. Planer mills are notoriously noisy. Their saws that finish lumber make a continuous and high-pitched sound. This penetrating sound pierces, and frequently damages, an unprotected ear. Unfortunately for Norman, he worked before today's use of earplugs and earmuffs, safety measures that protect sensitive ears.

CHAPTER 6 - FAMILY

Commenting on why and how he and his male siblings got into the business early, Norman said, "Dad was interested in continuing the business he had worked so hard to build. He looked to his three sons for the continuity of the business. He brought us in at an early age." [17]

Norman Kittell Martin

After his discharge from the Army in 1946, Norman joined his brothers already working in the company. His first major responsibility was with the forestry division, supervising that group while also working with logging operations. In this time before the company had begun actively acquiring land, Norman aided in land acquisition, surveying prospective land purchases and marking boundaries of purchased property. His introduction of applying bright yellow paint and bold "ROM" lettering on trees to mark property boundaries is still used by the Martin Companies today.

LIFE BY THE BOARD FOOT

Yellow "ROM '04" identifying Martin property and dating the property line

Implementing techniques learned from an experiment station in Crossett, Arkansas, Norman led in active improvement of the company's timber tracts. Known as timber-stand improvement (TSI), this process is one of girdling undesirable hardwoods to encourage pine growth. Claiming to be one of the first (if not *the* first) in Louisiana to follow that practice, Norman trained the Martin's first crew to work on TSI.

Reforestation was also a part of his responsibility. Much early land the Martins purchased was cutover, near-barren land. Often it was in small tracts of twenty to forty acres. Martins planted these properties in pine trees, allowing hardwood stands to be reforested by natural regeneration. Norman also oversaw the cottonwood plantation project on Raccourci Island in the Mississippi River.

In 1962 Norman became manager of Colfax Creosoting. He stated that in 1963 Ellis, Roy, Jr., and he divided professional responsibilities when they saw that their father, whose brilliant mind had become ravaged by a degenerative disease, could no longer function effectively. Ellis worked in Castor running that plant and all retail yards. Roy, Jr., ran the Alexandria mill. And Norman managed Colfax Creosoting.

CHAPTER 6 - FAMILY

After Norman left the company in 1967, he did not relinquish his shares in the business even though he no longer worked in it. He explained that his father had always been generous in giving shares in the business to the five children. He kept his stock, but he was no longer actively involved in daily affairs of the business. Like Roy, Jr., after his departure from the presidency, he continued serving on the board of directors. Norman resigned from his position on the board in 1996. He recommended, and the board agreed, that his son-in-law, Walter Jacobs Smith, succeed him as one to represent his family's interests.

Norman learned construction while working with the Martin Development Company, Inc., the entity which built low-cost housing to sell to Martin employees. After leaving the family business, Norman created his own company, Southwood Development Corporation, and built houses, mainly in underprivileged sections of Alexandria.

From construction, Norman widened his business interests to include apartment development and ownership. He also had mini-storage operations.

Although he no longer worked with the Martin Company, Norman worked. He developed a successful business enterprise of construction, apartment construction and management, and mini-storage operations on his own. He, too, practiced estate planning. Since none of his children followed in either his business or the Martin family enterprise, Norman sold his operations.

Norman has a deep spiritual sensitivity. One longtime observer of the Martin family recognized that Norman "had a tendency for religious matters."[18] This "tendency for religious matters" has kept Norman actively involved in Baptist churches in the Alexandria/Pineville area and in Baptist church life. He generously supports a mission school in Mexico, as well as other mission activities.

This religious and humanitarian impulse has doubtlessly contributed to some of his additional benevolent activities in the community. Norman was directly involved in establishing a Habitat for Humanity chapter in Alexandria. He wanted to use some of his building skills to help provide housing for those who could not afford it without outside help. Habitat for Humanity accepts no government aid and has a self-help aspect to it in that all applicants seeking a house from Habitat for Humanity have to put some "sweat equity" into the house themselves. Norman led in the organization of the Central Louisiana chapter. In 2004 he was not actively involved in it although he continues to support it financially.

LIFE BY THE BOARD FOOT

He also was instrumental in forming the Inner City Revitalization Corporation. The purpose of this organization is the revitalization of blighted, run-down areas in the community. In an effort to redevelop those neglected areas, this Inner City Revitalization Corporation accepts government aid and works with the city of Alexandria to create new, vibrant urban communities in existing neighborhoods.

Norman was also one of the organizers of the Central Louisiana Community Foundation. Working in twelve Central Louisiana parishes, this foundation manages individual donor's funds for charitable purposes. Hand-in-hand with community agencies, it offers opportunities for agencies with limited funds and for individual donors so that they have professional management for their philanthropic purposes.

Roy O. and Mildred renovated a frame building on the Louisiana College campus and gave it the name of the Martin Fine Arts Building. In 1992 Norman and Lorraine gave $1,000,000 to Louisiana College to complete monies needed to claim a gift of challenge from the Kresge Foundation and to construct a performing arts center. This was the largest individual gift that had ever been given to Louisiana College to that time. Following through on its challenge, the Kresge Foundation matched the Martins' gift, making the combined funds the largest benevolent grant ever received by the college. The result of that gift was the Martin Center for Performing Arts. Norman stated that it completed what his parents had begun sixty years before.

Martin Center for Performing Arts

CHAPTER 6 - FAMILY

The Martin Center for Performing Arts was dedicated on November 12, 1992. Patterned after an acclaimed theater facility at Vanderbilt University, this performing arts center contains 22,340 square feet of space. The center houses the school's Department of Communication Arts. Included in the Center are a performance area, classrooms, a video lab, debate research and practice space, and offices.[19]

Although the first of the Martin sons to leave active involvement in the Martin company, Norman is a successful businessman, an active churchman, and a major contributor to community humanitarian causes. He is active in civic affairs. In addition to his many community causes, he is a member of the Downtown Rotary Club in Alexandria. In late 2003, Norman and Lorraine purchased a home in Kansas City, Kansas, to live near their son Robert.

ESTHER MARTIN FLOYD

The youngest Martin child, Esther Louise Martin, was born in Alexandria on August 7, 1928. Also graduating from Bolton High School, she attended Kalamazoo College and Louisiana College before graduating from Louisiana Tech with a major in organ. As the other Martin children, she had begun music lessons at age four, Mildred's prescribed age for initiating piano lessons.

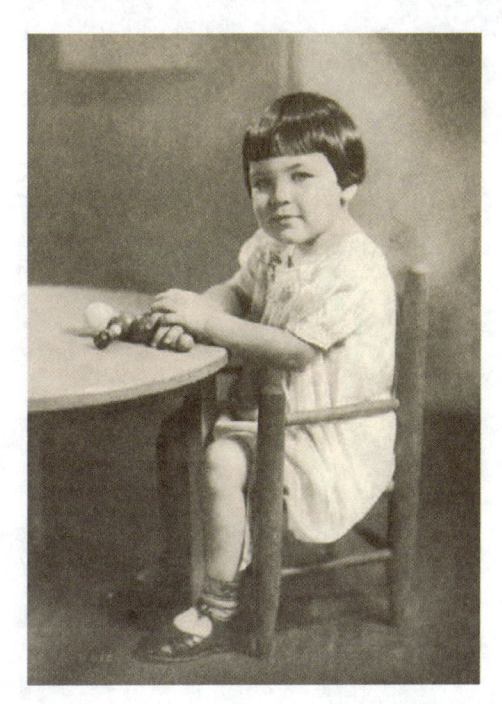

Esther Louise Martin
age 2-3

LIFE BY THE BOARD FOOT

Esther as a teenager

On February 23, 1952, Esther married John Claiborne Floyd, Jr., a medical doctor who has since retired from diabetes research at the University of Michigan. They live in Ann Arbor, Michigan.

Mr. and Mrs. John Claiborne Floyd
with
Mildred and Roy O. Martin

CHAPTER 6 - FAMILY

The Floyds have four children: Esther Elizabeth, Jennifer Marie, John Claiborne III, and Sara Melissa. Melissa Floyd Whittington currently owns the Martin family home on Edgewood Drive in Pineville, where she lives with her husband and two daughters.

Esther remembers moving from the house that she really liked in Alexandria to the Pineville property when she was 4 ½ -5 years old. That Pineville house, which began as a camp or retreat, still is home for a Martin and her young family. Chances are a visitor to the home-place might hear one of Esther's two granddaughters (fourth-generation Martins) practicing piano in its wood-paneled music room. [20]

The current structure has dramatically improved from its humble beginning in the early 1930s.

Circa 1930

2003
(front of Edgewood Drive house)

2003
(back entrance)

227

LIFE BY THE BOARD FOOT

Like Roy O. who fulfilled his professional vision of a successful company into the generations so, also, did Mildred realize her personal vision of establishing a family home in a beautifully serene rural setting.

The Edgewood Drive property originally had twenty acres, which housed their farm of animals, including at times chickens, pigs, goats, cows, geese, and horses. Esther remembers that every afternoon after school she had chores to do, tending animals or raking leaves in the fall. If friends were to come home from school with her, they got to help in her chores. According to Esther's remembrance, Mildred looked upon her youthful friends as additional persons to help with work rather than as guests of her youngest daughter. Since Esther is also the youngest child, she was the only child at home for a while. As a result, she had increasing responsibilities about the place until she, too, left for college.

The family also owned a cottage on Lake Michigan. Each summer, Mildred and children generally would spend at least one month at the cottage, which was close to both Mildred's and Roy O.'s childhood homes. Roy O. rarely spent much time at the cottage. Although he would travel to the vacation home with his family, he would soon become nervous with inactivity, returning to Louisiana, usually by train. Getting to the cottage with Roy O. was always a harrowing experience, said Esther. Her father's driving made her seasick with his starting and stopping, speeding up and slowing down in his hurry to get someplace. Apparently, he never learned to drive a consistent speed when behind a steering wheel.

Roy O. gradually, first because of business responsibilities and later because of physical incapacitation, let his grandchildren take his place behind the wheel on these annual trips to Michigan. Johnny remembers that driving Mildred to Michigan was a Martin rite of passage, especially for older grandchildren, as they received their drivers' licenses.

Cottage on Lake Michigan
Linden Hills, Michigan
1997

CHAPTER 6 - FAMILY

Esther suggested that the family was not really accepted locally when she was growing up in Central Louisiana. She cited that her father was not on church boards or committees even though he was the wealthiest man in the church. She also noted that she had never been in the home of other leading lumber families and that those families refused to do business with the Martins. Other family members are not as sensitive to that as is Esther. The major factor, cited by both family members and non-family members, is that these two Martins simply did not socialize with other people. Roy O. did not hang out with the lumber crowd. He and Mildred neither gave parties nor attended parties. They did not smoke or drink and did not associate with people who did. They worked and paid attention to business. They tended to their family and their home. And they went to church. That was the extent of their social activity.

Neither Esther nor her husband has been actively involved in the business. For most of their marriage, they have lived in Michigan. Obviously, she has shared in the stock and property that Roy O. gave to his children and has been involved in the same estate-planning program as the other Martins. But she has not been a part of the business itself.

FAMILY CHARACTERISTICS

From this review of the family of Roy O. and Mildred, family characteristics emerge.

Strong Will. The Martins are a strong-willed people. One does not have to have a close association with them to know that each one of them is strong willed. The trait is recognizable in both Roy O. and Mildred. That trait is simply in the Martin genes, and it shows up in many ways—even three generations removed.

Work Ethic. Their work ethic is a characteristic that is immediately noted in all Martins. Norman stated it: "We had a strong work ethic. Both our mother and father handed down a strong work ethic to us."[21] Both Martin progenitors were hard-working people. When Virginia gave her senior recital at LSU, Mildred arranged to have it broadcast in Alexandria over radio station KALB. Later, when the proud pianist got home, she found out that her father had been too busy working to listen to her recital over the radio.

Impetuous. The combination of their strong wills and their work ethic make the Martins appear impetuous. Often, their action is not so much from impetuousness as from impatience. A number of observers stated that Roy O. always knew what he was doing. While it might appear to others that he acted hastily or recklessly, he knew what he wanted to accomplish all the time. That characteristic likely had a lot to do with the dismissal of Roy, Jr. from his position as company president. While to outside observers the action was precipitous, obviously Ellis carefully (and surely painfully) planned it so the transfer of power would be as professionally seamless as possible. When Norman left the company, impatience was doubtlessly a factor. In each situation, these brothers must have been impatient with the way division of responsibility was working. Sibling rivalry had to play a part in both cases.

Performance Oriented. The Martin business is performance oriented, and individual Martin lives are performance oriented. They want to see results. Roy O. was impatient. He never stood still. When he did stand still, he jiggled coins in his pocket. They want to be doing rather than waiting. Martins want to see results.

Tension. One of the second-generation Martin children said there was always tension in the home. With that many strong-willed people around, tension is bound to occur, manifesting itself perhaps in terse words or short tempers. To survive contentedly in this Martin family, each member has to work out his or her place and learn how to relate to the others, remembering that most abrupt words or minor outbursts spring from an immediate situation and will be forgotten just as quickly as they were expressed. Apparently a situation that Mildred could not easily overlook was her inability to have an active role in the company. Several family members concurred that she felt she should have played a larger part in the business decisions. Tension certainly resulted.

The family does not seem to be an especially close family outside the office. They maintain good relationships. They keep up with one another. They are able to work well together. But they do not spend a great deal of time together. When it comes to business decisions, there is little sentimentality. If a hard decision involves a family member, so be it. However, an obvious paradox exists here because Martins seem to genuinely care for each other, for the good of the corporate family and for the good of each individual. They support each other in times of difficulty (such as illnesses and deaths), and they come together in times of celebration (such as weddings and anniversaries). Perhaps their annual stockholder/family meetings are building familial ties among the third and fourth generations that somehow became strained during the first and second generations.

CHAPTER 6 - FAMILY

Focus. Each of the Martins is a focused individual. Whether the focus is on business, music, or humanitarian efforts, each has the ability to focus. As already cited, Martin men seem to focus on business, family, and church.

Stewardship. The Martins have a strong sense of stewardship. Both Roy O. and Mildred, according to Esther, were interested in leaving the world a better place than they found it. Having the resources to do so, Martins as individuals and Martins as a family have generously contributed to both community and church. When asked if they were consciously taught philanthropy, the reply is that it was more by example. The original Martin parents apparently never lectured the family on philanthropy.

Faith. The Martins are people of faith. They are responsible church people who practice their Christian faith. As with philanthropy, faith was more "caught" than "taught." Norman said that church was where the car went on Sunday. Local churches, Christian missions, and church-related organizations have benefited from their financial support, their active involvement, and their leadership.

When the Martins come to mind, the Martin business success is what may first be considered. But the Martin business success would not have been possible without the Martins. Both individually and collectively as a family, the Martins are capable, caring, and contributing people. In business, community, and church, these Martins have made a difference.

Life By the Board Foot: 7

FORTUNE

Let a man so account of us, as . . . stewards . . . . Moreover it is required in stewards, that a man be found faithful (*1 Corinthians 4:1-2*).

Most Martins do not seem to draw a great line of distinction between "fortune" and "stewardship." By definition, "fortune" is success measured by possessions or money. A "steward" is one who manages the affairs of another. "Stewardship," then, is the act or attitude of managing one's life and possessions in a responsible way to conserve resources and contribute to society, based on the understanding that, no matter how much one has, he does not ultimately own it. All that a person has, he only manages while alive. At death all possessions are left behind. What remains is the result of how that person used life, influence, and possessions to better the world.

The Martin family consistently practices stewardship with the fortune they have amassed.

As confessing Christians and responsible church people, they generally view their financial success as a gift from a gracious God who has blessed their endeavors. As a result, most practice Christian stewardship in tithing their income (giving ten percent to their individual churches or church-related causes). But they have generously gone beyond that in supporting civic causes, institutions, and organizations.

Actions show that the Martins' sense of stewardship extends past their practice of Christian stewardship. They have been faithful stewards in the community. Individually and through the Martin Foundation, the Martin family has put their fortune to good use in contributions they have made to their local area. Daughter Esther said that both Roy O. and Mildred's idea was "to leave the world better than you found it."[1] Through numerous community contributions as varied as their individual family members, the Martins are indeed leaving the world better than they found it.

Until 1994 Martins, as a business entity, contributed to their community or to individuals as a need arose, basically at the whim of the particular Martin who was approached for a donation or who was made aware of a situation that needed financial support. Through the years, this Martin generosity had touched many institutions, many agencies, many lives, but the giving was sporadic and occasional.

LOUISIANA COLLEGE

Louisiana College (LC), operated by the Louisiana Baptist Convention, and the Martins have a long history. There in 1942 at this local college in Pineville, Roy O. and Mildred made one of their first significant philanthropic gifts. That gift provided for the renovating, decorating and furnishing of a two-story, frame building that would become the Martin Fine Arts Building.

Although this facility housing the music and art departments has been razed and replaced with a more modern structure, it served students well for several years as it honored the memory of Roy O.'s mother, Susie B. Martin.

A few years later, Roy O. and Mildred funded the remodeling of and an addition to Ware Hall, the oldest women's dormitory on the campus.[2]

CHAPTER 7 - FORTUNE

Then decades later in 1992, through their generous gift, Norman and Lorraine made possible the Martin Performing Arts Center.

Although this local, private Christian college has been a philanthropic recipient of choice, it has not always been an *alma mater* of choice for the Martins—perhaps simply because it was too close to home. Both Martin daughters, Virginia and Esther, did attend classes there for a while, but neither graduated from Louisiana College. Virginia Slaughter Martin who had been enrolled in LC when she met and married Ellis in 1941 returned to complete her degree in music there in 1978. Robert Keith Martin, Ph.D., son of Norman and Lorraine, received his undergraduate degree from LC in 1981.

Two Martins have even held adjunct teaching positions at Louisiana College: Virginia Martin Howard in the Music Department from fall of 1947 through the spring or 1950 and Maggie Burnaman Martin, Ph.D., wife of Johnny, in the English Department from the fall of 1985 through the fall of 1992.

THE MARTIN PUBLIC LIBRARY

Although Rapides Parish surely and eventually would have created a permanent home for its library in Pineville, the Martins certainly expedited and simplified that process. Donating property, (fronting Shamrock Street), finances ($14,000), materials (wood and paneling), and furnishings (all-inclusive), the Martin Public Library quickly became a reality when building restrictions were lifted after World War II.

Now serving as a living memorial to Roy O. and Mildred who made that vision a reality, the library continues to open its doors to the Pineville community. When the library observed its Golden Anniversary in 2000, the words spoken by Thomas Howell, Louisiana College faculty member, historian and Pineville native, described part of the legacy these two left to their community:

> The Martin Library was both a resource and a refuge for me during that portion of my childhood spent in Pineville. A generation later it lent the first library books to my two daughters. As an adult I continue to be a most frequent visitor. I am personally grateful for the opportunities provided. Countless others of all ages, races, levels of literacy, and diversity of interests have been encouraged, informed, inspired and entertained. The gift of the Martin family indeed has kept on giving, decade after decade, generation after generation – to paraphrase Roy O. Martin's words, enriched many lives, enlarged many horizons.[3]

Roy O. and Mildred saw a need in their community; they realized they could make a difference; and they used their personal resources to do so.

LIFE BY THE BOARD FOOT

PEABODY PARK

Peabody Park, Peabody High School, and Peabody Junior High School originally came into being, in great part, through the concerted efforts of Mildred Martin. Wanting to make her community better for everyone, not for just a select few, Mildred worked tirelessly to provide a place for African-American children to play in their own neighborhood and to learn in their own schools.

MARTIN FOUNDATION

Louisiana College, the Martin Pubic Library, and Peabody Park with two of its surrounding schools are only a few public institutions that have benefited from the philanthropy of those first-generation Martins. Their gifts were made mostly from personal financial donations, with some material donations made through the business. Martins continued to support their community in this manner through the next four decades. That method of philanthropy changed, and greatly improved, in 1994 with the Martin Foundation. Because it does not have a corpus of money invested through which it funds projects from the interest earned each year, it is not a foundation in the technical sense of the term. That is, the foundation does not meet the regulations of the federal Internal Revenue Service for foundations. Instead, it is the designated vehicle through which today's Martin Companies systematically and annually fund community, social, and educational activities in Central Louisiana. Through the Martin Foundation, Martins now exercise their community stewardship in a way that certainly would please their ancestors Roy O. and Mildred.

During its semi-annual meeting in October 1994, at the suggestion of Johnny, the board of directors appointed Lorraine Martin to head a two-person committee (she and one other) to determine and then to distribute charitable contributions for Roy O. Martin Lumber Company. This committee could enlist two other persons to help them in determining the entities to receive all distributed monies.

CHAPTER 7 - FORTUNE

Lorraine Martin
1997

Lorraine and her committee impressed stockholders and board members with their progress when they gave their first report at the annual meeting in April 1995. This report states that the committee would screen all requests for charitable contributions and would operate under the trade name of the Martin Foundation. The executive committee of the board of directors approved the annual budget for the foundation, whose designated focus is to assist charities that address individual's needs in five categories: social programs, cultural programs, education, civic programs, and disaster relief as well as some discretionary funds to meet charitable needs that occur during the year. The Martin Foundation confines its activities to the five Louisiana parishes in which the Roy O. Martin Lumber Company operates. By the time of the 1995 report, scholarships were set up at Louisiana College, Louisiana State University at Alexandria, and Northwestern State University. That number had tripled by 2004.

Money is provided through a budgeted item in the Martco Partnership. Its annual outlay of funds is recommended by a charitable contributions committee and approved by the company board of directors. Although originally conceived as a percentage of annual profits, the amount is actually a decision made each year by Martin's board of directors.

Since inception of this foundation in 1994, it has dispersed back into its community more than three million dollars. Its largest single beneficiary annually has been the United Way of Central Louisiana. Today, about thirty-five percent of its annual budget goes to this umbrella organization. In addition to the

LIFE BY THE BOARD FOOT

United Way, some individual social programs are also funded. These include organizations such as the Boy Scouts, the Girl Scouts, the Boys and Girls Club, the Hope House, both the YMCA and the YWCA, the Shepherd Center Ministries, the Habitat for Humanity, and the local food bank. The biggest contributions of the Martin Foundation are to social programs.

Education is its next leading beneficiary.

College scholarships were the first educational items funded by this philanthropic arm. By 2004, scholarships available first to children of employees were provided to nine colleges and universities throughout Louisiana: 1) Louisiana State University in Baton Rouge, 2) LSU at Eunice, 3) LSU at Alexandria, 4) University of Louisiana in Monroe, 5) University of Louisiana in Lafayette, 6) Northwestern State University in Natchitoches, 7) Louisiana College in Pineville, 8) Louisiana Tech University in Ruston, and 9) Southeastern Louisiana University in Hammond. If children of employees do not apply or qualify, other deserving students receive these educational benefits.

Matching funds for annual gifts to colleges and universities is another way Martins contribute to post-secondary education. The Martin Foundation will match employees' donations to area colleges up to a maximum of $5,000 per employee. Essentially, this means that one who works for any Martin company can double his or her personal donation to an area college through a matching gift made by the Martin Foundation.

Not only does the Martin Foundation fund college scholarships for children of employees, in 2001 scholarships were also made available for employees who want to further their education. This program grew out of Martins realizing that investing in the futures of their employees is an investment in the future of their company.

Public school education is a part of Martin benevolence through Partners in Education. For a number of years, the Martin Foundation has paired with Martin Park Elementary School in Alexandria through the Partners for Education program. For most of those years, the foundation gave a sum of money to the school, which the school could use at its discretion. Maps, globes, and teaching materials were provided to the school in this way. In addition, items for the use of the school are purchased through the company's purchasing agents. The Martin purchasing department will find good deals on needed items through the internet or will locate a more economical source for supplies or materials. Since schools can

CHAPTER 7 - FORTUNE

purchase these items without paying sales taxes, money is provided and information shared so the school can make those more cost-efficient purchases. Horseshoe Drive Elementary School in Alexandria has more recently become a Martin partner-in-education.

In 2000 the Martin Foundation bought thirty-three computers for Alexandria Senior High (ASH) in Alexandria. Because ASH did not have a room equipped for these high-tech machines, Martin also donated materials and paid for building a computer lab in this area school.

Aid to schools may take forms other than monetary gifts or guides to beneficial purchases. It sometimes is manifest in a more personal touch. Palmetto Elementary School is located near the Martco OSB plant and sawmill at LeMoyen. Each year the Foundation provides a birthday party for each child in that neighboring school.

Although not a part of the Martin Foundation, another contribution the Martin Company makes to the education of its employees and dependents comes through the ConSern program. Administered through the United States Chamber of Commerce, this "Loans for Education" program offers competitive interest rates, extended pay-back times and other unique features not found with conventional bank loans or institutional financing arrangements. The Martin Company is a sponsor of the program, allowing many of its employees to use ConSern as a financial source to provide education for their dependents.

In what could possibly be considered an employee benefit through the Martin Foundation, company employees may participate in an adult literacy program or a GED (graduate educational diploma) class. Both adult-literacy classes and GED classes are taught at Colfax Treating Company and Martco Partnership plants at both LeMoyen and Chopin. Through partnerships with Adult Education divisions from both Rapides and St. Landry Parish School Boards, classes in adult literacy and GED preparation are taught at Martin manufacturing facilities.

Adult literacy and GED preparation classes are usually two hours long and meet once or twice a week. Classes are taught on-site at the facilities. Instructors travel to and from Martin facilities for classes so that employees do not have to travel after work. Plant managers adjust work schedules for those employees taking courses, accommodating workers in establishing class times and dates. In the spring of 2001 courses offered were GED preparation, Literacy for Learning to Read or Reading to Learn, and English as a Second Language. Thirty-three Martin employees participated in that program in the spring

LIFE BY THE BOARD FOOT

2001 semester. Thanks to Mary Fowler who spearheaded both adult literacy and GED preparation classes, some in Martin's workforce are being provided an opportunity for personal and educational betterment that was never before offered them.

In addition to social programs and educational interests, the Martin Foundation contributes to its local community through both cultural and civic programs. Supporting public radio and Louisiana Public Broadcasting, Rapides Symphony, and Alexandria Museum, Martins address cultural interests in their community. Civic programs include building pledges for such projects as the Central Louisiana Performing Arts Center, Alexandria Museum of Art, Habitat for Humanity, Cenla Affordable Housing, Alexandria Housing Authority, Louisiana Baptist Children's Home, and Budget Management Services. The Red Cross and Angel Care have also been recipients of Martin Foundation beneficence. Fourth-generation Spencer Martin, who is the company's information systems programmer-developer, currently directs the Martin Foundation.

Some individual Martins have their own personal foundations through which they fund charitable causes. Others put their energies into creating or assisting other foundations. One example is Norman who participated in organizing the Central Louisiana Community Foundation and served as its president. Serving all twelve Central Louisiana parishes, this foundation accepts funds from smaller donors and organizations and, with professional expertise, manages those funds to help meet community needs. Martins give back to their communities in multiple ways and through various charitable conduits; however, the Martin Foundation is the official charitable arm of the Martin Company. Though not a foundation in the strictest sense of the term, it is the means by which the company leaves their community a much better place than they found it.

CONSERVATION CONCERNS

As major landowners – about six hundred thousand acres in 2004 - Martins have a vested interest in conservation. Conservation of natural resources, including the trees upon which they base their business and the land that produces those trees, is an absolute necessity for the Martin Company. Adherence to forestry Best Management Practices (BMPs) is one means of practicing conservation and sustainability of timberlands. But with leasing company land for hunting, their interest in wildlife conservation is also

CHAPTER 7 - FORTUNE

paramount. Conservation practices are additional contributions that Martin Companies makes to their larger community.

Reforestation is an obvious means of conservation. For years the Martin Company has aggressively practiced replanting harvested tracts of land. Their goal is to create a sustainable forest of trees—for today and for the future. In 1999, for instance, forest crews in their pine districts planted 7.5 million loblolly pines and .7 million slash pines, covering 14,700 acres.[4] Replanting occurs from November to March.

Planted seedlings

Planting a pine plantation or developing a tree farm is not just a matter of sticking a seedling in the ground and hoping it will grow. A tree farm requires intensive cultivation. After final harvest on a piece of property, the site may be treated with prescribed chemicals to kill any undesired, invasive species that may be present. If the site is on heavy clay soils, the area is then cultivated with plows attached to bulldozers. Root growth of tender seedlings is enhanced by planting trees on beds created by the ripping and bedding of plowing. Young trees are specifically spaced from each other to give growing room for each plant. Chemicals may again be applied to control invasive plants if deemed necessary. Also if needed, additional treatments are applied at years three or four. The site and seedlings are fertilized in order to replenish all naturally occurring nutrients in the soils. These tree-farming practices result in a quality product. Like any farmer, the Martin tree farmer strives for the highest possible yield on each acre of land.[5]

Another conservation practice that both protects and improves the environment is their voluntary adoption of Streamside Management Zones (SMZs) along waterways. Included in the Best Management Practices for forestry as developed by the Louisiana Forestry Association, SMZs are those areas adjacent to waterways (streams, lakes, rivers, bayous, and canals) that are left natural (not cleared of trees) when an area is harvested. The soil type, slope, vegetative cover, and character of each stream determine the width of a specific zone. Maintaining SMZs results in preserving shade for natural streams, maintaining water temperature, and reducing sediment entering the stream through erosion. This voluntary practice by the Martin Company helps to improve water quality in Louisiana, in and around the six hundred thousand acres it actively manages.

Mallards in flight

Night heron

CHAPTER 7 - FORTUNE

As its name implies, the Nature Conservancy is a non-profit national organization whose purpose is conservation of scenic land. Lands owned by this ecologically aggressive group are taken out of production, removed from development and managed in such a way as to preserve their indigenous pristine states. In 1998 the Martin Company donated to the Nature Conservancy a 160-acre tract of land that is located in both Rapides and Evangeline parishes.

RUBY-WISE SCHOOL FOREST

Ruby-Wise School, an elementary school in Rapides Parish just east of Pineville near the community of Kolin, was a junior high school in 1951. Martin owns a twenty-acre tract of timberland on Kastanek Road, near the school. In 1951, Roy O. Martin Lumber Company harvested that tract and gave its proceeds to the school.

Roy O. thought that replanting the property would teach those young school children basic principles of reforestation and would give a demonstration that reforestation would work. Acting on that belief, he devised a plan to educate a new generation: let those school children learn to be part of a future generation of tree farmers. Between 1952 and 1955, with help from Martin foresters, students at Ruby-Wise School replanted the twenty-acre tract. When this plantation matured, Martin harvested that tract again in 2000, giving more than $100,000 to the school.

LIFE BY THE BOARD FOOT

To continue to press home the message of reforestation, to emphasize that trees are an important renewable resource, Martins again assisted students of Ruby-Wise School in replanting the twenty-acre piece of ground. In some cases, grandchildren of some of the children who planted the first plot in 1952-1955 participated in replanting the same land nearly fifty years later.

District 1 Forest Manager
John Dunn
Assisting in Planting Pine Seedling

November 2000

CHAPTER 7 - FORTUNE

Roy III was quoted in the Alexandria Daily Town Talk, "Sound forest practices just reap so much more out of the land than Mother Nature could provide." He noted that while reforestation was not unknown in 1952-1955, it was not commonly practiced. Of his grandfather's action, Roy III said, "He knew it was a renewable resource, and you never took more from the land than you gave back."

Their monetary gift along with a plaque made from a cross section of the first tree milled from the timber donation was presented to the school in mid-November 2000. School principal, Debra Lucas, observed that it was appropriate at Thanksgiving. "It's like a gift from God," she said. The school planned to use the donated money to update its computers, automate its library system, replace its intercom system, and buy equipment for the students. "It really is a godsend," she said. And she further stated that, "Our school definitely needs some upgrades. We're hoping to spread it in a lot of directions to help the kids."

At a ceremony connected with the presentation, the Martin family announced that they would again dedicate future proceeds from that tract to the school for the next fifty years. [6] Visionary Martins continue to look to the future.

DONATION OF OFFICE BUILDING

Martin Companies moved into their ROMEX World Trade Center in Alexandria in November 2001. Its dedication and open-house celebrations were on November 23, 2001, the day after Thanksgiving.

taxpayers the costs of purchasing a piece of property and building a new facility for education and community events, Martins offered their Mill Street structure.

When first built on the site of the original mill on Fenner Street, the location of this administrative office complex had made sense. But by the time of the donation of the building to the city, it was no longer near a Martin facility. Rather, it was located in a rather out-of-the-way spot in a minority residential neighborhood. In vacating that property, the Martin Company left an area it had occupied continuously since 1923. However, needs had changed, and another opportunity had once again "knocked" on Martin's door.

The former Martin corporate office is now Martin Community Center. Officially dedicated on February 4, 2004, its more than twenty-one thousand square feet of building space on almost two acres is now home to "classrooms and meeting areas inside, a place to play basketball outside, and a playground protected within a courtyard."[7] Combining Martin's physical donation with $1.2 million in a Community Development Block Grant and property tax-supported, capital expenditure funds, the remodeled structure showcases what can happen when public and private sectors team together to improve their community. Even Martins attending the dedication were impressed with the results.

"All I can say is 'Wow!'" Roy Martin III said of the renovated building. "We are just so grateful that God has blessed us and that God presented us the opportunity to do something useful with this building."[8]

Martin Community Center
2301 Mill Street

CHAPTER 7 - FORTUNE

While this donation saved the City of Alexandria several million dollars in purchase price and construction costs, it likewise immeasurably rewarded Martin Companies. Johnny said almost immediately after occupying their new space, in ways that perhaps cannot be quantified, employees assumed a new level of professionalism, working more efficiently at their jobs and commanding greater respectability from customers and peers within their business community.

COMMUNITY INVOLVEMENT

Both the Martin Company and the Martin family are consciously involved in the life of their community. A part of their stewardship is this active involvement in making their community a better place to live. Their corporate culture as well as family tradition does not allow them to take from their local area without returning something both in terms of benevolent support and personal involvement. Community involvement, however, is as varied as are the individual Martins.

Most Martin family members are active church members. As confessing Christians, church is an important part of their lives. After all, when Roy O. returned from Beaumont, Texas, to South Bend, Indiana, he became reacquainted with Mildred whom he first met at business college when he spotted her sitting a few rows ahead of him in the Methodist Church. As active church people, Martins not only attend church services and activities regularly but they also sing in the choir, teach in Sunday school, serve on committees, minister as deacons or elders, and tithe their incomes.

A quiet, but nevertheless expressive, show of Christian commitment from both the family and the company is a Christian flag, one of four flags (Christian, federal, state, and company) that flies each day in front of their ROMEX World Trade Center. (See photo on page 245.)

While obviously a part of the business community of Alexandria/Pineville, Martins have also been involved in professional organizations that reach beyond their own business. Organizations such as the Chamber of Commerce and the Better Business Bureau receive their support. Roy O. served on the board of directors of the Rapides Bank and Trust Company. Roy, Jr., succeeded him on that board. That tradition continued until 2000 while Roy III served on the local board of Bank One, which acquired Rapides Bank and Trust in 1998.

LIFE BY THE BOARD FOOT

Through generous gifts to the United Way via its Martin Foundation, the company supports community social organizations. But community benevolence goes farther than that; Martins also serve on boards of directors of some of these organizations. The Salvation Army is but one example. Roy O. was a member of the Salvation Army board of directors, followed by Roy, Jr. Roy III currently serves on that board. Norman was one of the founders of the Habitat for Humanity chapter in Central Louisiana and also was a founding member of the Central Louisiana Community Foundation.

The Martin family identifies with their community through membership in civic clubs. Roy O. was a member of the Kiwanis Club. Roy, Jr., is a Lions Club member. Norman is a member of the Alexandria Rotary Club. Roy III has served on boards of the local United Way and Rapides Regional Medical Center. He is an active member of the Lion's Club.

Education in Central Louisiana benefits greatly from Martin involvement. The Martin Foundation actively participates in improving education in elementary, high school, and post-secondary institutions. Both Mildred and Virginia Slaughter Martin made significant contributions to public school music in Rapides Parish. Roy, Jr., his wife Vinita Johnson Martin, and Virginia Martin Howard are three of only seven persons who have received the LSUA Distinguished Service Award, the highest honor the university bestows on members of the Central Louisiana community.[9] Virginia Howard and Roy and Vinita all have endowed professorships at LSUA.

The local community benefits from the presence of the Roy O. Martin Lumber Company and its related companies. Both the company collectively and family members personally contribute significantly to their community. Martins are good neighbors, both corporately and individually. They understand the concept of stewardship and consistently practice it. They use their family fortune responsibly.

Life By the Board Foot: 8

FUTURE

According to the grace of God, which is given unto me, as a wise masterbuilder, I have laid the foundation, and another man buildeth thereon. But let every man take heed how he buildeth thereupon. . . . If any man's work abide which he hath built thereupon, he shall receive a reward. (1 Cor. 3:10,14).

What is the future of the Roy O. Martin Lumber Company and its related companies? The sawmill Roy O. bought in 1923 on Fenner Street in Alexandria is no longer there. The administrative office building adjacent to the mill that was occupied by the company for twenty-five years now belongs to the City of Alexandria. The sawmill at Castor was sold, then closed, and now stands as an empty reminder of the bustling activity at that site for many years. The dozen retail outlets scattered across Louisiana, the one in East Texas, and the one in Southern Arkansas no longer exist as Martin businesses. Only one of Roy O.'s children, four of his grandchildren, and three of his great-grandchildren work for the company in 2004.

Standing (left to right): Spencer Martin, Roy Martin III, Carole Martin Baxter, Nicole Robbins Harris and Johnny Martin
Seated (left to right): Natalie Martin Monroe and Mary Martin Fowler

LIFE BY THE BOARD FOOT

While the foregoing statement is true, it is also true that the company employs almost eleven hundred employees and operates four manufacturing facilities at three sites. Each of these plants is state of the art. The company owns about six hundred thousand acres of land and is still strategically acquiring land. In late 2001 the company moved into its new ROMEX World Trade Center, its office and administrative complex. Although a limited number of descendents of Roy O. and Mildred are directly involved in the company, included in these are the chairman of the board and CEO and the president and CFO. Most members of its board of directors are family members. In addition to this board, a six-member advisory board has been formed. Two of the six members of this board are Martins, Johnny and Roy III. Unequivocally, Martins still run the company.

However, since the number of Martins actively engaged in the daily work of the company is limited, a move to professional management is not just underway, it is being aggressively implemented. In typical Martin fashion, none of the operations is sentimentally held; as history indicates, the possibility of moving into new areas of operation in the forest products industry is always open. Today, employees receive a great deal of attention from management. Martins realize their employees are their greatest assets. As a result, their desire to make the Martin Company employer of choice in Central Louisiana is strong. As a privately held company, the Martin group is both poised and willing to make any necessary changes to stay competitive and profitable in a rapidly changing industry. Company leaders continually review their management processes and actively seek to be both effective and efficient.

As this successful organization completes the eightieth year of its existence, the future of the Martin Company is quite bright and promising, thank you.

REORGANIZATION

The second major reorganization of this company became official on December 29, 1999. Because Roy III devoted much of that year to this very expensive and inordinately massive task, it is most commonly referred to as the "reorganization of 1999." Working with Pete Marwick of KPMG, he completely restructured all existing Martin companies into limited-liability formats. To do so necessitated liquidating those original companies. All assets were then transferred tax-free into their new counterparts.

CHAPTER 8 - FUTURE

When queried about the reason for maintaining multiple companies through this restructuring of the corporation, Roy III responded that it allows more favorable tax consequences. In addition, "Each tub sits on its own bottom." Each idea or business enterprise is given its own identity so it can stand on its own. He asserted that the company does not have favorites. One company does not subsidize its sister companies. This approach obviously works because, overall, the corporation consistently makes money. For instance, if the plywood plant is not profitable, the sale of pine timber to the plywood plant by the woodlands division would make money for the woodlands division and, therefore, the company would profit.[1]

Their organization is continually being refined. With moving to their new administrative office building, ROMEX World Trade Center, various functions of the business were consolidated. Sales, for instance, of all Martin entities are handled from that central center rather than from their outlying sites, as they had been previously. All manufacturing operations have been put under the Martco Limited Partnership.

One group of nine managers for the current Martin Companies now directs these various businesses. Five managers are Martin family members, one representing each of the five second-generation Martin children: Gene Howard (Virginia Martin Howard), Johnny Martin (Ellis Spencer Martin), Roy Martin III (Roy Otis Martin, Jr.), Walter Jacobs Smith (Norman Kittell Martin), and Elizabeth Floyd, Ph.D. (Esther Martin Floyd).

Martin Family Managers

Standing (left to right):
Walter Smith, Elizabeth Floyd and Gene Howard

Seated (left to right):
Roy III and Johnny Martin

LIFE BY THE BOARD FOOT

The remaining four managers are professionals from outside both family and company.

This team of outside advisors grew out of Johnny and Roy III envisioning a group that could offer innovative direction. They thus created a board of advisors in the spring of 2002, which, with the 2003 restructuring, placed them alongside the former family board. The full group of nine managers meets twice annually, with the outside advisors meeting several additional times to discuss items in greater detail.

In those additional meetings, the advisory team offers strategic thinking and suggests long-range planning for today's Martin Companies. Each person on the board of advisors has a particular field of expertise. This group is composed of Johnny, chairman and CEO; Roy III, president and CFO; Charles S. (Charlie) Weems III, Esq., of Alexandria, company attorney and legal advisor; James J. (Jim) Davis of Atlanta, Georgia, sales and marketing expert in forest-products industries; Dr. William (Bill) Slaughter of Baton Rouge, former management professor at LSU and management consultant with SSA Consultants, Inc.; and Buford W. Price, consultant from the wood-products industry. Their purpose is to help company management strategize effectively and innovatively, for the long term. They evaluate key people working in the organization, encouraging each to think "outside the box." They also consider ways to upgrade skills. Essentially, and importantly, this group acts as a contrarian body whose primary role is to keep Johnny and Roy III from getting tunnel vision.[2]

Martin Executive Advisory Group
(Left to right: Bill Slaughter, Buford Price, Jim Davis and Charlie Weems)

CHAPTER 8 - FUTURE

These executive advisors search for creative resources to glean information and implement new ideas. A professional, experienced group, the board of advisors serves its purpose. For instance, Vision 2004 grew out of their discussions. Bill Slaughter helped create two important interchanges between management and employees: 1) professional management training for supervisors and 2) "town hall" meetings. At the annual "town hall" gatherings, Johnny meets every shift within every manufacturing division. The two to four weeks necessary to complete this yearly goal are grueling as he makes both early and late shift changes at each plant. However, the results are more than worthwhile as company chairman/CEO interacts personally with every front-line employee in small groups, answering questions that would otherwise be unheard. Because of these innovative "town hall" meetings, an important dialogue is forged between management and personnel.

Jim Davis, another executive advisor, suggested the name "The GRID" for the company's new product. The advisory group then outlined its marketing program, which has already proven successful.

Working closely as a unified team, these advisory and family managers pursue a common goal: perpetuating and growing today's Roy O. Martin Lumber Company for the benefit of future stakeholders.

LIFE BY THE BOARD FOOT

LEADERSHIP

The current team of first cousins works well together. According to Johnny, he and Roy III have a good relationship. They are both committed to seeing the company continue for another four or five generations of Martins.[3]

Jonathan Ellis Martin and Roy Otis Martin III

Others agree with Johnny's assessment. Paul Hood, accountant, observed that they function well. They have a line of command in the company - and they follow it.[4] Attorney Charles Weems is of the opinion that their similar engineering backgrounds make the two uniquely qualified to achieve results.[5] Bob Chown of Perforex, a management consultant firm with which they worked, observed that Johnny and Roy III are very complementary in the way they run the organization. He sees Johnny as perhaps more intuitive, observing that he has an almost-innate understanding of operations. Roy III, on the other hand, has a good (some call it phenomenal) grasp of numbers. Working with company information technology personnel, he pulls the myriad threads together with numbers. Roy III then puts those numbers together in a usable

CHAPTER 8 - FUTURE

format. Chown believes that Johnny and Roy III have a high level of mutual respect for one another, which is both good and necessary in a privately held company.[6] Johnny asserted that both he and Roy III do their core competency, whatever the title.

Both Johnny and Roy III came up through Martin ranks to their present places of leadership. Obviously, they each had a leg up on other people by virtue of being the grandsons of Roy O. and the sons of Ellis and Roy, Jr., respectively. But in the Martin manner, had they not been able to produce, they would not have remained in their positions. The Martin company culture is performance oriented. And that even includes all chief administrative officers of the company.

Johnny was born October 3, 1948. From an early age, he seemed to prepare for his future role in leading the family company, following the career path of his grandfather Roy O. Martin, Sr. Indeed, similar genetic qualities survive through two generations to link the founder to the current CEO. Roy O.'s complex dichotomy in character flourishes in this grandson. Johnny is demanding in his expectations, while generous in his actions; tough in negotiations, while sensitive to the needy; driven to succeed, while perpetuating close family ties.

Jonathan Ellis Martin
(circa 1952)

LIFE BY THE BOARD FOOT

Born twelve years after his first cousin on June 29, 1960, Roy III seemed equally destined to "drive" his family's Martin Companies to even greater fiscal greatness than that experienced by corporate leaders in the previous two generations. Like his grandfather, this Roy also has indefatigable energy. Thanks to the computerized era of laptops, cell phones, and Blackberrys, Roy III can multitask in ways unavailable to Roy O.

Roy Otis Martin III
in a company truck
(circa 1963)

Johnny began working in the mill at Castor while in high school during summers and school vacations. He testified that he loved it and that working in a sawmill was all he ever wanted to do.

Graduating Cadet
Jonathan Ellis Martin

Culver Military Academy
1966

CHAPTER 8 - FUTURE

After completing his engineering degree at Louisiana State University in January 1971, he immediately began working under the tutelage of his dad Ellis at the Castor sawmill. Thirty-three years later, he still insists that there is nothing he would rather do than get up and go to work each morning.

Jonathan Ellis Martin
(circa 1970)

On June 4, 1971, he married Maggie Ruth Burnaman, native of Etoile, Texas. The two had met at LSU where she finished her master's degree in English the month before their wedding at Broadmoor Baptist Church in Baton Rouge.

Johnny and Maggie Martin
1977 and 2004

LIFE BY THE BOARD FOOT

From 1971–1981 Johnny worked at the mill in Castor, assuming, like his predecessors, heavy responsibilities early in life. When Ellis moved from Castor to Alexandria in 1974, Johnny, at only twenty-four, became manager of Martin Timber Company sawmill at Castor. He left his managerial post there in 1981 to build the OSB plant at LeMoyen. With the exception of Colfax Treating Company, Johnny built each of the company's current manufacturing facilities. He became company president in 1994 when Ellis became chairman of the board of directors. The 2003 reorganization made Johnny chairman and CEO.

Roy III also entered the ranks of company employment when he was in high school. His first official experience came from working in the woods during one of his annual vacations. Another summer he worked at Basile. He also stacked the stacking sticks at the Fenner Street mill in Alexandria. Not afraid of gritty, hard work, this dashing teenager could, when opportunities required, impress with his good looks.

Early photo of Roy III
(in high school)

Just as impressive was his expertise on the tennis courts, a sport he energetically continues today as an adult.

Roy III graduated from LSU in 1982 with an engineering degree. He then began working at the LeMoyen facility in that same year with the construction group building the OSB plant, while he simultaneously entered the MBA program at LSU.

CHAPTER 8 - FUTURE

He and Kathy Sue Kilpatrick of Baton Rouge married on June 9, 1984.

Roy III and Kathy Martin
1984 and 2004

Roy III earned the coveted MBA degree in 1985. Kathy, an accomplished vocalist, received her MBA, also from Louisiana State University, in 1986.

Roy III
Early days at ROM
(Amid his typically cluttered desk)

259

LIFE BY THE BOARD FOOT

At Zack Woodard's retirement, Roy III moved into the corporate office to handle company finances. The following year, he was elected to the executive committee of the board of directors. In late 2003, he became president, maintaining his position as CFO. Like Johnny, Roy III followed in the professional steps of his father and grandfather.

Three Generations:
Roy Otis Martins
(circa 1964)

What about the leadership style of today's tandem of Martin overseers? Johnny states that management of today's Martin Companies is a shared responsibility between him and Roy III. On an organizational chart, Johnny may be at the top of the ladder of command. In practice, though, both he and Roy III run the company. Roy III emphasizes the concepts of responsibility and accountability, proven tenets of the Martin operation. Managers are given a great deal of responsibility to manage their areas, but they are also held accountable for their results. He maintained that company owners are very much in tune with daily details of the business. In addition to being result oriented, they are detail oriented. They know what is going on. Expanding on that, Roy III said that the real secret is going out into the mill itself. While it may take a million questions to learn the truth, it often takes only one visit to a plant to zero in on the problem. Both Roy III and Johnny regularly visit the mills, ensuring continued familiarity with operations of the various facilities.

CHAPTER 8 - FUTURE

Both Johnny and Roy III also pay attention to details. Roy III said that some professional managers who have joined their company are not as detail oriented as he and Johnny are. But, he added, Martins historically have made money by paying attention to the details. Certainly a key to their success, they set all standards of responsibility and accountability even higher for themselves than for their managers.

Chown agreed with their concepts of responsibility and accountability as descriptive of today's management style. Referring primarily to Johnny, he noted that Johnny specifically outlines expectations. When those expectations are met, other expectations will be put in place. Continuing the practice of his grandfather, he holds employees accountable for their performance. While he delegates responsibility to a manager, if that manager does not deliver, he will get directive. "And," added Chown, "you don't want Johnny Martin to get directive." The style of both Johnny and Roy III is to delegate myriad responsibilities, then to demand accountability – from their employees but, perhaps even more so, from themselves.

One need look only as far as their executive staff to find proof that this management style works. One vice president was quoted as saying, "I've never worked harder than these few years I have worked for the Martins, but I've never enjoyed coming to work as much as I have here." When queried to explain this seeming contradiction, a professional oxymoron, he quickly explained. "It's because of our boss." Could this process of delegating responsibility and then expecting results be contagious? Apparently it can be, as evidenced in Martin's sequential layers of management. And that contagious attitude permeates the Martin workforce as employees learn that their hard work will reap results for them personally and professionally.

Although both Johnny and Roy III would probably balk at the comparison, their management style is similar to that of Vince Lombardi, revered coach of the Green Bay Packers.

> Striving for excellence was everything to Lombardi.
> As with all great leaders, Lombardi was exceptionally adept at communicating his philosophy and vision to the members of his team. It is instructive to note that when the time came to call the final, fateful play that day [of the famous ice bowl against the Dallas Cowboys], Starr and the rest of the Packers offense all know that playing for the tie was not an option. As Maraniss describes the scene in his Lombardi biography, 'After playing for Lombardi for nine seasons, Starr knows exactly what his coach is thinking. He is conservative, he goes by the book, but he's a winner. "Run to win."'
> Maraniss' narrative reveals something else about Lombardi's approach to leadership. Over the years, we have come to think of Lombardi as the ultimate iron-willed manager, an avatar of the now-discredited command-and-control style of management. Yet when Starr ran back to the huddle after conferring with his coach, Lombardi admitted to Packers personnel man Pat Peppler that he had no idea what play Starr was going to call.

LIFE BY THE BOARD FOOT

> The coach was content to trust his quarterback's judgment, even at this crucial moment, when the game—and the entire season—was on the line.
>
> This, according to Maraniss, is the real essence of Lombardi's management style. 'There are many aspects to what could be called the Lombardi philosophy, but to me the most lasting and important was the concept of freedom through discipline. That is, you practice and refine and perfect something so that it becomes second nature to you, and once you have that discipline, you can react more freely when obstacles or troubles arise. Another way of saying it is that if you construct a solid foundation, you can withstand more.'
>
> Once you get past the stereotypes and the things you think you know about Lombardi, you are left with a great, even inspirational, leader who stood for nothing so much as passion, integrity, discipline, and a willingness to adapt to changing circumstances. . . . They are the keys to effective leadership. [7]

Communicating company philosophy, providing freedom through discipline, and encouraging through example that same passion, that same integrity and that same willingness to adapt to changing circumstances exhibited by their fathers and grandfather, Johnny and Roy III are effectively leading their company into the twenty-first century. To stay competitive in a rapidly changing industry, they encourage, no they require, their managers to "think outside the box." Realizing industry paradigms of past generations may no longer apply universally in today's work environment, they necessarily have developed motivational tools and operational strategies that keep them, in Johnny's words, "moving the rock" a bit farther every day. One or two people alone are not adequate to the task; however, a committed and focused team of managers, line supervisors and hourly workers can budge that rock just enough to stay ahead of rival manufacturers.

Realizing, too, that nothing, not even industry experience, is a substitute for intelligence and commitment, they have recently hired high-ranking managers and supervisors who, before joining the Martin team, had little or no professional experience in the lumber industry. Probably unthinkable for their fathers and grandfather, this willingness to recruit creative, motivated and intelligent individuals from other professional disciplines has helped raise their bar of excellence. Because they are willing to develop and work within a fluid, progressively changing paradigm, these two Martin men have gained respect from peers, from employees, from friends and from family.

How long will company leadership remain in Martin hands? That, of course, is a question for which no one really has an answer. At the time of this writing both Johnny and Roy III are relatively young. They each have good backgrounds and good reputations in the forest-products industry through family, training, and experience. They are performance oriented, but at the same time, they give a lot of

CHAPTER 8 - FUTURE

attention to their employees. New Martin business talent could well come to the surface from unexpected sources. After all, it is in the genes.

INTENTIONALITY IN MANAGEMENT

In speaking of managing the business, Ellis once said that he had "no training in that stuff"; he "just did what had to be done." Johnny observed that in earlier days "everything was run by the seat of the pants." That is no longer true. Certainly, as a privately held company, the Martin Company is able to move more quickly to implement change than would a corporation answerable to stockholders. They do not have cumbersome layers of management to wade through before deciding a course of action. Johnny and Roy III have shown themselves not only open to change but to be initiators of change. With a freedom they both appreciate and guard, they can make decisions about an issue more quickly than other companies. They can also commit resources to a project more quickly than most. And they have proved themselves capable of doing both. When a proposal comes up, a sound process can quickly be implemented if it meets with favor from management. An issue is not just about cutting costs; all issues are about getting results. However, with an organization as large as today's related corporations within the Martin Companies, management must be more professional, more specialized, and more intentional than perhaps it was in earlier years.

Johnny leads the way in intentionality in management. He and Roy III obviously inherited some of those genes that determine leadership, but they also have had more administrative tutoring than earlier managers. Johnny's training began as on-the-job education. Ellis' method of teaching company management to his son was to put a desk alongside his in his Castor office, allowing the young novice to hear and observe his mentor/father. Perhaps not scientific, but the process worked for Johnny, giving him invaluable, immediate insight to the many ups and downs of manufacturing.

With an MBA from LSU, Roy III's management training was more formal. Melding textbook principles from MBA classes with real-world issues, Roy III quickly made his mark with the company. Undoubtedly, his financial acumen and technological applications moved the company to new, ever-progressing levels of fiscal efficiency. Management consultant Chown observed that Johnny is committed to making any changes necessary for the company to be consistently productive. Speaking of this privately

LIFE BY THE BOARD FOOT

held business, Chown said that the only security they have is the ability to change and to adapt. Johnny and Roy III are willing to make any and all adaptations necessary for the continuing good of the company.

Johnny notes that his plan for moving from an entrepreneurial style of management to a professional style of management is well underway. Because he and Roy III have recognized the Martin gene pool may have run out of individuals who are either qualified or interested in running the business, they have recruited professional vice-presidents who are neither Martins nor stockholders but who are highly capable persons who operate the company in a professional manner. Company leadership is dedicated to thoroughly understanding the various layers of management within the company, and they are equally committed to improving each layer in ways available to them. Specifically, they start by improving their profitability with the assets (the people) they already have in place. Under Johnny's leadership the company is "leaving the fold of parental guidance and moving to professional management."[8] As part of this evolution, the company needs to continue its current course, changing from being driven by a few to executing from a broader range within a bigger scope. To achieve this, Martins must continue to recruit people who can operate on that level. These new professionals then have to be trained in the corporate culture. Borrowing an in-house expression, they have to be "Martin-ized." When successfully Martin-ized, they necessarily understand the vision and values, the ideals and goals of the company, which they can then communicate throughout the organization--from top management to line supervisors to hourly workers.

This long-range plan proved successful with the 2003 appointment of Scott Poole to the position of chief operating officer. Having been vice president of forestry and having completed the executive MBA program at LSU in March 2004, Scott validated himself and his commitment, his expertise and his loyalty to Roy O. Martin Lumber Company.

Scott Poole

CHAPTER 8 - FUTURE

Not only does the company develop its executive team, it also trains its lower-level employees. Johnny asserted that they spend a lot of money on training. He observed that in the manufacturing process "you are only as good as the front-line supervisors."[9] Today, Martins train hourly workers to become supervisors. Supervisors also have periodic training to increase their supervisory skills. An example is the company's "Advanced Supervisory Leadership" program. Running from September 2000 until February 2002, this interactive program provided leadership tools to twenty-eight supervisors representing all divisions of the Martin organization. With twelve training sessions, subject matters included workplace safety, effective communications, and employee training and development. This program focused on giving supervisors tools they could actually use on the job.[10]

To encourage longer tenures among employees and to foster company loyalty, the Martins implemented a Promotional Opportunity Program (POP) in 2001. Every job in the company is now available to someone already employed in the company. Johnny feels that if an employee wants to grow in knowledge and experience, that person should be encouraged to do so. He also observed that those employees who are lost to a Martin division by their moving to other jobs with other companies are usually the best performers. Martin Companies thus intends to encourage these best performers by allowing them opportunity for advancement within the corporation.

This means their executive organization has a renewed focus on the employee. Johnny indicated that, in the last decade, they have taken a totally different attitude toward their employees. They now realize how much attention they previously had paid to capital – machinery, plants, and the like – and how little attention they had paid to human capital – company employees. A current goal is to make their Martin Companies the employer of choice in Central Louisiana. All employee-benefit programs now grow out of concern for those who work for them; as a result, their focus is on the employee. Johnny told of his personal experience with a front-line employee at one of the plants who came up to him and hugged him, with tears in his eyes, thanking his boss for helping him learn to read. This incident illustrates the success of emphasizing employees and shows the Martin personal touch: an employee felt comfortable enough with the president of the company to hug him as he walked through the plant.

LIFE BY THE BOARD FOOT

Johnny also cited the chaplaincy program, MARTIN CARES, as an indication of their focus on the employee. After realizing they had little control over the many extraneous personal circumstances of their employees, Johnny contracted with Marketplace Ministries in Dallas, Texas, to provide on-the-job counseling to their workforce.

This chaplaincy program shows that their company cares for each individual, that each worker is viewed as more than a machine. A regular, job-site presence of fourteen chaplains encourages Martin employees to live by Judeo-Christian principles. This, in turn, creates a workforce comprised of better persons who usually become better employees.

MARTIN CARES
Chaplains
2004

CHAPTER 8 - FUTURE

Loyal, long-term employees are not new with the Martin Company. Through the years many employees have served long and well, some as long as forty-two years. One example is Jeff Morrison who retired after that many years from the Castor mill without missing a day of work. When he retired, Ellis gave him a gold pocket watch. Times have certainly changed. Today, they regularly reward employees and divisions as well-defined goals are met. This more focused approach toward employees as individuals is paying off, benefiting both employer and employee.

Training a workforce, offering opportunity for advancement, and focusing on employee's needs are all aspects of intentionality in management. All of these are directed to employees, but Johnny and Roy III realize they, too, need to participate proactively in the process, keeping themselves abreast of latest trends and open to new opportunities. They do this through membership in professional organizations. While mentally stimulating and personally affirming, these groups also allow Johnny and Roy III to share their expertise and wield their influence. Johnny belongs to an organization composed of chief executive officers of successful Louisiana companies.

Involvement with managerial groups has served to widen the boundaries of "community" for the current Martin leaders. As professional and civic peers interact and network with these problem-solving, decision-making Martins, they have come to respect the many contributions the two cousins have made, and can continue to make, in the world around them. As a result, Johnny and Roy III now have an opportunity to influence, not just Alexandria and its surrounding area, but the state of Louisiana. Roy III is a member of Louisiana's Committee of 100 for Economic Development, a group of respected CEOs whose function is to address quality-of-life issues in Louisiana—education, housing, transportation, environment health care, public safety, libraries, recreation, arts and social services. This group quietly, but effectively, operates from the premise that an economically healthy state not only makes good business sense, but that it also contributes to an improved lifestyle for all Louisiana citizens.

As today's Martins continue to give back to their local communities, they receive recognition and respect in return, affirming the principle of the Golden Rule. When the Louisiana Wildlife Federation named Roy O. Martin Lumber Company its "Company of the Year" in 2001, it recognized their

LIFE BY THE BOARD FOOT

organization as the "most environmentally friendly company" in Louisiana. Martins realize that environmentally sound principles result in good business practices.

In July 2003 Johnny, on behalf of his company, accepted the prestigious Lantern Award. Presented by the Louisiana Economic Development, this award recognized the company's efforts in agriculture and forestry. Lantern Award recipients are Louisiana businesses that help the state achieve a vibrant, balanced economy, a fully engaged, well-educated workforce and a quality of life that places Louisiana among the top ten states in the country. Today's Martins are widening their sphere of influence as they continue to improve their world.

Johnny Martin (center)
accepting
Lantern Award
from
Kelsey Short, LED Director of
Agriculture/Forestry (left)
and
Don Hutchinson, Secretary LED (right)
June 2003

Reflecting their intentionality in management, the current administrative team of all Martin Companies sets specific goals and objectives for what they intend to achieve. The 2004 SALT team (Strategic Action Leadership Team) is composed of company chairman (Johnny), president (Roy III), executive vice president and CEO (Scott Poole), vice president for human resources (Ray Peters), treasurer (Curtis Meaux), vice president of manufacturing (Mark DiCarlo), vice president of sales (John Rogalski), information services manager (Jesse Bolton), manager of engineering and construction (Adrian Schoonover), vice president of land and timber (Mickey Rachal), and executive administrative assistant (Evelyn Smith).

CHAPTER 8 - FUTURE

Top row (left to right): Adrian Schoonover, Scott Poole,
Curtis Meaux, John Rogalski and Jesse Bolton
Bottom row (left to right): Mark DiCarlo, Roy III,
Johnny and Ray Peters
Not pictured: Evelyn Smith and Mickey Rachal

These eleven in-house professionals have defined the vision and values of the Martin Companies.

Their vision statement is known as the ROM Vision 2004. This four-pronged directive is well circulated in the company and beyond. A visitor to any of their offices will find it displayed on computers, doors, books and bulletin boards as a reminder of the principles that guide their corporate family:

- Roy O. Martin Lumber Company intends to be one of the top five plants in each manufacturing division as measured by cost, margin, safety and customer satisfaction.

- Roy O. Martin Lumber Company intends to be the employer of choice in central Louisiana resulting in a committed, competent and contributing workforce.

- Roy O. Martin Lumber Company intends to maximize value from timberlands while maintaining Forest Stewardship Council certification.

LIFE BY THE BOARD FOOT

- Roy O. Martin Lumber Company intends to ensure its long-term viability as a privately held, ethically based, professionally managed company.

Outlining a clear view of what the company intends to be for at least a five-year period, these concepts were not just adopted, then quickly forgotten. Rather, they spell out specific intentions, clear goals that company management keeps before itself and others.

Along with its vision statement, SALT also developed a set of values the organization holds dear. Supporting the ROM 2004 Vision statement, they form an acronym RICHES:

- Respect
- Integrity
- Commitment
- Honesty
- Excellence
- Stewardship

In a president's newsletter sent to all the employees on December 6, 2001, Johnny gave his interpretation of those values. His words have since been synopsized and distributed throughout the company:

- **Respect** for each other as human beings uniquely created by God.
- **Integrity** in what we do and what we say we will do, regardless of the cost, legally and ethically.
- **Commitment** to the business, to our employees, to our customers, and to each other.
- **Honesty** in our interaction with our fellow employees, our supervisors, our customers, our vendors, and our families.
- **Excellence** in product quality, employee training and development, and process improvements.
- **Stewardship** of our land, timber, and plant assets.[11]

If the four intentions in ROM's Vision Statement 2004 are the mantra reverberating throughout the ranks of Martin employees, these six values are the mantle, which envelops that vision and allows it to become a reality by the year 2004. Martin executives and managers, certainly, and most supervisors and other employees understand the vision before them, and they embrace the values that will allow them to reach their lofty goals.

CHAPTER 8 - FUTURE

All Roy O. Martin companies operate with a distinct understanding of their values and their goals. This is definitely not management "by the seat of the pants" but management with particular purposes in mind. These values and goals are regularly communicated to the entire company workforce, hourly workers as well as supervisory and management personnel.

SIGNIFICANCE OF THE LAND

Paul Hood, accountant, referred to the "all powerful land." Both Johnny and Roy III unequivocally agree with that assessment. Roy III expounded further, observing that the land is "the soil from which the company grows, literally." Johnny emphasized even more, saying that the business is what keeps the family together. To sell the land would be to sell the family heritage. He illustrated his statement by saying that if they sold the business, all they would have is a pile of money. Money would not keep the family together. But by having the land, Martins maintain a thriving, respected business while fostering goodwill that can continue to connect a family, reminding them of their special heritage.

Production of timber and manufacturing of lumber continue to be big business in Louisiana. A brochure distributed by the Louisiana Forestry Association states that forests cover 13.8 million acres or forty-eight percent of the land area in the State of Louisiana. Fifty-nine of Louisiana's sixty-four parishes contain land capable of producing sufficient timber to support forest industries as well as providing habitat for wildlife, recreational opportunity, scenic beauty, and other benefits. In 1995 trees accounted for sixty-eight percent of the total value of all plant commodities in Louisiana. But even as mature trees are harvested, more trees are replanted. The forest products industry plants at least twenty-five trees for each Louisiana citizen each year – more than one hundred million new trees annually. This thriving industry represents twenty-nine percent of the one hundred thirteen thousand owners of forestlands in Louisiana. Its economic impact in Louisiana in 1995 was $5.1 billion.[12] Unequivocally, forest products have a future in Louisiana's economy. And today's Martin Companies intends not only to be a part of that future but also to play an increasingly significant role in it.

Owning land is a major factor in any future success of the company. Substantial ownership means they are not dependent on other people for timber. Neither are they dependent on other people for timber prices. Naturally, then, controlling timber costs is essential for any--and all--future success of the company.

LIFE BY THE BOARD FOOT

Timber on Martin land is treated as a crop, as a very precious crop. Through TSI (timber stand improvement), their timber crop is carefully cultivated. Trained and experienced foresters practice silviculture, the art and science of growing and managing forest crops, and genetic improvement of trees. In the words of Roy III, "We can grow a tree faster, taller, straighter than Mother Nature."[13] Both Johnny and Roy III indicate that they are constantly looking for ways to increase the value of their timber.

When urban population grows into company-owned timberlands, then the company goes into real estate. Their latest residential development is Coulee Crossing, south of Alexandria. This thriving subdivision joins several others throughout the state beginning, decades earlier, with Martin Park in Alexandria. Martin Development, which initially was run by David Martin, Ellis' son and Johnny's brother, is the development arm of the company. It was merged into the Roy O. Martin Lumber Company in 1988.

Manufacturing is Martin's primary means of converting timber into cash. Quite literally, all timber on company-owned lands can be used by one of the four manufacturing divisions within its organization. Pine timber goes into making poles and plywood. Hardwood timber is turned into lumber at LeMoyen's sawmill. Even previously discarded "trash" trees can now be milled into OSB (oriented strand board) at LeMoyen. Virtually no standing timber on Martin company lands is wasted.

Not content with acreage they now own, the company makes strategic purchases of land each year. Today's primary goal, however, is to consolidate their land holdings. Many of their land purchases are of smaller parcels, from twenty acres up. Obviously, there have been some exceptions to this because the company has made several large purchases of land in the past. Quite significantly, since the 1960s, the various Martin enterprises have rarely borrowed money for land purchases. If borrowing is necessary or fiscally prudent, any loan generally is of short duration. Such was the case in 2002 when the Martins purchased a total of 59,800 acres from Louisiana-Pacific. These two transactions included a 37,000-acre parcel in north-central Louisiana and a 22,800-acre parcel west of Oakdale. Then in early 2003, again from LP, they purchased another 50,000 acres on the Texas-Louisiana border in southwest Louisiana.

These were certainly significant purchases, a deviation from the way Martins have historically increased their land holdings. An industry magazine, <u>Timber Harvesting</u>, comments on the method that perhaps best describes most of Martin Company's land purchases:

> Martin purchased some timber during the 1930s, but it was not until after World War II that timber acquisitions became a significant effort to insure [sic] a permanent timber

CHAPTER 8 - FUTURE

supply . . . . Starting at such a late date meant very few large tracts were available. Thus, ROM holdings have taken the shape of whatever has come on the market over the years. The company's patchwork timber holdings dot the maps from the northernmost parish all the way down the Red River and into the Atchafalaya Basin in parcels ranging from 20 acres to several thousand. Species range is as varied as the patchwork itself.[14]

Along with buying land, the company also swaps land. Through the years they have participated in some very sophisticated swapping. Always legal, these swapping techniques are sometimes very innovative, satisfying both parties. Roy III is quite insistent that they stay within the spirit of the law as well as the letter of the law.

Hood maintained that land is the real foundation of the company's success. Roy III followed up by saying that today's third-generation managers know that money comes from the land. Whatever they can do to convert trees to cash is to the long-term benefit of their stockholders, the Martin family. For these reasons, Johnny maintains that they will at least always keep the land privately held; that land keeps the family together.

ROMEX WORLD TRADE CENTER

The company broke ground for its new administrative office center, ROMEX World Trade Center, on December 26, 2000. Located at 2189 Memorial Drive in Alexandria, corporate headquarters finally moved away from the vicinity of Roy O's original sawmill. Adjoining Alexandria Mall, this modern structure is at the epicenter of Alexandria's business district, in Business Park, which was developed by the Martin Company.

ROMEX World Trade Center is certainly a showcase for the numerous wood products the company manufactures. As one might expect, wood is a central focus of the building with pecan floors and cypress millwork and beams.

LIFE BY THE BOARD FOOT

The Romex board room, named after founder of the original Martin company, contains a pecan and walnut table specially designed and crafted for the area.

The
Roy O. Martin, Sr.
Board Room

CHAPTER 8 - FUTURE

The MilMar Library is a daily reminder of Mildred Martin's legacy of, and love for, libraries.

MilMar Library

The reception desk is made of red gum. Several executive offices are paneled with magnolia. An impressive display of various woods manufactured by the company is located in the east corridor of the first floor.

Reception Desk

LIFE BY THE BOARD FOOT

And, affirming the Martin's musical heritage, a grand piano is positioned under the first-floor stairway.

Grand Piano
donated by
Virginia Martin Howard

Essentially, all wood in the building was produced from each of the company's manufacturing operations.

Even treated poles support the covered entrance to the building.

Covered entrance with treated poles

CHAPTER 8 - FUTURE

This headquarters building is called a "World Trade Center" because Martin exports worldwide, according to Roy III. Martin Companies export wood products to Pacific Rim countries, Mexico, the Caribbean, and Europe. In fact, their Karimoku Conference Room reflects a sound, long-standing business relationship Martins have with one of their Japanese customers. Martin shipped pecan wood to Karimoku who then built furniture for their impressive executive conference room. In true Japanese style, these leather-cushioned conference chairs are lower than American-made counterparts. Their subtle premise is that goodwill is more easily fostered when adults confer in a more casual, relaxed atmosphere.

Karimoku Conference Room

The goal-oriented, purposeful management style of the Martin Company can be well executed through corporate headquarters. Efficient spaciousness of the ROMEX World Trade Center consolidates their corporate structure.

LIFE BY THE BOARD FOOT

CONTINUING EMPHASES

As today's Martin Company (restructured into Martin Companies, L.L.C., ROM) completes its eightieth year with the third generation of Martin leadership, some continuing emphases are clearly evident.

Land. Martin Companies is still intent on increasing its land base. Roy III described land as the cash cow. Manufacturing plants, he observed, are the means of converting timber to cash. Roy III also maintains that Martin is one of only a few timber companies still aggressively buying land. An interesting phenomenon of Martin's land base is that, with the exception of one relatively small plot in Texas, all of their land is in Louisiana. And while they negotiate with some larger lumber companies for bigger plots of land, they also continue to buy smaller parcels from private landowners. Roy III says that land is important because the company will never grow larger than the land will allow. Having adequate land makes the company self-sufficient into the future, thus helping perpetuate the Martin Companies while providing much-needed jobs within the state.[15]

This land is not just held by the Martins, it is made productive by and for the Martin Companies. One goal in their Vision Statement is to "maximize value from timberlands." To accomplish such an ambitious undertaking, their further task is to make every acre of land productive. Through growing trees, furnishing gravel or dirt, leasing minerals, hunting, or providing recreational and aesthetic values, each acre of Martin-owned or Martin-controlled land is made productive in one or more ways. The main purpose, of course, is growing trees on the land. As John Dunn wrote, "Without the trees, no value can be realized whether as raw materials for our plants, as recreational value for our hunters, or as aesthetic value for nature-appreciating stakeholders. Although timber is our main objective, our forestry staff never loses sight that many other activities and values are attached to the lands we manage."[16]

Exports. Exporting lumber and other forest products is not new to Martin Companies. As evidenced by his stamped passport, Roy O. missed a meeting of the board of directors in the late 1930 due to being in Mexico on a lumber-selling trip.

CHAPTER 8 - FUTURE

That the new administrative office building is named the **ROMEX** *World Trade* Center (italics mine) indicates today's Martin business is not confined to its local area but that it reaches a global market, annually expanding its international sales. An export sales manager makes up a part of the sales division. Roy III stated that, in the foreseeable future, the company would like to export thirty to thirty-five percent of the total value of its manufactured products.[17]

Just as the Roy O. Martin Lumber Company participated in the World War II effort by supplying lumber for building military camps and constructing Higgins landing crafts, so has the current company joined in the War on Terrorism launched by President George W. Bush after the September 11, 2001, terrorist attack on New York City. In January 2002 the Martins sent ten truckloads of plywood (more than 6,000 sheets) through a vendor in Virginia to the U. S. Naval Base in Guantanamo Bay, Cuba. This plywood was used to build shelter for U. S. troops and the Taliban and al-Qaida detainees. Along with the plywood, Martco employees added stick-on American flags to the containers and inserted one hundred twenty signed messages thanking U. S. personnel for the good job they were doing in protecting freedom.[18]

Emphasis on Employees. Johnny asserted that their current emphasis on employees began in the 1990s. He recognizes that his generation of stockholders – grandchildren and great-grandchildren of Roy O. and Mildred Martin – are more interested in personally affirming and professionally growing Martin personnel than were some of the older family members.[19] He realized this is just one of the necessary changes any company must make to remain competitive in a rapidly changing business environment.

That emphasis on employees is recognition of contributions employees make to Martin's continued success. And it also demonstrates a concern for them as persons. They are not machinery; they are human beings with worth and value, with abilities and feelings, with needs and problems, with skill and potential. Growing out of Christian commitment, today's company leadership appreciates each employee as a person. Canadian OSB equipment consultant Rob Zaytsoff said of Johnny, "He is pro-active for people. People are valuable resources."[20] Johnny repeatedly states that he wants each person to be as good as he or she can be.

This continuing regard for employees acknowledges that fewer Martins will be employees and managers in the future. A necessary shift to professional managers rather than family managers is part of that acknowledgement. Future managers will need to be developed and encouraged in order for them to stay with the company over long periods of time. As Johnny observed, "We have to face the fact that there are no more Ellis Martins and Zack Woodards out there." In some cases, two or three persons have to be hired to replace one of these experienced, talented individuals who leaves the company.[21] Today's employees, especially those in administrative positions, are the new breed of Martin management. Already, they are more involved in crucial decisions than were their predecessors. As they continue to assimilate into current corporate culture, they will benefit from learning crucial stories of Martin's company history. Only then can they understand what this family-owned company stands for; only then can they appreciate those personal sacrifices and professional struggles of previous generations who paved the way for today's success.

Innovation. The company has been very innovative. Each of its manufacturing plants is state of the art. Equipment is changed periodically to take advantage of innovations in technology.

Company leadership is not only open to change, but it is looking for ways to change to increase productivity and profitability of the company. Zaytsoff characterized Johnny as very forward thinking. He observed that Johnny is never afraid of the future. He is always thinking ahead and asking, "How can I make a better product?"[22]

CHAPTER 8 - FUTURE

When asked about future business ventures, Johnny replied that they are more concerned with enhancing existing products than in undertaking new ventures. He stated that they are doing more fine-tuning of existing products rather than starting anything brand new. By enhancing what they already produce, for example, by using different glues in plywood and OSB and treating some of their products with fungicides and insecticides, they can get a better return on their investment.[23] Roy III basically agreed, saying that they can add value to their plywood by selling more sanded plywood, cutting to measure, or by adding tongue and groove to the plywood.

In 2002 and 2003, the Martins introduced two new value-adding products to their customers: The GRID® panel system and Eclipse™ radiant-barrier panels. Designed for builders and carpenters to cut without measuring, the patented GRID® panel system saves time and money while building quality. Each panel is stamped "with a crisp, printed dimensional pattern for ease of installation."[24]

LIFE BY THE BOARD FOOT

Radiant-Barrier products, used primarily on roof decks, are manufactured with a foil overlay. Marketed under the name Eclipse™, these panels provide insulation and roof decking in a one-step process for builders and carpenters, again saving time and money for Martin's many customers.

Eclipse™
Radiant Barrier

Martco's OSB plant continues experimenting with products that will provide value-adding options to their customers. Soon, customers can have their panels treated with "fungicides, pesticides, water-repellants, and decay-resistant compounds." Additionally, Martco is developing and testing Moldshield™. When marketed, this product will add value while targeting mold resistance. Chemicals used in this process are "all water based and contain no heavy metals or arsenic. The three key ingredients are items commonly found in cosmetics, soaps, and shampoos. Two of the three ingredients are pesticides; the unique mixture they form provides the surface treatment for OSB that is mold resistant."[25]

Since the Martin Companies is privately owned, innovative decisions can be made more quickly than in publicly owned corporations. Zaytsoff opined that Johnny knows what "the numbers are" before he begins any project. He never once heard Johnny say, "I'll have to check on that and get back in touch with you." His answers are always direct and forthcoming, pointedly so. Roy III explained it by saying that Martin decision-makers are still in charge. They can act quickly, and they can act decisively. Then they stick with their decisions. He admitted, though, that sometimes the Martins in charge may turn a little too fast.[26]

CHAPTER 8 - FUTURE

One example of an action that moved even faster than the Martin norm for expediting decisions is the donation of their Mill Street office to the city of Alexandria. Johnny and Roy III had been discussing a future move to a modern facility in a more suitable location, but they had not finalized plans to do so. Almost by accident, late one afternoon Roy III learned that Alexandria's city council was meeting that night to authorize purchase of a lot at the corner of Vance and Winn, just a few blocks from the company's Mill Street location. Seizing this narrow window of opportunity, literally a few hours, Roy III quickly worded a proposal outlining a tentative option for Martin to donate their office to the city. He requested confidentiality from his recipient, intending for council members simply to consider his proposal privately and, at that night's meeting, to table a decision about purchasing the Vance/Winn lot. Apparently, though, the one who received his fax failed to notice his request for confidentiality. At the council meeting a short time later, an official announcement was made. And, later that night on the local 10:00 news, a reporter further confirmed that Martins had donated their office to the city! Roy III quickly called Johnny to prepare him for the next morning's headlines. All was well. Roy III's quick action had simply accelerated an idea he and Johnny had frequently discussed and eventually planned to implement. "Eventually" simply came sooner than either expected.

The company has been creative and innovative from its beginning. Roy O. was able to see business opportunities and move into them. Ellis carried forward that pattern of taking advantage of available opportunities and adapting as necessary. Under the current company leadership of Johnny and Roy III, innovation is a continuing emphasis. They are constantly seeking new ways to convert timber into cash. Since nothing is sentimentally held, they could sell any manufacturing plant at any time if their business plan changes. They could, by the same token, move into new areas of productivity and create new products if an opportunity arises for that.

Results Orientation. The Martin Companies is oriented toward results. They want to see something happening. Bob Chown characterized the Martin organization as "very clearly a performance culture." He observed that company leadership would accept an error of commission before they would an error of omission. They want people to be doing something.[27] Johnny agreed with that observation. He added that they want to attract the kind of people to work with them who are high on ethics, high on professionalism, high on getting things done.[28]

LIFE BY THE BOARD FOOT

Johnny maintains that they are trying to position the company to continue far into the future. He added that the purpose of the company is not to employ Martins or near-Martins (in-laws) but to hire those best qualified for each and every job, whoever they may be. He further recognizes a distinct line between ownership and management. Properly running the business is in the best interest of all Martins. He also said, "Our job is to keep the business going." Preservation of the business is their major concern. For that to occur, performance is important.

References to *stakeholders* show up frequently in company publications, indicating that while employees may not be stockholders in the company, they are stakeholders. They have a stake in what happens in the company. Their performance makes a difference in the profitability of the company and, therefore, in the continuance of jobs. This is communicated to all employees. For instance an article in *ROM Today* discusses changes in the LeMoyen facility, "With all these changes, I am proud to know that some things will never change. Even in the midst of dramatic modifications, our primary goals remain constant. We strive towards safety, efficiency, and productivity. Our employees work as a team. They are very loyal, dedicated to making Martco a better, safer, and more profitable business."[29] To this Mary Erdoes, Global Head of Investments with J. P. Morgan Company, adds:

> What I have found across all family members is passion for the business that is paralleled with a warmth for stakeholders. As a financial provider to the company, the family has taken me in as a "part of the family." In doing this, just as they do with all other stakeholders, they create an alignment of what I provide that better matches the ROML long-term strategic goals. Embracing me as a stakeholder allows me to make better long-term decisions for the shareholders.[30]

Employees at all levels are made to understand that performance counts and results matter.

Private Ownership. The Martin Companies is one of the largest privately owned forest products industry businesses in the nation. In fact, J.P. Morgan reports that Martin ranks twenty-eight among the largest forestland owners in the United States. All stock is held by Martin family members. In earlier days, minimal shares were given to certain employees as equity bonuses. Since then, the company has found other ways to benefit key employees. Shares are no longer distributed to persons other than family members.

Johnny recognizes, however, that the time may come in the not-too-distant future that Martins do not run the company. The company would then be much like a public company, run by professional managers. But its ownership would still basically be in family hands. He sees a distinct line between

CHAPTER 8 - FUTURE

ownership and management. Today's two leaders are positioning the company to grow. Both Johnny and Roy III profess that they will continue to operate the business in the best interests of their shareholders – the Martins.

This current company leadership, Johnny and Roy III, are very aware of their role as stewards for the family firm. Roy III stated that he hoped they could take the values of the first-and-second-generation Martins and carry them on. Johnny said that he hoped that they have thus far conducted themselves (and will continue to) so that those who come behind them will have found them faithful to the legacy given them. He hoped that those who follow them will find them faithful to their business, to their family, and to their faith.

To say that the Martin Companies is privately held is to describe company ownership in business terms. In personal terms, however, today's Martin Companies grew from a particular family with a unique heritage. An integral aspect of that heritage is not only having ideas but also outlining specific steps that will allow today's ambitious vision to become reality for future generations.

Today's Martins in charge are actively consolidating their personal visions into a combined plan of action. Building on Johnny's succession plan for each key position in the company, Roy III is, in 2004, developing a "family-governance succession plan." Working with fourth-generation Martins, he seeks to create a family committee who will help answer critical questions:

> 1) Who in the family will participate in the governance of the Company in the next generation?
>
> 2) Who are our next family group leaders?
>
> 3) How will the next generation pick our family leaders in the fifth and sixth generations?
>
> 4) What family members want to work in our business, and how should we objectively evaluate their talents?
>
> 5) What other areas exist for member participation not directly involved in daily operations, such as philanthropy?

He writes to his fellow stockholders, "As a family, we cannot be expected to produce competent plant managers, engineers and factory supervisors for the long-term, but we can expect to have family members involved in choosing the right people. With a sense of vision, our family will have a common goal and a unified reason to stay together rather than offer excuses for growing apart. I believe if we incorporate these ideas into our culture, we will be able to change and grow as a company far into the future. Cooperative families are profitable families."[31]

Johnny asserted that their profitable business holds the family together. Therefore, they intend to keep the business, particularly the land, to keep the family together. This is their primary long-term goal: maintaining family unity through their business. And that business is successful, privately held, and ethically run. As they continue to apply these generational principles, Johnny assessed, "We have been frugal with the resources God has given us."[32] Hollis McNully, who has supplied equipment to Johnny for two decades, agreed that an ingredient of the company's success is that they are frugal. But when they spend money, they spend it wisely. And they are not afraid to spend money when new technology will enhance the product.[33]

PROSPECTS

Prospects for the Martin Companies are positive.

Company leadership of Johnny as chairman and CEO and Roy III as president and CFO is that of capable, committed Christian business leaders. They are third generation Martins who are universally described as ingenious, intelligent, self-motivated, and personable. While exacting in their expectations, they relate as friends to those with whom they conduct business, often developing long-term personal relationships from initial business contacts.

Jonathan E. Martin
and
Roy Otis Martin III
2004

CHAPTER 8 - FUTURE

Both Mike Knerr of USNR and Hollis McNully stated that Johnny remembers what one says to him in a business proposal. Then he expects that person to keep his word. They both agreed that Johnny keeps his word and expects others to do the same. McNully added that if a supplier follows contractual stipulations and delivers on time, he "gets hit in the back with a check." [34] In other words, the company promptly pays its bills.

McNully described Johnny as an interesting dichotomy; basically, he is the toughest businessman he ever met, but he has a heart of gold. These are the same traits, almost verbatim, employee/poet Les Evans ascribed to Roy O. in 1954, almost fifty years earlier:

They say he's rough at times! Alas!
His drive is strong and fierce,
That mighty men oft quake and fall,
Before his eyes that pierce.
But many know that 'neath the steel,
Beats one Big Heart of Gold--[35]

Roy O., Sr.
Jonathan Ellis Martin
(circa 1949)

Genetics obviously have contributed to Martin success. However, genetics alone do not guarantee success. They must be paired with motivation and hard work. And a vision, if it succeeds, must be paired with determination. This successive group of Martin leaders has developed a formula that works for them.

Both Johnny and Roy III have a keen awareness of the business principles necessary to conduct a business the scope and size of theirs. Through both training and experience as well as through conferences, workshops, and organizations, they are well-trained executives. By placing more professional managers than family members in leadership positions, the company definitely knows its business. Both Johnny and Roy III have used their engineering skills to organize themselves and their company. Practically all interviewees characterized the Martin Company as extremely well run.

Johnny and Roy III are forward thinking in their outlook, seeking ways to improve their business so as to stay ahead of the curve in an ever-changing, highly competitive industry. More than one interviewee described Johnny as visionary. McNully said that Johnny sees where things are going, then is there waiting with a smile to greet his competitors when they get there. He also stated that larger companies track the Roy O. Martin Company. They are known for maximizing value from their materials, what raw materials go in and what comes out as the finished product.

Johnny and Roy III have a real sense of stewardship to family as they keep their business successful and growing. But to do that, the company will have to move to new levels of operation. Buddy Tudor of the Alexandria/Pineville construction firm of Tudor Enterprises observed that whereas the first two generations of Martins were more focused on building the business, the third generation, specifically Roy III, is interested in leading the business to another level. They are aggressively "moving the rock," pushing their continually growing and consistently profitable enterprise into the twenty-first century with more focus on image and community involvement. [36]

As a privately held business, the Martin Companies is well situated to take advantage of opportunities before them. They, for instance, buy land when other, larger lumber companies sell land. They can make decisions quickly and move into new or innovative activities quickly. And they are always open to new opportunities.

They are goal-oriented. They want to be the price setter in their industry for each product they manufacture. With only one facility for each product they manufacture, this may be difficult. However, they continually strive to reach ambitious goals.

These Martins are also results-oriented. They expect to get results for the work they do.

Martin Companies is stable, solid, and fiscally sound. Using contemporary methods and professional management, this company certainly is a business model for a privately held corporation in the forest-products industry.

All their manufacturing facilities are state of the art. And with their innovative approach to company leadership, they are improving all the time. McNully is of the opinion that Johnny is primarily responsible for those technological advances that have brought the company from a "peckerwood" sawmill to a world-class force. And Knerr observed that Johnny is always involved in every technological improvement. McNully cited one situation, which he said brackets the way their company conducts business. His then-partner sold Castor sawmill a state-of-the-art scanning system. But the mill was run by

CHAPTER 8 - FUTURE

an old steam engine; one motor ran the whole operation. On the front end of the mill was old, even outdated, technology. On the back end of the mill was the new, highly modern, technology. He observed that this reflects the company philosophy of keeping something if it works and is paid for; however, if something newer comes along that can produce faster and better, install it.

A company culture of competence and competitiveness has developed. The statement that "You can't go broke making money" (paraphrase of the advice "Pop" Hill gave Ellis more than sixty years ago) is something of a company slogan. Two family members who are in the business unwittingly made it to the same banker in one week. Bill Moore, who with American Wood Dryers has sold the company twenty kilns, said that Johnny seeks out the best people and inspires them to do their best.[37] To that McNully added that not only does Johnny know how to build a team and inspire them with his vision, he also knows how to motivate them to excellence. Interviewees were unanimous in saying the Martin Company is well run, from top to bottom.

In recent years, the company has also moved to more community involvement and development. Of course, Roy O., Ellis and Roy, Jr., necessarily were intent on establishing the business, then stabilizing it. They did that well. Today with an established, stabilized and successful business, present leadership can become more involved in community and civic affairs. Johnny cites Bob's Candy in Albany, Georgia, which tithes its company profit. His personal goal is to move toward that standard. As Christians, most family members tithe their income individually. As a Christian-oriented business, they would like to reach that standard for their business, also. At the present time, their contributions through the Martin Foundation are based on dollar amounts rather than percentages.

Wayne Denley, president of Hibernia Bank in Alexandria said of Roy III, "As a businessman Roy III reflects the physical and mental toughness one usually associates with the early timber barons. Fortunately, he also provides for the family business a new age of enlightenment, though, with regard to social responsibilities, community development, and philanthropic leadership."[38]

Mary Erdoes adds:

> Today's combined management team of Johnny and Roy Martin is one of the most dynamic partnerships I've ever seen across businesses in the United States. The "Ying and Yang" that exists between Johnny's aggressive, non-conformist day-to-day management style and Roy's intense financial savvy is the key ingredient in the re-shaping of the company to succeed into and through the next century. It is this unique

combination that has taken them so briskly through the turbulent financial conditions over the past few years. [39]

As an indication of the positive effects of the concerted efforts and efficient work of the twenty-first century Martin Companies, in April 2002 the Roy O. Martin Company and its Martco Limited Partnership divisions received certification by SmartWood under the Forest Stewardship Council (FSC) for both responsible management of its timberlands and chain-of-custody of its finished products. SmartWood is a forest-certification program funded by the Rainforest Alliance, a leading international conservation organization based in New York, New York. The mission of the Rainforest Alliance is to protect ecosystems and the people and wildlife that live within them by implementing better business practices for biodiversity conservation and sustainability. Companies, cooperatives and landowners that participate in their certification programs meet rigorous standards for protecting the environment, wildlife, workers and local communities. Another validation of their concern for their world, the Martin Companies is the first in Louisiana to receive this coveted SmartWood stamp of approval, which is based on a company's ecologically sound principles, social awareness and consciousness, and economic impact in the community. By thus showing its forestry accountability and receiving certification, the company now displays an appropriate logo on all its products.

CHAPTER 8 - FUTURE

In a news release announcing the certification, Johnny was quoted as saying:

> FSC certification of our company timberland, manufacturing facilities and products is the culmination of our commitment to stewardship and responsible forest management. Since our company's founding by my grandfather almost 80 years ago, we have grown our timberland base using the utmost care and company-developed forestry practices to ensure the optimal long-term environmental, social and economic benefits to the company and surrounding communities."[40]

After only two short years, having proved their commitment to FSC values, Johnny and Roy O. Martin Lumber Company were honored at the annual meeting of the Rainforest Alliance. This May 2004 gala event in New York City recognized individuals and corporations that proactively practice conservation and environmental principles. Further evidence of the Martins widening their net of influence and recognition, Johnny accepted this prestigious award along with other CEOs from across the globe. Johnny, standing among professional peers from Time, Inc., Anderson-Tully Company and Kinko's, Inc., to name a few, was a proud testimony that his grandfather's gamble those many years previously had indeed been worthwhile. That vision, that will, that determination, and, of course, that hard work--genetic DNA--continue to garner respect and success for the Martins.

Photo from Rainforest Alliance Gala

Ever conscious of their role as stewards of the land, also in the spring of 2004, the Martins completed a nature trail on the company's Hixson-Simmons tract near Kolin, Louisiana. Johnny had envisioned a "place to educate non-foresters on the beauty and diversity of a natural forest . . . a place we should use to educate employees, politicians, students and the general public on forestry, wildlife and fauna in our native Louisiana."[41] This scenic walk with designated stops along the way will eventually include plots showing various stages of reforestation. Currently, it is available, by appointment, to interested groups—another tool the Martins can now use to affirm their commitment to conservation while educating the public to the importance of the State's timber industry.

Although Johnny and Roy have moved their company steadily into a managerially run corporation, they recently once again proved the same entrepreneurial spirit as that of their grandfather who first charted his (and their) future by moving to Alexandria and purchasing that fledgling sawmill in 1923. On June 24, 2004, in Houston, Texas, they were named Ernst & Young Entrepreneur of the Year for the Houston and Gulf Coast region. Three generations of Martins working hard, committing to goals, envisioning possibilities, creating their best, and, yes, daring to be different, allowed Johnny and Roy III to achieve this coveted award in the retail and consumer-products division. In November 2004, they will be inducted into the Ernst & Young Entrepreneur Hall of Fame at its annual conference in Palm Springs, California, where they will be eligible to compete in one of several categories.

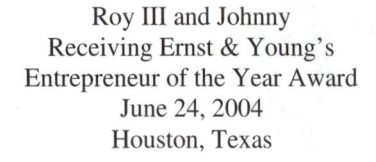

Roy III and Johnny
Receiving Ernst & Young's
Entrepreneur of the Year Award
June 24, 2004
Houston, Texas

CHAPTER 8 - FUTURE

These two Martins firmly believe it has been their dedication to shared family values and uncompromising commitment to high standards of corporate excellence that account for their continuing success, reporting revenues of close to $270 million in domestic and international sales. Their "riches," those core values of respect, integrity, commitment, honesty, excellence and stewardship, factor in to all decisions, enabling their company to reach its vision of ensuring long-term viability while maximizing value from its timberland.

Today, times are good for the Martins—and today's Martins know how to have a good time among their peers as they did at the Rainforest Alliance gala in New York and the Entrepreneur of the Year gala in Houston. However, they know that economic winds are subject to sudden change. The flourishing OSB, lumber and plywood markets of early 2004 could abruptly reverse before year-end. Nevertheless, if history is an indication, like their predecessors, Johnny and Roy III will make sure their company can weather the often-unpredictable market fluctuations.

They are already hedging their bets on the future. On July 26, 2004, their board of advisors unanimously approved a major expansion of its Martco Limited Partnership manufacturing division. This expansion will enable Martco to modernize its existing plywood plant at Chopin, Louisiana, so that it can use smaller diameter timber while increasing production. They will also construct a new OSB plant at a company-owned site near Oakdale, Louisiana. When completed in late 2006, this plant will utilize small-diameter pine pulpwood and will employ one hundred forty hourly and thirty salaried personnel. All of these modernizations and expansion plans are in keeping with Martco's stated Vision to be one of the top five plants in North America in each of its divisions as measured by cost, margin, safety and customer satisfaction. An ambitious goal, certainly, but few who know these Martins doubt that it will be achieved.

Through their years as industry leaders, the Martins have been able to put both life and business in perspective. In the 1980s during the fiscal downturn of that period, a young salesman visited with Ellis in his office in Alexandria. During the course of that conversation, this unseasoned vendor mentioned the bad economy and asked Ellis if he had ever seen the manufacturing market as depressed as it was then. Ellis replied, laconically, that "business had been pretty bad back in '31." Like the instinctive squirrels who in summer store their nuts for the winter, the Martins know they can weather certain future difficult times by making provision during the good times.

LIFE BY THE BOARD FOOT

    Management specialist Peter Drucker once wrote: "To establish, maintain, or restore a theory [of business] does not require a Ginghis Khan or a Leonardo da Vinci in the executive suite. It is not genius; it is hard work. It is not being clever; it is being conscientious."[42] While not at all discounting their intelligence or their ability to see and seize opportunities before them, the Martin family has well demonstrated Drucker's observation. They have been willing to work hard. They have been conscientious in their efforts. In embracing these concepts and integrating them into their corporate psyche, these Martins have established and maintained a successful business.

For the family of Roy O. and Mildred Brown Martin, money **does** grow on trees. And life **is** by the board foot.

LIFE BY THE BOARD FOOT   ROY O. MARTIN COMPANIES

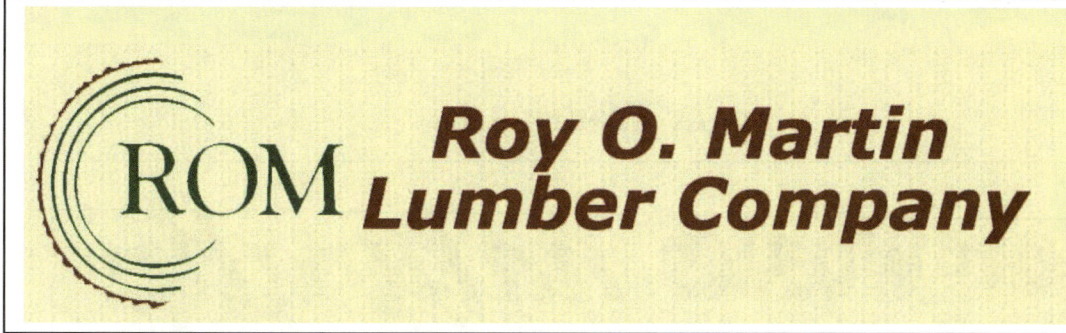

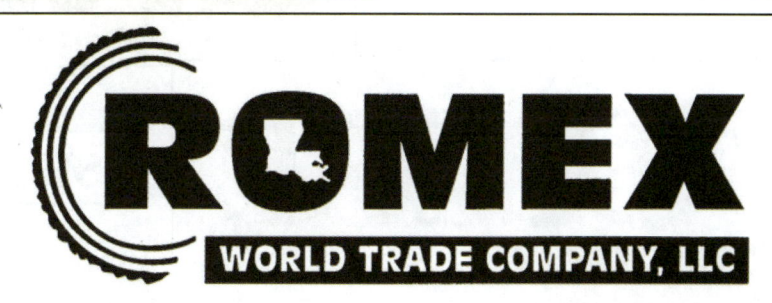

ROM Roy O. Martin Lumber Company

ROM

Stewardship · Respect · Integrity · Excellence · Honesty · Commitment
ROM — Roy O. Martin Lumber Co., L.P.

ROMEX
WORLD TRADE COMPANY, LLC

MARTCO LIMITED PARTNERSHIP

MTC

PERFOREX
FOREST SERVICES

LIFE BY THE BOARD FOOT

Company Trademarks

Wood works naturally™

TuffStrand OSB™

THE GRID™ Panel System

SMARTCORE PLYWOOD™

SHUGA BERRY®

"SCIG"™ SmartCore® Industrial Grade Plywood

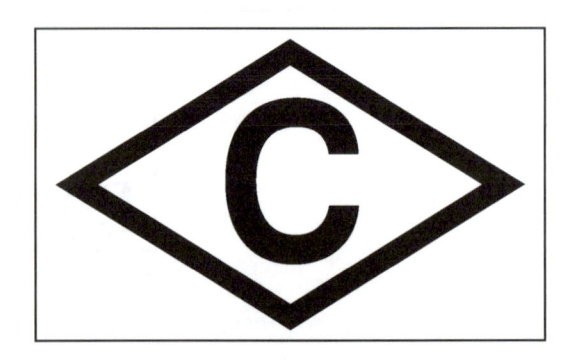

eclipse™ Radiant Barrier Panels by Martco
Available in OSB and Plywood.

◇C

296

INDEX

2003 reorganization, 180, 258
288 North McLean Street, 37
305 North Montgomery Street, 38
Abandoned Mills Report, 15
Acadiana Place, 139
Albany, Georgia, 289
Alexandria, i, ii, iii, v, 3, 7, 14, 18, 39, 40, 41, 43, 44, 45, 46, 47, 48, 52, 53, 54, 56, 57, 58, 59, 61, 62, 64, 65, 69, 70, 72, 77, 78, 82, 83, 84, 89, 92, 93, 95, 96, 97, 100, 102, 104, 105, 107, 111, 112, 113, 114, 115, 119, 120, 121, 123, 124, 125, 139, 142, 143, 149, 150, 152, 157, 166, 167, 169, 170, 175, 178, 179, 192, 193, 194, 196, 201, 202, 204, 205, 206, 207, 208, 209, 213, 218, 219, 222, 223, 224, 225, 227, 229, 237, 238, 239, 240, 245, 247, 248, 249, 252, 258, 267, 272, 273, 283, 288, 289, 292
Alexandria Daily Town Talk, 64, 113, 245
Alexandria First Methodist Church, 47
Alexandria Golf and Country Club, 139
Alexandria Housing Authority, 240
Alexandria Mall, 273
Alexandria Museum of Art, 240
Alexandria Senior High School, 208
Alexandria, Louisiana, i, 3, 40, 102, 143
Alley, John G., 62, 150
American Forest Products, 124, 297
American National Bank, 84
American Steel and Wire Company, 106
American Wood Dryers, 289
Angel Care, 240
Arbor, Inc., 141, 215
Arcadia, Wisconsin, 207
Armac Industries, Incorporated, 184
Artificial regeneration, 155
ASH, 239
Atchafalaya River Basin, 156, 161, 163
Austin, Texas, 203
Avoyelles Parish, 75
Avoyelles Parish, Louisiana, 75
Bank One, 52, 247
Barbara Lee Morros, 214
Baton Rouge, iv, 170, 205, 238, 252, 257, 259, 297
Baxter, Carole Martin, 149, 215
BBCC, 161
Beaumont, Texas, 26, 46, 53, 102, 191, 247
Bentley Lumber Company, 8
Bentley, Lorraine Dorothy, 220
Benton Harbor, Michigan, 203
Best Management Practices, 154, 240, 242
Better Business Bureau, 247
Bible Memory Association, 199
Bienville Parish, 78, 184
Bishop, Lottie, 19
Black Bear Conservation Committee, 161
Black Lake, 44, 74, 75, 78, 96, 162, 205, 206
BMA, 199
BMPs, 154, 240

LIFE BY THE BOARD FOOT

Bodcaw Lumber Company, 8
Bolton High School, 202, 205, 214, 220, 225
Bolton, J. W., 83
Bolton, Jesse, 268
Bolton, Robert, 52, 83, 121, 122, 297
Bordelonville, 75, 76
Bork, David, 146
Boy Scouts, 198, 199, 238
Boys and Girls Club, 238
Broadmoor Baptist Church, 257
Brown, Henry and Nettie, 26
Brown, Mildred, 28, 191, 293
Brunswick, 139
Buchanan, William, 8, 297
Buckner, Jerry, 126
Budget Management Services, 240
Burnaman, Maggie, 257
Burns, Anna C., 297
Bush, President George W., 279
Business Park, 139, 273
Cairo, Illinois, v, 31
Calvary Baptist Church, ii, 62
Calvin Center, Michigan, 24
Camp MilMar, 197, 198, 199
Carter, James E., 3, ii, 297
Castor, 44, 45, 64, 75, 78, 82, 84, 86, 87, 88, 89, 91, 92, 93, 94, 95, 96, 113, 120, 125, 139, 150, 152, 167, 177, 184, 190, 205, 206, 207, 208, 209, 210, 212, 217, 222, 249, 256, 257, 258, 263, 267, 288
Castor mill, 45, 78, 82, 84, 86, 87, 88, 89, 91, 92, 93, 94, 95, 96, 120, 152, 267
Castor sawmill, 96, 257, 288
Castor, Louisiana, 44, 184
Castro, Fidel, 140
Caterpillar Company, 203
CCA, 108
Cenla Affordable Housing, 240
Central Louisiana, 1, 3, 7, 8, 15, 17, 50, 54, 61, 64, 105, 112, 118, 139, 196, 198, 223, 224, 229, 236, 240, 248, 250, 265
Central Louisiana Community Foundation, 224, 240, 248
Central Louisiana Performing Arts Center, 240
Chamber of Commerce, 170, 239, 247
Chicago, Illinois, 119
Childers, William T., 15, 297
Chown, Bob, 254, 283
Colfax, 46, 65, 106, 107, 108, 109, 110, 111, 116, 118, 150, 166, 177, 182, 222, 239, 258
Colfax Creosoting Company, 46, 65, 106, 107, 108, 111, 118
Colfax Treating Company, 47, 107, 108, 109, 111, 239, 258
Colfax, Louisiana, 107
Committee of 100, 267
Community Development Block Grant, 246
ConSern, 170, 239
Cooley Crossing, 139
Cottonwood, 156
Creston Lumber Company, 40, 67
Crossett, Arkansas, 154, 222
Crowell, C. T., 7
Crowell-Spencer Lumber Company, 7
Cumberland Presbyterian Church, 199

Index

Dallas, Texas, 266
Davis, James J.(Jim), 252
Davis, Jim, 252, 253
D-Day Invasion, 89
Denley, Wayne, 289
Des Moines, Iowa, 93, 106
DiCarlo, Mark, 268
Divine Guidance, 18
DNA, iii, 44, 148, 291
Drucker, Peter, 292
Ducks Unlimited, 162
Dunn and Bradstreet, 142
Dunn, John, 278
Dura-Wood Treating Company, 47
E. B. Norman Company, 70
E. Sondheimer Company, 3
EBT, 169
Eclipse™, 281, 282
Edenborn Estate, 46, 106, 107, 177
Edenborn, William, 106
Edgewood Drive, 47, 60, 62, 193, 216, 227, 228
Edwardsburg, Michigan, 24
Eisenhower, Dwight D., 89
Elkhart, Indiana, iii, 19, 21
Ellis, 30, 37, 57, 64, 65, 71, 82, 86, 87, 88, 89, 91, 92, 93, 94, 95, 96, 99, 104, 108, 109, 111, 113, 116, 118, 119, 120, 121, 122, 123, 124, 125, 126, 132, 139, 141, 143, 145, 149, 150, 151, 152, 157, 167, 175, 176, 177, 178, 180, 183, 184, 188, 190, 196, 197, 198, 202, 204, 205, 206, 207, 208, 209, 210, 212, 213, 215, 217, 218, 222, 230, 235, 251, 255, 257, 258, 263, 267, 272, 280, 283, 289, 292, 297
Ellis Investments, Inc., 141
Employee Focus, 172
Environmental Protection Agency, 109, 212
EPA, 109
Erdoes, Mary, 284, 289
Estate planning, 182
Esther, 37, 184, 194, 217, 225, 226, 227, 228, 229, 231, 233, 235, 251
Etoile, Texas, 257
Eunice, 44, 56, 73, 148, 170, 238
Eunice Band Mill Company, 44, 73
Eunice, Louisiana, 73
Evans, Les, 5, 63, 287
Exports, 278
Felger, Otis A., 41, 67
Fenner Street, i, 14, 18, 40, 45, 56, 62, 67, 69, 71, 72, 74, 86, 93, 104, 112, 115, 116, 119, 122, 123, 124, 125, 143, 150, 166, 179, 190, 196, 216, 246, 249, 258
Fenner Street sawmill, 69, 104, 123, 166, 179
Ferguson, John L., 297
First Baptist Church, i, 48, 49, 207, 219
First National Bank of Chicago, 34, 121
First United Methodist Church, 47, 199, 219
First United Methodist Church of Pineville, 199
Floyd, John Claiborne, Jr., 226
Forest Park, 139
Forest Stewardship Council, 269, 290
Forests and People, i, 96, 179, 297
Fowler, Mary Martin, 149
Fox Chase, 139

FSC, 290, 291
GED, 170, 239
Georgia-Pacific, 124
Girl Scouts, 198, 199, 238
Glankler, Gene, 77, 166, 205
Golden Age of Forestry, 1
Good Pine Lumber Company, 8
Goudeau, Clyston, 94
Grand Rapids, Michigan, 30, 41
Grant Timber and Manufacturing Company, 8
Great Southern Lumber Company, 6, 7
Green Lumber Company, 102
Greenwing, 162
Guantanamo Bay, Cuba, 279
Habitat for Humanity, 223, 238, 240, 248
Hammond, 170, 238
Hardtner, Henry E., 7
Hardwood, 125, 155, 272, 297
Harris, Nicole Robbins, 150
Hartford, Michigan, 26, 30, 192, 297
Hibernia Bank, 289
Higgins boats, 90, 91
Higgins Industries, 89
Higgins, Andrew Jackson, 89
Hill, Marvin, 206
Hillyer-Deutsch-Edwards Lumber Company, 8, 153
Hixson-Simmons tract, 292
Hodge, Louisiana, 44
Hodges, A. J., 107
Home Place Land Company, 70
Hood, Paul C., 58, 150
Hope House, 238
Hopkins, J. F., 40, 67, 72
Howard Associates, Inc., 141
Howard Building Center, 102
Howard Lumber & Supply Company, 102
Howard Lumber Company, 45, 99, 100, 101, 102, 203
Howard, Gene, 56, 251
Howard, Mark, 45, 113, 114, 204, 217
Howard, Mark Eugene, 99, 203
Howard, Mark Eugene II, 203
Howard, Virginia, 204, 248
Howard, Virginia Martin, 61, 99, 113, 147, 204, 235, 248, 251
Howell, Thomas, 51, 235, 297
Hunt Forest Products, Inc., 96
Hunting club, 161
Hunting clubs, 161
Industrial Lumber Company, 8
Inner City Revitalization Corporation, 224
Interlocken, 197, 219
International Paper Company, 94
J. A. Bentley Lumber Company, 7
Jeffress, Charles, 57, 60, 100, 218
Jeffress, Charles H., v
Jennings, Louisiana, 102

Index

Johnny, iv, 96, 120, 125, 142, 143, 147, 148, 149, 150, 151, 172, 180, 190, 207, 212, 228, 235, 236, 247, 250, 251, 252, 253, 254, 255, 256, 258, 260, 261, 262, 263, 264, 265, 266, 267, 268, 270, 271, 272, 273, 279, 280, 281, 282, 283, 284, 285, 286, 287, 288, 289, 291, 292
Johnson, Carl, 109, 110
Johnson, Vinita Grace Strackeljohn, 215
Jones, Governor Sam Houston, 51
Julliard, 202
Kankakee, Illinois, 192
Karimoku Conference Room, 277
Kees, Ralph, 57, 100, 166, 187
Kellogg, Walter W., 297
Kerr, Ed, i, 54, 96, 297
Key Result Areas, 181, 182
Kilpatrick, Kathy Sue, 259
Kincaid Lake, 139
Kisatchie National Forest, 15
Kittell, Susie Belle, 19, 20, 49
Kiwanis Club, 52, 248
Knerr, Mike, 287
Kojis, Richard, 111
Kolin, Louisiana, 292
KPMG, 141, 181, 250
Kresge Foundation, 224
Lafayette, 71, 102, 139, 170, 238
Lafayette, Louisiana, 102
Lafourche Lumber Company, 102
Lake Charles Lumber Company, 102
Lake Charles, Louisiana, 102
Land Craft Vehicle Personnel boat, 89
Landry, Richard, 53, 54, 176, 297
Lantern Award, 268
LC, 142, 234, 235
LCVP, 89
LDEQ, 109
LeMoyen OSB, 134
LeMoyen, Louisiana, 125
Lincoln Road School, 208
Literacy for Learning to Read, 239
Lombardi, Vince, 261
Long Leaf, Louisiana, 7
Long Pine Lumber Company, 45, 74
Louisiana Baptist Children's Home, 240
Louisiana College, i, 49, 50, 51, 57, 166, 169, 170, 199, 202, 204, 206, 224, 225, 234, 235, 236, 237, 238
Louisiana Department of Environmental Quality, 109
Louisiana Department of Wildlife, 159
Louisiana Forestry Association, i, 65, 154, 179, 242, 271
Louisiana Public Broadcasting, 240
Louisiana State University, 169, 170, 202, 205, 237, 238, 257, 259
Louisiana Tech University, 170, 238
Louisiana-Pacific, 104, 122, 123, 124, 125, 153, 218, 272
Louisiana-Pacific Corporation, 104, 123
Louisville, Kentucky, 70
LP, 104, 123, 124, 125, 272
LSUA Distinguished Service Award, 248
Lucas, Debra, 245
Lunding, Franklin J., 168

LIFE BY THE BOARD FOOT

Magnolia, Arkansas, 46, 100, 102
Marcus, Ira, 119, 184, 185
Mark Howard, 45, 113, 114, 204, 217
Marketplace Ministries, 170, 266
Martco, 105, 124, 125, 126, 130, 131, 132, 133, 134, 135, 136, 139, 141, 142, 172, 174, 175, 178, 179, 180, 181, 213, 237, 239, 251, 279, 282, 284, 290
Martco Limited Partnership, 251, 290
Martco Partnership, 105, 124, 125, 126, 134, 139, 141, 178, 179, 237, 239
Martco Plywood, 135, 136, 172
Martco sawmill, 132, 134
Martin Building Materials, 102
MARTIN CARES, 170, 171, 266
Martin Center for Performing Arts, 224, 225
Martin Community Center, 246
Martin Companies, 3, 6, i, 65, 83, 111, 141, 142, 143, 145, 146, 147, 149, 151, 153, 156, 167, 180, 183, 184, 185, 186, 218, 219, 221, 236, 241, 245, 247, 251, 252, 256, 260, 263, 265, 268, 269, 271, 277, 278, 282, 283, 284, 285, 286, 288, 290
Martin Distributors, 105
Martin Fine Arts Building, 49, 224, 234
Martin Foundation, 169, 233, 236, 237, 238, 239, 240, 248, 289
Martin Home Center, 102, 104, 122, 124, 138
Martin Home Centers, Inc., 104
Martin Park, 46, 139, 238, 272
Martin Public Library, 50, 235
Martin Timber Company, 44, 78, 93, 94, 96, 100, 118, 124, 141, 142, 184, 185, 210, 215, 258
Martin Timber Company, Inc., 141
Martin, Albert Andrew, 19
Martin, Albert DeWitt, 20
Martin, Eddie, 48
Martin, Ellis, 30, 123, 141, 208, 280, 297
Martin, Ellis Spencer, 37, 204, 251
Martin, Esther, 251
Martin, Esther Louise, 37, 225
Martin, Johnny, iv, 251, 261
Martin, Jonathan Ellis, 96, 254
Martin, Lorraine, 236
Martin, Maggie, ii, iv, 172
Martin, Maggie B., Ph.D., 3, iv
Martin, Mildred B., 41, 67
Martin, Mildred Virginia, 37, 200
Martin, Norman Kittell, 37, 251
Martin, Roy O. III, 52, 135, 141, 145
Martin, Roy O., Jr., 13, 113, 122
Martin, Roy O., Sr., i, iii, iv, 1, 3, 64, 65, 78, 113, 143, 182, 186, 255
Martin, Roy Otis, Jr., 37, 251
Martin, Spencer, 150, 240
Martin, Susie Kittell, 19
Martin, Virginia Slaughter, 196, 235, 248
Martin, Wallace Beardsley, 20
Martin,Esther Louise, 37, 225
Martin-Wilkie-Hopkins Company, 44, 71, 72
Marwick, Pete, 141, 181, 250
May Brothers, 44, 73
Mayflower, 26
MBA, 258, 259, 263, 264
McNully, Hollis, 286, 287

Index

Meeker Mill, 69
Meeker, Louisiana, 43
Memphis Bank of Commerce and Trust Company, 41
Memphis, Tennessee, i, v, 31, 37, 38, 74
MHC, 104, 105, 124, 138, 139, 141, 142
MHC Properties, 104, 105, 138, 139, 141
MHC Properties, Inc., 105, 138, 141
Michigan College of Mines and Technology, 99
MilMar Library, 275
Milroy Mercantile Company, 45
Minden Lumber Company, 8
Minden, Louisiana, 102
Miracle Camp, 199
Missouri Pacific Railroad, 44, 71
Mobile, Alabama, 84
Moldshield™, 282
Moncrief, W. A., 209
Monroe, 14, 102, 170, 238, 297
Monroe, Louisiana, 102
Monroe, Natalie Martin, 150
Moore, Bill, 289
Moravian Music Foundation, 204
Morgan City Lumber Company, 102
Morgan City, Louisiana, 102
Morgan, J. P., 107, 284
Morgan, J. P. Company, 284
Morgan, James P., 65
Morton, J. Sterling, vi
Mouton, Maurice, 107
Munsterman, John, 58, 97, 126, 152, 166
Natchitoches, 45, 46, 59, 74, 99, 100, 101, 102, 117, 118, 134, 135, 139, 157, 163, 169, 170, 203, 204, 238, 297
Natchitoches Parish Police Jury, 118, 135
Natchitoches, Louisiana, 59, 102
National Recovery Administration, 77
Nature Conservancy, 243
New Orleans, 5, 89, 107, 126, 196, 214, 297
New Orleans, Louisiana, 89
New South Business College, 26
New York, New York, 290
Newell Lumber Company, 44, 73
Nickey Brothers, i, 32, 37, 38, 39, 58, 70, 166, 192
Nickey Brothers Lumber Company, i
Norman, ii, 37, 49, 54, 56, 64, 65, 91, 98, 100, 108, 109, 113, 117, 118, 122, 143, 150, 153, 155, 166, 184, 190, 199, 208, 218, 219, 220, 221, 222, 223, 224, 225, 229, 230, 231, 234, 235, 240, 248, 251, 297
Norman Kittell Martin, 37, 251
Norman Martin, ii, 297
Norman Oil and Gas Company, 117
Northwestern State University, 59, 166, 169, 170, 237, 238
Norton, Clyde, 108, 116, 166, 181, 182
NRA, 77
Nutt, Haywood, 107
O'Quin, Chester, 59, 100, 166, 176, 187
Oak Shadows, 139
Oakdale, 8, 153, 166, 272
Oakdale, Louisiana, 153

LIFE BY THE BOARD FOOT

Oberlin Conservatory of Music, 202
Occident Flour, 28
Opelousas, Louisiana, 102
OSB, 124, 125, 126, 128, 130, 131, 132, 135, 139, 142, 150, 175, 178, 212, 239, 258, 272, 280, 281, 282, 292
Partners for Education, 238
Payne, Moore, and Herrington, 58
Peabody High School, 197, 236
Peabody Junior High, 197, 236
Pelican State Lumber Company, 102
Peoria, Illinois, 100, 203
Perforex, 181, 254
Peters, Ray, 268
Peterson, Keith, 60, 83, 151
Peterson, Keith D., 83
Pine Wood Lumber Company, 8
Pineville, i, 46, 47, 48, 49, 50, 51, 53, 56, 57, 65, 77, 86, 107, 110, 139, 166, 169, 170, 193, 195, 196, 197, 198, 199, 201, 202, 204, 205, 208, 213, 219, 223, 227, 234, 235, 238, 243, 247, 288, 297
Pineville Elementary School, 48, 196
Pineville Lumber Company, 77, 86
Pineville, Louisiana, i, 49
Plaquemine, Louisiana, 39
Pleasant Hill, Louisiana, 92
Poole, Scott, 147, 212, 264, 268
POP, 175, 265
Press, 297
Price, Buford, 252
Price, Buford W., 252
Promotion Opportunity Program, 175
QDMA, 161
QMD, 161
Quality Deer Management, 161
Quality Deer Management Association, 161
Railroads, 117
RailWorks Corporation, 47, 117
Rainforest Alliance, 290, 291, 292
Rapides Bank and Trust Company, 52, 82, 218, 247
Rapides Parish Library, 50
Rapides Parish Library Board, 50
Rapides Regional Medical Center, 248
Rapides Symphony, 240
Reading to Learn, 239
Reagan, President, 130
Red Cross, 240
Red River, 48, 56, 74, 135, 157, 163, 164, 202, 216, 273
Reforestation, 155, 156, 222, 241
Replanting, 241
Retail lumberyards, 99
RICHES, 147, 270
Ringgold, 87, 199, 206, 207, 208, 209
Rockefeller, John D., 65
Rockford, Illinois, 32, 34, 192
Rogalski, John, 268
ROM Today, 172, 181, 284
ROMEX, 139, 140, 141, 147, 180, 245, 247, 250, 251, 273, 277, 279
ROMEX World Trade Center, 139, 140, 180, 245, 247, 250, 251, 273, 277, 279

Index

ROMEX World Trade Company, 139, 141
ROMEX World Trade Company, L. L. C., 139, 141
Roosevelt, Franklin D., 77
Roy III, 52, 135, 141, 142, 143, 147, 148, 149, 151, 167, 185, 190, 215, 219, 245, 247, 248, 250, 251, 252, 254, 255, 256, 258, 259, 260, 261, 262, 263, 264, 267, 268, 271, 272, 273, 277, 278, 279, 281, 282, 283, 285, 286, 287, 288, 289, 292
Roy O., 3, 5, 6, i, ii, iii, iv, v, 1, 3, 8, 13, 14, 17, 20, 21, 22, 23, 24, 26, 27, 28, 29, 30, 31, 32, 33, 34, 36, 37, 38, 39, 40, 41, 42, 43, 44, 45, 46, 47, 48, 49, 50, 51, 52, 53, 54, 55, 56, 57, 58, 59, 60, 61, 62, 63, 64, 65, 66, 67, 68, 69, 70, 71, 72, 73, 74, 75, 76, 77, 78, 82, 83, 84, 85, 86, 88, 91, 92, 93, 95, 96, 97, 98, 99, 100, 104, 105, 106, 107, 112, 113, 114, 115, 119, 122, 123, 124, 125, 126, 135, 139, 140, 141, 142, 143, 145, 148, 149, 150, 151, 153, 157, 162, 166, 167, 168, 170, 172, 175, 176, 177, 180, 182, 184, 185, 186, 187, 188, 190, 191, 192, 194, 196, 197, 198, 200, 205, 209, 210, 212, 213, 215, 216, 217, 219, 224, 228, 229, 230, 231, 233, 234, 235, 236, 237, 243, 247, 248, 249, 250, 253, 255, 256, 264, 267, 269, 270, 271, 272, 278, 279, 283, 287, 288, 289, 290, 291, 293, 297
Roy O. Martin Industries, 104, 119, 141, 185
Roy O. Martin Lumber Company, i, ii, iii, iv, v, 1, 3, 17, 41, 43, 44, 64, 65, 67, 69, 70, 71, 72, 73, 75, 76, 77, 83, 84, 86, 88, 91, 92, 93, 96, 99, 100, 104, 105, 106, 112, 113, 115, 122, 123, 124, 125, 139, 140, 141, 142, 143, 145, 148, 149, 157, 170, 186, 191, 192, 215, 217, 236, 237, 243, 248, 249, 253, 264, 267, 269, 270, 272, 279, 291, 297
Roy O. Martin Profit Sharing Plan, 169
Roy Spur, 75, 78
Roy, Jr., 13, 42, 45, 52, 56, 58, 64, 65, 71, 91, 113, 114, 115, 118, 122, 123, 143, 145, 150, 178, 184, 186, 190, 197, 202, 208, 214, 215, 216, 217, 218, 219, 222, 223, 230, 247, 248, 255, 289
Ruby-Wise School, 243, 244
Ruston, 91, 96, 170, 238
Safetygas, 45, 84, 85
Safetygas, Incorporated, 45
SALT, 181, 268, 270
Salvation Army, 51, 218, 248
Sanders, D. B, 54, 92, 97, 152, 297
Scalers, 11
Schoonover, Adrian, 268
Selective cutting, 14
Shafer Company, 29, 30, 31
Shafer Lumber Company, 29
Shafer, Cyrus C. Lumber Company, i, 29, 30, 39
Shepherd Center Ministries, 238
Shreveport, 46, 83, 84, 107, 117, 199, 208
SHUGA BERRY®, 132
Simington Lake, 21, 22
Slaughter, Bill, 252, 253
Slaughter, Dr. William, iv
Slaughter, Dr. William (Bill), 252
Slaughter, Virginia Ruth, 206
SmartCore®, 136
SmartWood, 290
Smith, Evelyn, 268
Smith, Walter Jacobs, 186, 223, 251
SMZs, 154, 155, 242
Snowden Estate, 75
Somerset, Ltd., 141
South Bend Business College, 24, 26, 27
South Bend, Indiana, i, v, 24, 28, 51, 53, 191, 247
Southeastern Louisiana University, 170, 238
Southern Bag and Paper Company, 44
Southern Chevrolet, 59, 166

Southwood Development Company, Inc., 141
Spence, A. B., 7
Springhill, Louisiana, 94
SSA Consultants, iv, 252
St. Landry Parish, 239
St. Louis, Missouri, 106
Stamps, Arkansas, 8
State of Louisiana, 135, 141, 271
Stearns Foundation, 204
Stephens College, 202
Stevens, Cora Belle Martin, 20
Strategic Action Leadership Team, 181, 268
Streamside Management Zones, 154, 242
Studebaker, 25, 26
Studebaker Corporation, 26
Subchapter S, 142
Sulphur, Louisiana, 102
Superior Lumber and Supply Company, 102
Swampers, 11
Taliban, 279
Tall Timber Lumber Company, 8
Technology, 203
Texaco Oil Company, 152
The Glade, 139
The GRID, 132, 253, 281
The GRID™, 281
The Sawdust Gazette, 172, 174
Thibodeaux, Joyce Martin, 297
Thibodeaux, Louisiana, 102
Thomas, J. Elliston, 27, 31
Time, Inc., 291
Tremont Lumber Company, 183
Trout Creek Lumber Company, 8
TSI, 54, 93, 153, 222, 272
Tudor, Buddy, 288
Turner Lumber Company, 125
Tuscaloosa Sands, 209
U. S. Forest Service, 157
United States Coast Guard, 214
United Way, 237, 248
United Way of Central Louisiana, 237
University of Louisiana, 170, 238
University of Michigan, 204, 226
Urania Lumber Company, 7
USNR, 287
Vanderbilt University, 225
VanPly, 153
Vernon Parish Lumber Company, 105, 106
Virginia Martin Howard, 61, 99, 113, 147, 204, 235, 248, 251
Vision 2004, 253, 269
Vision statement, 270
Vision Statement 2004, 270
VMH Foundation, 204
Walker, Martha Avodna, 208
War on Terrorism, 279
Ware Hall, 49, 234

Index

Watertown, New York, 110
Weems, Charlie, 208, 252
Wilkie, W. I., 44, 72
Wilmar Plywood, 118
Woodard, Zack, 100, 104, 119, 120, 167, 176, 184, 187, 209, 260, 280
World War I, 46, 50, 54, 61, 88, 89, 92, 93, 94, 97, 112, 149, 152, 196, 207, 214, 235, 272, 279
World War II, 46, 50, 54, 88, 89, 92, 93, 94, 97, 112, 149, 152, 196, 207, 214, 235, 272, 279
Woychuck, N. A., 199
Wysocki, Lewis, 117
YMCA, 26, 28, 238
YWCA, 238
Zaytsoff, Rob, 280

ENDNOTES

ENDNOTES

Chapter 1

[1] Anna C. Burns, A History of the Louisiana Forestry Commission (Natchitoches, LA: The Louisiana Studies Institute, Northwestern State College, 1968) 21.

[2] Walter W. Kellogg, The Kellogg Story: Fifty Years in the Southern Hardwood Business (Monroe, LA: Thomas J. Moran's Sons, Inc., 1969) 52.

[3] Archer H. Mayor, Southern Timberman: The Legacy of William Buchanan (Athens, GA: The University of Georgia Press, 1988) 12.

[4] Ibid., 13

[5] Ibid., 13-14.

[6] Ed Kerr, "History of Forestry in Louisiana," Tales of the Louisiana Forests (Baton Rouge: Claitor's Publishing Division, n. d.) 1-2, 4-5.

[7] Ibid., 2-7.

[8] Mayor, Southern Timberman 37-41.

[9] William T. Childers, Echoes from the Millpond: A Brief History of the Louisiana Central Lumber Company, Clarks, LA, 1902-1953 (Columbia, LA: 1987) 2, 39.

[10] Ibid., 2.

[11] Ibid., 113.

[12] Mayor 43-44.

Chapter 2

[1] Ed Kerr, "Behind the ROM," an in-house advertising brochure noting the thirty-year history of Roy O. Martin Lumber Company, circa 1953, 8.

[2] John L. Ferguson, American Forest Products Industries, New Orleans, LA: 3. Press release found among Martin archives.

[3] Autobiography 5.

[4] Joyce Martin Thibodeaux, The Browns of Hartford, Michigan. Houma, LA: Professional Printers (1984), 39.

[5] Autobiography 16.

[6] Ibid., 17.

[7] John L. Ferguson, "How to Make a Million," Sunday: The Indianapolis Star Magazine, 20 November 1960: 30. Included in the Autobiography.

[8] Personal interview with Ellis Martin by James E. Carter, October 26, 2000.

[9] Autobiography 14.

[10] Cited in Browns 56.

[11] Ed Kerr, "Behind the ROM," an in-house advertising brochure noting the thirty-year history of Roy O. Martin Lumber Company, circa 1953, 8.

[12] Autobiography 42.

[13] Ibid.

[14] Ed Kerr, "Behind the ROM," an in-house advertising brochure noting the thirty-year history of Roy O. Martin Lumber Company, circa 1953: 5-6.

[15] Personal interview with Norman Martin by James E. Carter, November 3, 2000.

[16] Thomas Howell, "Speech at the Golden Anniversary of the Martin Library in Pineville, September 17, 2000," 7.

[17] Personal Interview with Robert Bolton by James E. Carter, September 27, 2000.

[18] Personal Interview with Richard Landry by James E. Carter, March 5, 2001.

[19] Personal Interview with D. B. Sanders by James E. Carter, December 11, 2000.

[20] Autobiography 34.

[21] Personal Interview with D.B. Sanders by James E. Carter, December 11, 2000.

[22] Ed Kerr, "Success by the Board Foot," Forests and People, First Quarter 1958; reprinted in Autobiography and Tales of the Louisiana Forest.

[23] Comments from Gene Howard, March 23, 2004.
[24] Personal Interview with Charles Jeffress by James E. Carter, January 19, 2001.
[25] Personal Interview with John Munsterman by James E. Carter, September 20, 2000.
[26] Personal Interview with Paul C. Hood by James E. Carter, May 9, 2001.
[27] Personal Interview with Chester O'Quin by James E. Carter, March 21, 2001.
[28] Personal Interview with Keith Peterson by James E. Carter, September 14, 2000.
[29] Ed Kerr, "Behind the ROM," an in-house advertising brochure noting the thirty-year history of Roy O. Martin Lumber Company, circa 1953: 8.
[30] Ibid, 6.
[31] Personal Interview with Virginia Martin Howard by James E. Carter, July 16, 2001.
[32] Personal Interview with John G. Alley by James E. Carter, September 27, 2000.
[33] Les Evans, "To ROM." Among personal papers, dated 1954.
[34] <u>Alexandria Daily Town Talk</u>, Alexandria-Pineville, Louisiana, 14 June 1962.
[35] The Louisiana Forestry Association <u>Newsletter</u>, February 1973, reprinted in <u>Autobiography</u>.

Chapter 3
[1] Charles H. Jeffress, ed., <u>An Autobiography of Roy Otis Martin (Alexandria, LA: Printing Dept. of Roy O. Martin Lbr., Co.)</u> 37-43.
[2] Ibid., 37, 42, 44.
[3] Personal interview with Ellis Martin by James E. Carter, October 26, 2000.
[4] Personal interview with Roy O. Martin, Jr. by James E. Carter, December 11, 2000.
[5] Ibid., 49.
[6] Personal interview with Ellis Martin by James E. Carter, October 26, 2000.
[7] <u>Autobiography</u> 55.
[8] "To the Stockholders of the Roy O. Martin Lumber Company, Inc." Annual meeting 1930. Minutes book of the Roy O. Martin Lumber Company. The pages in the Minute Book of the Roy O. Martin Lumber Company are not numbered consecutively. References to the Minutes Book hereafter will be to the date of the meeting.
[9] Minutes Book, 20 January 1934.
[10] Personal interview with Robert Bolton by James E. Carter, September 27, 2000.
[11] Personal interview with Keith Peterson by James E. Carter, September 14, 2000.
[12] Minutes Book, 29 January 1937.
[13] Kellogg 149.
[14] <u>Autobiography</u> 60-63.
[15] Personal interview with Ellis Martin by James E. Carter, October 26, 2000.
[16] Ibid.
[17] Melanie Torbett, "Higgins Boats: The Wooden Boats that Won the War," <u>Forests and People,</u> Third Quarter 2000: 4-5, 7.
[18] Minutes Book, 4 March 1947.
[19] Personal interview with D. B. Sanders by James E. Carter, December 11, 2000,
[20] James Morgan, "A Bit of History . . . Martin Dimension Plant – Castor." <u>The Sawdust Gazette</u> 1 July 1995.
[21] <u>The Shreveport Journal</u> 13 February 1950.
[22] Ed Kerr, "Success . . . By the Board Foot." n. p.
[23] "La. Lumber Mill Closing," Alexandria <u>The Town Talk</u> 13 November 2000, sec. A: 4.
[24] Personal interview with John Munsterman by James E. Carter, September 20, 2000.
[25] Zack Woodard, personal notes, March 6, 2004.
[26] Ed Kerr, "Behind the ROM," an in-house advertising brochure noting the thirty-year history of Roy O. Martin Lumber Company, circa 1953: 10.
[27] Zack Woodard, personal notes, March 6, 2004.
[28] Zack Woodard, "Martin Companies' History," December 22, 1997: 2.
[29] Eric J. Brock, "Shreveporter Edenborn Was Among Country's Wealthiest," <u>Shreveport Times</u>.
[30] <u>Autobiography</u> 42; Personal interview with Ellis Martin by James E. Carter, October 26, 2000.
[31] Personal interview with Clyde Norton by James E. Carter, January 29, 2001.

ENDNOTES

[32] Personal interview with Ellis Martin by James E. Carter, October 26, 2000.
[33] James Ronald Skains, "Colfax Creosoting Deals With Environmental Issues While Serving Utilities," The Piney Woods Journal, April 1998, sec. A: 3.
[34] Jane O'Neal, "The History of Colfax Creosoting," ROM Today, July 1996: 1.
[35] Ken Gardner, "Colfax Biopiles—Mounds of Environmental Responsibility," ROM Today, September 2003: 7.
[36] Gary R. Pinnell, "Helping Out, Colfax Creosoting Shipping Poles to Ice-Plagued Northeast," Alexandria Daily Town Talk 13 January 1988.
[37] The Piney Woods Journal, sec. A: 1.
[38] Alexandria Daily Town Talk, 13 January 1998; The Piney Woods Journal, sec. A: 1.
[39] Personal interview with Clyde Norton by James E. Carter, January 29, 2001.
[40] Charles Parsons, "A New Skin" and "Hot Wax at Colfax," ROM Today, May 2001: 1-2.

Chapter 4
[1] Personal interview with Roy O. Martin, Jr., by James E. Carter, June 22, 2001.
[2] "Roy O. Martin, Jr. Becomes President of Lumber Firm," Alexandria Daily Town Talk, 14 June 1962.
[3] Personal interview with Clyde Norton by James E. Carter, January 29, 2001.
[4] Personal interview with Norman Martin by James E. Carter, June 14, 1962.
[5] Zack Woodard, personal notes, March 8, 2004.
[6] Personal interview with Ellis Martin by James E. Carter, October 26, 2000.
[7] Personal interview with Ellis Martin by James E. Carter, October 26, 2000.
[8] "The Sheathing Masters," company video produced by VideoCorp, Inc., executive producer and technical consultant, Audrey Osborn, Roy O. Martin Lumber Company, 1994.
[9] Ibid.
[10] "From Boards to Boardrooms," company video produced by VideoCorp, Inc, executive producer and technical consultant, Audrey Osborn, Roy O. Martin Lumber Company, 1994.
[11] Jack Petree, "Roy O. Martin Lumber Stays on Leading Edge," TimberLine, October 2000: 7.
[12] "From Boards to Boardrooms," company video produced by VideoCorp, Inc., executive producer and technical consultant, Audrey Osborn, Roy O. Martin Lumber Company, 1994
[13] Roy O. Martin III, Notes on an Address to the Natchitoches Lion's Club, April 1996; "Roy O. Martin Makes Wood Plant Official," The Natchitoches Times, 9 June 1994.
[14] "One Billion Square Feet," ROM Today, June 2000: 3.
[15] John Rogalski, "A New Family Member," ROM Today, March 2000: 3.
[16] Steve Wagner, email to Jonathan E. Martin, February 4, 2002.
[17] Curtis Meaux, "ROMEX World Trade Center," ROM Today, May 2001: 3.
[18] Roy O. Martin III, email to Maggie Martin, February 3, 2004.
[19] Roy O. Martin III, email to Maggie Martin February 4, 2004.

Chapter 5
[1] Quoted by Francine Russon, "Growth Drives Family Firms Crazy," Time, March 2000, Your Business Section: B15.
[2] Ibid.
[3] Sharon Nelton, "Ten Keys to Success in Family Business", Nation's Business, April 1991: 44-45.
[4] Zack Woodard, "Martin Companies' History," December 22, 1997: 4.
[5] Charles H. Jeffress, ed., An Autobiography of Roy Otis Martin (Alexandria, LA: Printing Dept. of Roy O. Martin Lbr. Co., 1961) 64.
[6] Personal interview with Charles Weems by James E. Carter, July 26, 2001.
[7] Personal interview with Ellis Martin by James E. Carter, October 26, 2000.
[8] Personal interview with John G. Alley by James E. Carter, September 27, 2000.
[9] Personal interview with Paul C. Hood by James E. Carter, May 9, 2001.
[10] Personal interview with Ellis Martin by James E. Carter, October 26, 2000.
[11] Personal interview with John G. Alley by James E. Carter, September 27, 2000.
[12] Personal interview with Norman Martin by James E. Carter, November 3, 2000.

LIFE BY THE BOARD FOOT

[13] Personal interview with Keith Peterson by James E. Carter, September 14, 2000.
[14] Personal interview with Paul C. Hood by James E. Carter, May 9, 2001.
[15] Bill Wieger, "Perspective," <u>ROM Today</u> November 1996: 5.
[16] Personal interview with Norman Martin by James E. Carter, November 3, 2000.
[17] Greg Herbert, "The ABCs to BMPs and SMZs," <u>ROM Today</u>, March 1998: 5.
[18] Personal interview with Bill Wieger by James E. Carter, May 31, 2001.
[19] "Trees Replaced," <u>The Sawdust Gazette</u> 1 October 1993: 5; Steve Breaux, "The Work of Forestry," <u>ROM Today</u>, November 1996: 1.
[20] Mike Keatchum, "Time to Replant," <u>ROM Today</u>, March 1999: 5.
[21] "Lost Ground," Alexandria <u>The Town Talk</u>, 28 November 2001, sec. A: 7.
[22] Hank Smart, "Martin Hunting Lease Program," <u>ROM Today</u>, November 1996: 2.
[23] Chris Clayton, "Wildlife Tracks," <u>ROM Today</u>, September 2001: 5; advertisement: "Quality Deer Management Seminar," Alexandria <u>Daily Town Talk</u>, 5 August 2001, sec. B: 6.
[24] Greg Herbert, "The Bear is Back," <u>ROM Today</u>, September 2000: 5.
[25] Greg Herbert, "Martin Foresters Educate Greenwings," <u>ROM Today</u>, September 1997: 3.
[26] Scott Poole, "Martin Has State Champion," <u>ROM Today</u>, June 1997: 3.
[27] Jennifer McCrary, "Optimizing the Timber Factory," <u>Timber Harvesting</u>, March 1998: 14, 16.
[28] Personal interview with Richard Landry by James E. Carter, March 5, 2001.
[29] Roy O. Martin III, "Employee Loyalty: Key to Profits," <u>ROM Today</u>, May 1996: 3.
[30] Woodard, "Martin Companies' History," 1.
[31] Terry Garrett, "ConSern for Education," <u>The Sawdust Gazette</u>, 1 April 1995: 3.
[32] Kim Evans, "MARTIN CARES: A Chaplaincy Program," <u>ROM Today</u>, December 1997: 1.
[33] Heather Barron, "Feeling Better?" <u>ROM Today</u>, March 2001: 7.
[34] "Ten Good Reasons to Work At Martco," <u>The Sawdust Gazette</u>, 1 February 1994: 1.
[35] Personal interview with Chester O'Quin by James E. Carter, March 21, 2001.
[36] Personal interview with Richard Landry by James E. Carter, March 5, 2001.
[37] Personal interview with Zack Woodard by James E. Carter, June 27, 2001.
[38] Personal interview with Roy O. Martin, Jr., by James E. Carter, December 11, 2000.
[39] Personal interview with Ellis Martin by James E. Carter, October 26, 2000.
[40] <u>Forests and People</u>. Fourth Quarter 2000.
[41] Jack Petree, "Roy O. Martin Lumber Stays on Leading Edge," <u>TimberLine,</u> October 2000: 7.
[42] Griff Griffin, "Edger Optimization Vital to Hardwood Mill Upgrade," <u>Forest Industries</u>, March 1989: 11.
[43] Keith Barron, "Perforex at Martco," <u>ROM Today</u>, March 2001: 6.
[44] Ray Peters, "JEM's 'Key Result Areas,'" <u>ROM Today</u>, June 2000: 2.
[45] Ibid.
[46] "Keep Business Going With Succession Plan," Alexandria <u>The Daily Town Talk</u>, ---------.
[47] Woodard, "Martin Companies' History," 3-4.
[48] Roy O. Martin III, email to Maggie Martin, February 3, 2004.
[49] Ibid.
[50] Walter Smith, "The ROM Formula for Success," <u>ROM Today,</u> March 1998: 1.
[51] Personal interview with Roy O. Martin, Jr. by James E. Carter, June 21, 2001.

Chapter 6
[1] Charles H. Jeffress, ed., <u>An Autobiography of Roy Otis Martin</u> (Alexandria, LA: Printing Dept. of Roy O. Martin Lbr. Co., 1961) 64-65.
[2] Personal interview with Roy O. Martin, Jr., by James E. Carter, June 11, 2001.
[3] Personal interview with Esther Martin Floyd by Joe Abraham, January 19, 1999.
[4] Personal interview with Virginia Martin Howard by Joseph Abraham, May 26, 1998.
[5] Personal interview with Esther Martin Floyd by Joe Abraham, January 19, 1999.
[6] Ibid.
[7] Personal interview with Virginia Martin Howard by James E. Carter, July 16, 2001.
[8] Personal interview with Norman Martin by James E. Carter, November 3, 2000.
[9] Personal interview with Virginia Martin Howard by James E. Carter, July 16, 2001.
[10] Personal interview with Mr. and Mrs. Cob Cook by James E. Carter, June 27, 2001.

ENDNOTES

[11] Personal interview with Charles Weems by James E. Carter, July 26, 2001.
[12] Zack Woodard, personal notes, March 8, 2004.
[13] Ellis Martin, handwritten notes, n. d.
[14] Scott Poole, "Thoughts on Mr. Ellis and His 80th Birthday," ROM Today, December 1997: 2.
[15] "Lecompte couple gets LSU-A Service Award," Alexandria The Daily Town Talk, 4 January 2001, sec. A: 6.
[16] Personal interview with Roy O. Martin, Jr. by James E. Carter, June 21, 2001.
[17] Personal interview with Norman Martin by James E. Carter, November 3, 2000.
[18] Personal interview with Keith Peterson by James E. Carter, September 14, 2000.
[19] "LC Meets Requirements for $5,000,000 Kresge Grant," Baptist Message 7 May 1992 and "Louisiana College Sets Dedication of New Performing Arts Center," Baptist Message 12 May 1992: 3.
[20] Personal interview with Esther Floyd Martin by Joe Abraham, January 19, 1999.
[21] Personal interview with Norman Martin by James E. Carter, November 3, 2000.

Chapter 7
[1] Personal interview with Esther Martin Floyd by Joe Abraham, January 19, 1999.
[2] Ibid.
[3] Howell, "Golden Anniversary Speech" 7.
[4] Mike Keatchum, "Time to Replant," ROM Today, March, 1999: 5.
[5] Brent Deen, "Down on the Farm," ROM Today, March, 2000: 5.
[6] Melissa Gregory, "Mighty Profits from Tiny Saplings," Alexandria Daily Town Talk 17 November 2000, sec. A1-2: 8; "Martins Give $1000, to Ruby-Wise School," Forests and People, Fourth Quarter 2000: 32.
[7] William Taylor, "New Center Close to Home," Alexandria The Town Talk, 5 February 2004, sec. A: 1.
[8] Ibid., A-3.
[9] "Lecompte Couple Gets LSU-A Service Award," Alexandria The Town Talk, 4 January 2001, sec. A: 6.

Chapter 8
[1] Personal interview with Roy O. Martin III by James E. Carter, December 21, 2001.
[2] Personal interview with Jonathan E. Martin by James E. Carter, March 1, 2002.
[3] Personal interview with Jonathan E. Martin by James E. Carter, December 21, 2001.
[4] Personal interview with Paul C. Hood by James E. Carter, May 9, 2001.
[5] Personal interview with Charles Weems by James E. Carter, July 26, 2001.
[6] Personal interview with Robert M. Chown by James E. Carter, January 22, 2002.
[7] Dayton Fandray, "Lombardi's Lessons: Leading Well Is the Only Thing That Counts," Continental Magazine, January 2004: 27-28.
[8] Personal interview with Jonathan E. Martin by James E. Carter, December 21, 2001.
[9] Ibid.
[10] Ray Peters, "Advanced Supervisory Leadership," ROM Today, December 2000:2.
[11] Jonathan E. Martin, "President's Newsletter for Oct.-Nov., 2001."
[12] "Louisiana: A Peek at Our Future." Brochure produced by the Louisiana Forestry Association, the Southern Forest Heritage Museum and Research Center in cooperation with the International Paper Foundation, The Louisiana Pulp and Paper Industry, and the Louisiana Logging Council.
[13] Personal interview with Roy O. Martin III by James E. Carter, December 21, 2001.
[14] Jennifer McCrary, "Optimizing the Timber Factory," Timber Harvesting, March 1998: 14.
[15] Personal interview with Roy O. Martin III by James E. Carter, March 1, 2002.
[16] John Dunn, "Maximization of Forestlands," ROM Today, March 2002: 7.
[17] Personal interview with Roy O. Martin III by James E. Carter, March 1, 2002.
[18] Kalvin Hackney, "Martco Plywood Heads to Cuba," ROM Today, March 2002: 3. Incidentally, the article ended with these words: "This story will never hit the history books. However, when you are on your back porch with your grandchildren in your lap, you will have a great story to tell." That story hit this history book.

[19] Personal interview with Jonathan E. Martin by James E. Carter, March 1, 2002.
[20] Personal interview with Rob Zaytsoff by James E. Carter, March 1, 2002.
[21] Personal interview with Jonathan E. Martin by James E. Carter, March 1, 2002.
[22] Personal interview with Rob Zaytsoff by James E. Carter, March 1, 2002.
[23] Personal interview with Jonathan E. Martin by James E. Carter, March 1, 2002.
[24] Ken Gardner, "Moldshield™," ROM Today, March 2003: 4.
[25] Ibid.
[26] Personal interview with Roy O. Martin III by James E. Carter, March 1, 2002.
[27] Personal interview with Robert M. Chown by James E. Carter, January 22, 2002.
[28] Personal interview with Jonathan E. Martin by James E. Carter, March 1, 2002.
[29] Tracy Ann Kidder, "Some Things Never Change," ROM Today, December 1999: 4.
[30] E-mail from Mary Erdoes, J. P. Morgan Company, New York, New York, to James E. Carter, April 23, 2002.
[31] Roy O. Martin III. Letter to stockholders, January 28, 2004.
[32] Personal interview with Jonathan E. Martin by James E. Carter, December 21, 2001.
[33] Telephone interview with Hollis McNully by James E. Carter, April 5, 2002.
[34] Ibid.
[35] Les Evans, "To ROM." Personal archives, 1954.
[36] Telephone interview with Buddy Tudor by James E. Carter, April 4, 2002.
[37] Telephone interview with Bill Moore by James E. Carter, April 8, 2002.
[38] Telephone interview with Wayne Denley by James E. Carter, April 16, 2002.
[39] E-mail from Mary Erdoes to James E. Carter, April 23, 2002.
[40] "Roy O. Martin Company Certifies Timberland and Operations," News release from SmartWood, a program of the Rainforest Alliance, April 2002.
[41] Email from Johnny Martin to Chris Clayton, et. al., May 7, 2004.
[42] Peter Drucker, Managing in Times of Great Change (New York: Harper and Row, 19--), 37.

APPENDIX A

Glossary of Terms[1]

A FLAT™ - Martco Plywood's trademark.

B FLAT™ - Martco Plywood's trademark.

ADA – Americans with Disabilities Act.

APA – American Plywood Association.

Acknowledgment - A written verification of the acceptance of any order sent by a seller, such as a manufacturer, to a buyer and listing the details of the transaction.

Acre - A unit of land measurement equal to 43,560 square feet.

Adhesive - Any substance used to bond the surfaces of two materials. Adhesives are made from inorganic and organic sources, with the former used principally on materials that will be exposed to weather.

A-Frame Car - A railroad flat car with an A-shaped frame, running the length of the car, to which loads can be secured.

Agency Stamp - The grademark of an authorized grading agency.

A Grade – 1) In plywood, a smooth, paintable face with limited repairs. Suitable for natural finish in some applications. 2) A clear grade of lumber; in Redwood, A Grade allows some sound sapwood or medium stain and small checks that will not develop into splits.

Air Dried - Seasoned by exposure to the atmosphere, in the open or under cover, without artificial heat.

Air Shed - An unheated building used in air-drying lumber. Usually open on two or more sides to permit natural air movement.

---

[1] This glossary of terms was prepared by Mary Lambert for Martin company personnel who may not be familiar with forestry and lumber terminology.

LIFE BY THE BOARD FOOT

Alley - A parallel passage between the piles of lumber air-drying in a yard.

Along the Grain - In the same direction as the grain; the stronger and stiffer direction in wood. In plywood, the same direction as the grain of the face ply.

Anti-Sapstain Treated - A chemical treatment applied to lumber to prevent discoloration of the sapwood during storage or shipment.

Anti-Stain Treated - Lumber or other wood product treated with any of various chemicals to retard staining caused by exposure to weather or fungi.

APA Trademark - The registered trademark of the American Plywood Association. It is used as a grademark to signify that a panel has been manufactured under the association's quality supervision and testing program.

Arbor - An axle or spindle that supports cutting tools that spins or rotates.

BACT - Best available control technology.

BF (Bd. Ft.) - Board feet, or foot.

Bag House - A sander-dust collector in a plywood or OSB plant.

Balanced Panel - A plywood panel having face and back veneers of uniform thickness. A balanced panel is less likely to warp.

Band Mill - A sawmill using a toothed, endless steel blade for its saw.

Band Saw - A saw consisting of a continuous piece of flexible steel, with teeth on one or both sides, used to cut logs into cants and also to rip lumber.

Barcode - A label bearing a symbol consisting of a series of bars and spaces affixed to individual pieces of lumber or other merchandise. Used with scanning device at the point of sale, barcodes improve inventory control and the speed and accuracy of clerks at checkout lines.

Best Management Practices (BMP) - State of local regulatory or non-regulatory guidelines for protecting waterways as required by federal statutes. They include the Clean Water Act and the Water Pollution Control Act.

Best Opening Face System (BOF) - A computer program developed at the U.S. Forest Products Laboratory. The program determines the optimum sawing pattern to use on a log in order to maximize the lumber yield of the log.

APPENDIX A

Blanked Lumber - Lumber dressed to a size in excess of standard dressed size but scant of nominal size. It may involve any dressing from S1S to S4S. It is usually intended for later remanufacture.

Blender - A machine that blends wood particles and resin in the construction of panels such as particleboard and OSB.

Block - A log, to be used in veneer production, that has been cut to a designated length, usually 4 or 8 feet. Sometimes referred to as a bolt.

Block Conditioner - A vat or room in which veneer blocks are conditioned for peeling, usually by steaming or soaking in warm water.

Blue Stain - A discoloration of wood caused by a fungus; usually occurring in the sapwood. It is particularly troublesome in Ponderosa Pine logs during the warmer months.

Board - A piece of lumber less than two inches in nominal thickness and one inch or more in width.

Board Foot - The basic unit of measurement for lumber. One board foot is equal to a 1-inch board 12 inches in width and 1 foot in length. Thus, a 10-foot long, 12-inch wide, and 1-inch thick piece would contain 10 board feet. When calculating board feet, nominal sizes are assumed.

Bond - The adhesion between materials.

Borate - A chemical retardant/suppressant used to fight forest fires. Aircraft, often-reconditioned military bombers, "bomb" the fire with the chemical. Phosphate is more commonly used now.

Break Down - To reduce a log to lumber or plywood.

Breast Height - A standard height from average ground level. A point at which diameter, girth, and basal area of a standing tree are measured. Generally, 4.5 feet, or 1.37 meters, above ground level.

British Thermal Unit (BTU) - The amount of heat required to raise the temperature of one pound of water one degree Fahrenheit.

Broken Unit - A number of pieces of lumber or plywood less than the number in a standard unit or package.

Bucking Saw - A crosscut saw used to cut, or "buck," felled timber into log lengths.

LIFE BY THE BOARD FOOT

Bull Edger - The first and, usually, largest edger behind the head rig, to which low-grade cants are directed for ripping to widths suitable for further manufacture on a resaw or trimmer.

Bundle - A package of lumber, usually sorted by grade and/or size and most often consisting of narrow boards or strips.

Bung - A stopper for the opening of a barrel or cask.

Bunk - A cross support on a logging truck or railcar that supports the logs.

Butt - The lower end of a tree, or a log from that part of the tree closest to the stump.

Butt Cut - The first log above the stump.

Butt End - The end of a log nearest the butt, or stump end, of the tree.

Butt Flare - The swell of a log where a tree was cut close to the ground. Common in cypress.

CCA – Chromated copper arsenate.

CDX – CD plywood with exterior (X) glue line.

Cant – A large slab cut from a log at the head saw, usually having one or more rounded edges, and destined for further processing by other saws.

Cant Hook - A wooden lever with an iron hook at the lower end, used in turning logs or cants.

Carbide Tip Saw - A saw equipped with especially hardened teeth to resist wear.

Carload - A railroad car filled to normal capacity.

Carriage - The framework to which a log is fastened during manufacture at the head saw.

Carriage Dog - A device that holds a log steady while it is being passed by a saw on a carriage.

Car Seal - A device fastened to a lock on a rail car door that must be broken to open the door; a broken seal indicates that the car's contents may have been tampered with.

Cash Flow - The amount of money generated from the operation of a business. Cash flow is determined from the net income of the business, less depreciation and non-cash expenses. Cash flow information helps a company plan and control its cash needs.

APPENDIX A

Catalyst - In wood finishing, a chemical that, when added to conversion coatings, initiates chemical bonding.

Cat Face - A scar on a tree or log, caused by fire or injury to the growing tree.

Catwalk - Elevated grated walkway used by employees to avoid being on the floor with moving equipment.

Caul - In OSB production, the flat metal plate on which wood particles are formed into mats, conveyed, and processed.

Cherry Picker - A light log loader utilizing tongs or a grapple operated from a boom to pick up individual logs.

Chip - A small piece of wood used to make pulp. The chips are either made from wood waste in a sawmill or plywood plant or from pulpwood cut specifically for this purpose. Chips are of generally uniform size and are larger and coarser than sawdust.

"Chip-n-Saw" - A brand of chipping head rig. Although this is one of several brands, the name has come into common usage as applicable to all such types of machines.

Chipper-Canter - A machine that makes cants from whole logs using chipping heads only and no saws.

Chipper Knives - The knives that reduce wood to chips for use in pulping or for the manufacture of compressed-wood panels. The design of the knife contributes to the shape of the chip.

Chucks - A pair of metal spindles with prong "fingers" that grasp a peeler log in a veneer lathe, holding the log firmly at both ends so that it can be turned against the knives to produce veneer.

Circle Saw (AKA "rotary saw") - A round saw with teeth around the circumference.

Climb Cutting - A method of machining with a cutting tool. The tool rotates in the same direction as the material being cut is traveling.

Collapse - Irregular shrinkage in wood above the fiber saturation point; caused by the collapse of wood cells as free water is drawn out of the cell cavities without replacement with air or more water.

Composer - A machine that joins the edges of random-width veneer to form full sheets. Also called a Veneer Composer or Veneer Welder.

Conditioning – 1) The adjustment of the moisture content of wood to that existing in use, either through controlled drying in a kiln or by exposure to site conditions. 2) Steaming,

LIFE BY THE BOARD FOOT

in lumber to relieve the stresses present at the end of a controlled drying period, in plywood to prepare a peeler for a lathe.

Conditioning Vat - A vat, or room, in which hot water or steam is used to prepare a plywood peeler for a lathe. Veneer peels more readily and with less breakage from a conditioned block.

Conveyor - Device used to move waste or other product from point A to point B.

Cord - A unit of measurement equal to a stack of wood 4x4x8 feet or 128 cubic feet. Pulpwood is often measured in cords.

Core Gap - An open joint extending through or partly through a plywood panel, occurring when core veneers are not tightly butted. When center veneers are involved, the condition is referred to as "Center Gap."

Core Saw - A band saw used to cut stacks of core veneer to specific sizes.

Core Void - See Core Gap.

Creosote - A wood preservative consisting mainly of aromatic hydrocarbons obtained by distillation of coal tar. Used to preserve wood products such as utility poles, fence posts, and the like that come into contact with the ground.

Cross Grain - An area in a piece of lumber in which the grain of the wood is distorted so that it runs across the piece from edge to edge instead of along the length of the piece. An example would be the deviation of the grain around a knot. Cross grain represents a weakness in the piece.

Cross Tie - A cross member, usually of wood, used to support railroad rails in a roadbed.

Cup - Deviation flatwise from a straight line across the width of a piece of lumber, measured at the point of the greatest distance from the line.

Cured - Dried, seasoned.

Cutoffs - Short pieces, trimbacks.

Cut-to-Size - Lumber, plywood, or particleboard sawn to a specific size, usually designated by the buyer. Most often seen in items destined for remanufacture.

DISC – Domestic International Sales Corporation.

Dead Rolls - Rollers that are not power driven, as opposed to live rolls.

APPENDIX A

Debarker - A device that removes bark from a log by abrasion. The bark's bond with the wood is broken at the cambium layer as the log revolves while it passes through the machine; cylindrical abrading heads with conical projections and knives combine to remove the bark.

Decay (AKA "dote" or "rot") - Disintegration of wood substance due to action of wood-destroying fungi.

Deciduous - Trees that lose their leaves; usually broadleaved and usually classified as hardwood.

Defect - Any naturally occurring imperfection, or condition of wood, including decay, shake, checking, pitch seams, etc., that would make lumber or other finished wood products off grade.

Degrades - Pieces of lumber that on reinspection prove to be of lower quality than the grade originally assigned to them.

Dehumidification Drying - An alternative kiln-drying process in which moisture removed from lumber is condensed and then vented from the kiln.

Demurrage - A charge assessed by a carrier for holding a rail freight car, truck or ship.

Density - In OSB manufacture, the weight of a panel as measured in pound per cubic foot.

Dribble - A spade-like tool used to prepare planting holes for seedlings. Dribbles are most commonly used in the South, but their use has spread to other areas for the planting of containerized seedlings.

Dimensional Stability - The ability of a material to maintain its original dimensions under variations of temperature, moisture, and physical stress.

Dip Tank - A vessel holding wood preservative. Wood is briefly dipped into the tank where it receives a superficial treatment.

Dog - A device designed to bite into and hold something securely, such as "dogging" a log on a carriage.

Double-End Kiln - A dry kiln with doors at both ends and a track running through it; the charges are loaded through one end and unloaded through the other.

Double-End Trimmed (DET) - Passed through saws to be smoothly trimmed at both ends, commonly in length increments.

Doyle - A widely used log scale, particularly in the South.

LIFE BY THE BOARD FOOT

Dressed Lumber - Lumber that has been processed through a planing machine for the purpose of attaining a smooth surface and uniformity of size on at least one side or edge.

Drip Pad - A platform that units of treated lumber are placed upon to capture the drippage of chemicals not absorbed by the wood. The pads are designed to prevent seepage of treatment chemicals into the ground.

Drum Chipper - A type of chipper used especially to convert lily pads and trim ends to pulp chips.

Drum Debarker - A debarker made from welded steel channels or tubes, open at each end, and inclined toward the discharge end. Used principally to debark bolts up to eight feet long before they are chipped for pulp.

Dry Bulb – Used in kiln drying, a sensing device that indicates the temperature of the air.

Dryer - An oven-like apparatus used to remove moisture from green veneer by passing the veneer through a heated compartment on a moving set of rollers.

Drying Rate - The time it takes to dry lumber to a certain moisture content. The drying rate is affected by kiln conditions and the properties of the wood itself, including its propensity to develop defects from drying.

Drying Shed - A building in which green or treated lumber is placed for air drying.

Dry Kiln - A chamber in which wood products are seasoned by applying heat and withdrawing moisture.

Dunnage Bags - Bags made of rubber, plastic, or a combination of materials. The bags can be inflated to fill spaces between portions of a load, or between the load and the sides of the vehicle carrying it.

EBT - Employee Benefits Trust.

EEOC – Equal Employment Opportunity Commission.

ESA – Endangered Species Act.

EWP – Engineered wood products.

Edge – 1) The narrow faces of rectangular-shaped lumber. 2) To cut wood products to remove wane and other defects and to produce square edges.

Edger - A piece of sawmill machinery used to saw cants after they come off the head rig, squaring the edges and ripping the cants into lumber.

APPENDIX A

Edge Sealing - The application of a sealant, paint, or other type of coating to the edges of a wood panel to reduce water absorption by the panel.

Edging – 1) Waste wood produced by an edger when cutting and squaring lumber from a slab or cant. 2) The act of squaring a piece of lumber in the edger.

Electrostatic Precipitator (ESP) - A pollution-control device that uses electrically charged plates to remove particles from air emission sources.

Endangered Species Act (ESA) - The Endangered Species Conservation Act of 1969, designed to protect plant and animal species in danger of extinction.

Engineered Panel - A piece of plywood or other panel product designed to meet particular specifications concerning strength or rigidity and for use in particular applications, especially structural uses.

Environmental Protection Agency (EPA) - U.S. government agency charged with enforcing many of the nation's environmental standards.

Epoxy - A type of synthetic resin used in certain paints and adhesives.

Equilibrium Moisture Content (EMC) - The point at which wood is stable and in equilibrium with the humidity of its surroundings; it is neither taking on or giving up moisture.

Exterior - A type of plywood that is produced throughout of veneers that are of C grade or better and is bonded with a completely waterproof adhesive. Such a panel will retain its glue bond when wet, and is suitable for permanent exposure to the weather.

FAS – Firsts and seconds (sawmill grade).

FMLA - Family Medical Leave Act.

Face - The face of a piece of lumber of plywood is that side showing the better quality or appearance.

Fee-Owned Timber - Timber that is presently owned free and clear.

Fence - A straight-edge guide mounted parallel to a saw blade to guide a cant as it is passed through the saw.

Filer - A saw filer. The person who keeps the saws sharp in a sawmill or logging operation.

LIFE BY THE BOARD FOOT

Fire Scar - A burned or charred area on a tree or log, often entry point for decay-causing organisms.

First In, First Out (FIFO) - A type of accounting for inventory in which items purchased first are assumed to be the first to be sold. An accountant will compute the cost and profit on the oldest or first price in the inventory. Opposite of Last In, First Out (LIFO).

Fishtails - Strips of veneer with fishtail-shaped defect on one end.

Flaker (AKA "waferizer") - A machine that converts round wood and/or mill wastes into flakes for use as the raw material for particleboard or waferboard.

Flat Grain (FG) - Annual rings (grain) that form an angle of less than 45 degrees with the surface of a piece of lumber.

Fluted Butt (AKA "flared butt") - The asymmetrical butt of a tree in which the wood has grown from the ground to the bole to form long furrows or grooves, often enclosing earlier growths of bark.

Forestry - The science and practice of managing and using for human benefit the natural resources that occur on and in association with forested lands.

Forest Stewardship Council (FSC) - The certification of forestry practices by the organization. Currently the certification mechanism and standards utilized by the Martin companies for their timberland management practices. Generally considered the most stringent of all certification practices by environmental organizations.

Forklift (AKA "lift truck") - A piece of mechanized equipment used to move units of lumber or plywood. Steel blades, or "forks," slip under the load, which is then lifted hydraulically, moved to the desired location, and lowered into place.

Four-Quarter (4/4) - (See Quarter Measure) - A reference to the thickness of lumber, especially select, industrial, and board material, which utilizes a nominal one-quarter-inch scale. Thus, 4/4 is a nominal 1-inch, 5/4 is 1-¼ inches, 6/4 is 1 ½ inches, etc.

Free on Board (FOB) - A reference to the point to which the seller will deliver goods without charge to the buyer. Additional freight or other charges connected with transporting or handling the product become the responsibility of the buyer.

Full Sawn - A grading term used to describe rough lumber that has been cut to full nominal size.

Full Sheet - A whole veneer panel, such as a 4x8 sheet.

Gang Edger - An edger with multiple saws.

APPENDIX A

Gang Saw - A machine in which two or more saws are mounted together, either on the same arbor on or in the same sash and used to saw logs or cants.

Gap - A defect in plywood where an edge void occurs on an inner ply.

Glue-Bond Test - A test designed to determine the performance of a glue board. Samples of glued veneers are subjected to various tests, including soaking for interior glues and boiling or vacuum-press exposures followed by shear testing for exterior glues.

Grademark (GM) - A stamp or symbol indicating the grade, quality and/or intended use of a piece of lumber, plywood, or other wood product. To be recognized as "grade marked," the product must bear an official stamp issued by a grading agency and applied by a qualified grader or it must be accompanied by a certificate attesting to the grade.

Grader - A worker who examines lumber, plywood, or other wood products and assigns it a grade according to an established set of rules.

Grade Sawing - The practice of turning a log on the carriage in order to obtain the highest values or grades.

Grade Logs - Term generally used to describe hardwood logs whose grade or quality is sufficient for use at our LeMoyen hardwood sawmill.

Grade Stamp - A rubber stamp, issued by a grading agency or association to a client mill and used to indicate the grade of a particular piece of lumber or panel, along with other information. A typical grade stamp will include the species, the grade, the producing mill by name and/or agency number, the grading agency, and a designation (for lumber) of whether the stock was dry or green when surfaced.

Grapple - A heavy set of tongs with fine teeth on the inside edge.

Greenchain - A moving chain or belt on which lumber is transported from saws in a mill. The lumber is pulled from the chain by workers and stacked according to size, length, species, and other criteria.

Green End - A manufacturing facility that produces green veneer. "Green end" is used to describe a facility or portion of a facility that parks the logs, cuts them into block lengths, peels and clips the veneer, and sorts the veneer according to grade.

Guard - Device used to cover and protect employees from injury by moving mechanical parts.

Gullet - The space between two teeth in a saw.

HMA – Hardwood Manufacturing Association.

LIFE BY THE BOARD FOOT

Hammermill (AKA "Hog") - A machine for producing fibers from solid wood pieces by hammering or flailing them.

Hardwood - A general term referring to any of a variety of broad-leaved, deciduous trees, and the wood from those trees. The term has nothing to do with the actual hardness of the wood; some hardwoods are softer than certain softwood (evergreen) species.

Head Rig - The principal saw in a sawmill, where logs are first cut into cants before being sent on to other saws for further processing.

Head Saw - The principal break-down saw in a sawmill; part of the head rig.

Heartwood - That portion of the tree contained within the sapwood; this term is sometimes used to mean the pith. The heartwood is dormant and is unnecessary for the tree's continued life; the living part of the tree is contained in its outer parts.

Hog - A machine used to grind wood into chips for use as fuel or for other purposes; the wood used is usually waste wood unfit for lumber or other uses.

Hogged Fuel - Fuel made by grinding waste wood in a hog. Used to fire boilers or furnaces, often at the mill or plant at which the fuel was processed.

Honeycomb - A type of decay indicated by large pits in the wood.

Hot Deck - The supply of logs currently being used in a sawmill or veneer plant. Opposite of Cold Deck.

Hot Pond - A vat of heated water used to condition logs before peeling into veneer or before flaking to produce furnish for waferboard or OSB.

Hot Press - The method of producing plywood whereby adhesion of layers in the panel is accomplished by using a heat process, under pressure, to cure the gluelines.

Incising - Cutting slits into the surfaces of a piece of wood prior to preservative treatment to improve absorption.

Ink Stamp - A roll stamp that puts required information on a panel.

Internal Bond - The particle-to-particle bonding in reconstituted panel products, measured in pounds per square inch. Internal bond is tested by gluing metal blocks to the face of a panel and measuring the force needed to separate the particles.

Invoice - An itemized list of goods shipped, and their prices; a bill.

JIT – Just-in-time.

APPENDIX A

Jags - Odds and ends left in an inventory; quantities too small to make up a unit.

Juvenile Wood - The initial wood formed adjacent to the pith, often characterized by lower specific gravity, lower strength, higher longitudinal shrinkage, and different microstructure than mature wood. Also called core wood, pith wood, crown-formed wood.

KD – Kiln dried.

KDAT – Kiln dried after treating.

Kerf - The width of a saw cut. The size of a kerf is dependent on saw thickness, saw type, sharpness, and other factors.

Kickers – Mechanical arms that move logs from one conveyor to another conveyor.

Kiln - See Dry Kiln.

Kiln Dried - Lumber that has been seasoned in a kiln to a predetermined moisture content.

Kiln Stick - A thin piece of wood used between layers of lumber to improve air circulation within the pile.

Kiln Truck - A wheeled framework designed to hold a load of lumber for drying in a kiln. Used in kilns with tracks.

Knife Marks - Imprints or markings of machine knives on the surface of dressed lumber or on veneer, usually due to dull or chipped knives.

Knot - A branch or limb embedded in a tree or cut through in the process of manufacturing.

LA – Louisiana (postal code).

LC – Letter of credit.

LRF – Lumber recovery factor.

Laser Line - A line of light projected on a cant, used as a cutting guide at the edger.

Lathe - A machine upon which logs are peeled to yield veneer for plywood.

Lay Up - The process of manufacturing plywood. The term is used to describe the assembly of veneers into panels after glue has been applied in preparation for pressing.

LIFE BY THE BOARD FOOT

Lift Truck (AKA "Forklift") - A vehicle equipped with two sturdy arms, which can be slipped under a load to support it while it is being lifted.

Lily Pad - A round piece cut from the end of a log.

Linear Expansion - A measurement of the growth along the length and width of a particleboard panel when it is exposed to various humidity levels.

Linebar - A fixed, or moveable, metal plate or fence at the edge of a roll case, against which a piece of lumber rides as it goes through a resaw or edger.

Linebar Resaw - A resaw with a stationary bandsaw and a moveable linebar, which is set to determine the width or thickness of the piece of lumber being resawn.

Log - The stem of a tree after is has been felled. The raw materials from which lumber, plywood, and other wood products are processed.

Log Cut Up - Area where logs are cut to length.

Long-Term Lease - Properties on which the Martin companies have an extended period of time to grow, manage, remove and re-grow timber but includes no land ownership. Terms usually range from 49 to 99 years.

M – Thousand.

M^3 – Cubic meter.

MBF - The standard abbreviation for 1,000 board feet of standing timber, logs or lumber.

MCC Room - Motor Control Center.

MMBF - One million board feet.

MMSF - One million square feet.

MOR – Modulus of rupture (OSB, plywood).

MSDS - Material Safety Data Sheets.

MSF - The standard abbreviation for 1,000 square feet, surface measure, of plywood or other panel products.

Marguard – Martco Sawmill's trademark (Borate-treated lumber).

Mat - Layers of wood that are oriented to make an OSB panel.

APPENDIX A

Metal Detector - A device used in many mills to detect old metal, such as spikes driven into trees and subsequently overgrown, ahead of the saws.

Millwright - The person in a sawmill or plywood plant who maintains and repairs machinery and other equipment.

Modulus of Elasticity (MOE) - A measurement of stiffness in a wood product, found by determining the relationship between the amount a piece deflects and the load causing the deflection. Factors affecting the MOE include size, span, load and the species being tested.

Modulus of Rupture (MOR) - A measurement of the load required to break a wood product.

NHLA - National Hardwood Lumber Association.

O&ES – Oiled and edge sealed (plywood).

OSB - Oriented Strand Board.

OSHA - Occupational Safety and Health Administration.

Optimizer - Any of various pieces of sawmill equipment designed to maximize the yield from a log or cant by using scanners, linear positioning, and computers to determine the best way to saw, edge, or trim the wood. Among the types are small-log, edger, ripsaw, trimmer, and head rig carriage optimizers.

Oriented Strand Board (OSB) - Panels made of narrow strands of fiber oriented lengthwise and crosswise in layers, with a resin binder.

Ovendry - Containing no water, or a moisture content of 0%.

PO - Purchase order.

PPE - Personal Protective Equipment.

PSI - Pounds per square inch.

PTS - Price at time of shipment.

Package-Loaded Kiln - A trackless compartment kiln used to dry packages of lumber. It usually has large doors so that it may be loaded using a forklift.

Panel - A sheet of plywood, particleboard, or other similar product usually of a standard size, such as 4x8 feet.

LIFE BY THE BOARD FOOT

Patch - A piece of wood or synthetic material used to fill defects in the plies of plywood. Also, Plug.

Pecky - Characterized by peck, channeled or pitted areas or pockets found in cedar and cypress.

Peeler Core - That portion of a peeler block that remains after the veneer has been taken. Peeler cores are often used as raw material for the production of studs or landscape timbers.

Penta - Short for *pentachlorophenol*, a wood preservative.

Phenol - A product of the petroleum industry used in the production of phenolic resin, exterior plywood glue. Phenol is made from benzine.

Pike Pole - A long extension rod used to free a jammed product.

Pitch - An accumulation of resin in the wood cells in a more-or-less irregular patch. Classified for grading purposes as light, medium, heavy, or massed.

Pith - The small, soft core in the structural center of a log.

Pkg. - Package.

Planer - A machine used to surface rough lumber.

Ply - A single layer or sheet of veneer. One complete layer of veneer in a sheet of plywood.

Plyblocks - Pine logs that are cut 9 feet in length and utilized at our Chopin plywood mill.

Plylogs - Pine logs that are cut in multiples of 9 feet (18', 27') and utilized at our Chopin plywood mill.

Plywood - A flat panel made up of a number of thin sheets, or veneers, of wood in which the grain direction of each ply, or layer, is at right angles to the one adjacent to it. The veneer sheets are united under pressure by a bonding agent.

Poles - Pine timber that is utilized for telephone, electrical and miscellaneous utility needs. The stems suitable for poles are generally very straight and considered the most valuable use of our timber resource.

Powder Post Beetles - The larvae of lyctus beetles that bore through wood for food, leaving undigested powdery remnants in their burrows.

APPENDIX A

Predrying - A drying process used to accelerate the evaporation of free water. Stickered loads of lumber are placed in a building and heated air is circulated over the wood. The process is similar to regular kiln drying, except that much lower temperatures are used.

Prepress - A machine used to apply, without heat, pressure to a load of plywood, prior to the load being inserted into the hot press.

Quartersawn (AKA "Quartered Lumber") -The lumber sawn so that the annual rings form angles of 45 to 90 degrees with the surface of the piece.

RL – Random length.

ROI – Return on investment.
 -Roy O. Martin logo.

RW&L – Random width, random length.

Railroad Tie – A piece of industrial lumber used to support rails on a roadbed. In Britain and other countries, a "Sleeper."

Redry - To return material to a dry kiln or veneer dryer for additional drying when the material is found to have a higher moisture content than desired.

Relative Humidity - The amount of water vapor in the air as a percentage of the maximum amount the air could hold at a given temperature.

Resaw - 1) To saw a piece of lumber along its horizontal axis. 2) A bandsaw that performs such an operation.

Resin (AKA "Glue") - A natural vegetable substance occurring in various plants and trees, especially the coniferous species. Used in varnishes, inks, medicines, and plastic products. Also, any of a variety of synthetic products having many of the properties of natural resin and used in the production of plastics or other products.

Roller Bar - A round metal bar set in a channel across the head of a veneer lathe, parallel to the axis of the block, and driven so the surface speed of the bar is the same as that of the block.

Rotary-Cut Veneer - Veneer peeled from a round log by turning the log against a knife to produce a continuous sheet of wood of a uniform thickness. The common method of making softwood veneers.

Routing - The method of removing a defect when a router patch is to be inserted in a piece of plywood.

S2S - Surfaced two sides.

LIFE BY THE BOARD FOOT

SAP (AKA "RFN") - Soon as possible.

SBA – Structural Board Association.

SCIG™– Martco Plywood's Trademark (SmartCore Industrial Grade).

SYP – Southern yellow pine.

Sanded - Panel products that have been processed through a machine sander to provide a smooth surface on one or both sides.

Sander - A machine designed to smooth wood and to remove saw or lathe marks and other imperfections. Sanders range in size from hand-held to large drums or belts capable of resurfacing a full-size panel.

Sapwood - The outer layers of growth between the bark and the heartwood that contain the sap.

Sawline – Machines with saws that reduce the dimensions of a raw product, such as saws that cut 8'x16' mats into 4'x8' sheets of OSB.

Scanner - A device used to determine the dimensional aspects of logs, lumber, or veneer prior to any one of the steps in the manufacturing process.

Scant - Less than standard or required size.

Score - Waste from veneer production resulting from the trimming of the veneer at the peeling lathe. Peeler blocks are usually slightly longer than the length of the veneer that is to be produced from them. Spur-type knives at each end of the lathe cut into the block as it turns. This scoring will yield veneer of the desired length with straight edges and parallel sides. Also called spur trim.

Setworks - The portion of the head rig carriage that precisely positions the log or cant to be sawn.

Shake - A lengthwise grain separation between growth rings or a break through the rings (radial shake), usually the results of high winds.

Sheathing - Plywood, waferboard, oriented strand board, or lumber used to close up sidewalls, floors, or roofs preparatory to the installation of finish materials on the surface.

SHUGA BERRY ® – Martco Sawmill's trademark name for white hackberry.

Side Shield - A clear plastic safety device inserted onto the arm of prescription glasses to protect an employee's eyes.

APPENDIX A

SMARTCORE® – Martco Plywood's Trademark.

Sorter - A mechanical device that sorts lumber for thickness, width, or length by dropping or ejecting pieces into separate compartments.

Span Rating - The recommended center-to-center spacing of supports for structural panels. The rating is carried as part of the grademark and indicates the spacing in inches for various types of applications. For example, 32/16 in a sheathing panel shows 32 inches as the maximum spacing of supports when that panel is to be used as roof sheathing and 16 inches when it is used as subflooring.

Spindle - A shaft used as the axis of rotation; an arbor or mandrel.

Split - A lengthwise separation of a piece of lumber extending from one surface through the piece of the opposite surface or to an adjoining surface. Classified for grading purposes as short, medium, or long split. In plywood, a separation of wood fiber completely through a veneer.

Spreader - A machine that spreads glue on veneer prior to lay-up.

Sticker Stain - A stain on dry lumber resulting from the use of a sticker with a mineral or fungal content.

Strapping - Flexible metal bands used to bind lumber or plywood into units for ease of handling and storage.

Strips - Pieces of veneer less than 4 feet wide.

Sturd-I-Floor - A trade name registered by the American Plywood Association for a panel designed specifically for use as combined subfloor/underlayment in residential floor applications.

Summerwood - The dense fibrous outer portion of each annual ring of a tree, formed late in the growing period, although not necessarily in the summer.

Surfaced - Refers to lumber that has been dressed by a planing machine for the purpose of attaining smoothness of surface and uniformity of size. Surfacing may be done on one side or edge, or on all sides.

Synthetic Resin Patch (Plug) - A patch composed of a synthetic substance, such as epoxy, used to fill voids caused by defects in the veneers of the plywood panel.

T&G - Tongue and groove.

Taildrums - The tail end of conveying device.

LIFE BY THE BOARD FOOT

Tally - A numerical breakdown of the carious lengths and/or widths in a load of lumber.

Three-Eighths Basis (3/8" Basis) - A measurement of production used in the structural panel industry. Most often, it is used in describing capacity and production figures. The 3/8-inch basis describes a volume of panels as if all had been made 3/8-inch thick regardless of the actual thickness of the panels being described. This provides a common denominator when comparing capacities, volumes, and output figures.

Tie Logs - Term used to denote a poor quality log that is utilized by the railroad tie industry and is generally sold or delivered to points outside our company facilities.

Tight Side - The upper side of peeled veneer as it comes off the lathe. This side of the veneer was closest to the bark. When veneer is sliced, it is the side that is away from the knife. The tight side is usually the exposed side of a face or back ply.

Time Timber - Properties owned by the Martin companies that include only timber and provide a scheduled amount of time to remove the timber for our benefit. Periods of removal range from 12 months to 15 years.

Tongs - An implement used to pick up logs. Tongs usually have spiked points for biting into logs to establish a sure grip.

Tray - A conveyance used in transferring veneer from the lathe to the clipper. Trays are rubber belt conveyors that serve as temporary storage areas for veneers coming from high-speed lathes. Trays are loaded by a short conveyor, called a tipple, that can be raised or lowered at one end.

Trim Saw - A set of saws, usually circular, used to cut lumber to various lengths by lowering individual blades to make contact with the lumber as it passes beneath the saws on a moving chain.

TUFFCORE® - Martco's trademark plywood.

TUFF-STRAND® – Martco's trademark OSB.

UBC – Uniform Building Code.

UP – Union Pacific Railroad.

USA – United States of America.

Underlayment - Structural wood panels designed to be used under the finished flooring in a structure.

Unedged - Lumber whose edges have not been squared; waney.

APPENDIX A

Unscrambler - A piece of sawmill equipment that straightens out jumbled accumulations of lumber that collect on a transfer chain before the lumber is further processed. The lumber pieces are separated and delivered, one layer deep, to the machine in an orderly manner.

V-Belt - Power transmission device made out of rubber and poly cord that is manufactured in a V- shaped design.

Vats - Large containers used for steaming logs, or for submerging them in hot water prior to peeling or slicing them into veneer or cutting them into wafers. The steaming or heating of logs makes them easier to process and can increase recovery.

Veneer - Wood peeled, sawn or sliced into sheets of a given constant thickness and combined with glue to produce plywood.

Vendor Purchases - Timber purchased as it is delivered to our facilities, sometimes called "Gatewood." The Martin companies have no prior interest in either the timber or land from which the products are produced.

Wt – Weight.

Wafer - A relatively large, flat flake cut from wood in the manufacturing of waferboard or oriented strand board.

Waferizer - A machine that converts wood bolts to wafers for use in waferboard or oriented strand board.

Waferwood - Pieces of poor quality trees that are not suitable for use in either the sawmill, plymill or tie mills. Generally described as inferior in wood quality or as diseased. Can usually be identified by rot or holes somewhere along the stem.

Wellons – A furnace system that uses our wood waste to heat thermal oil. The oil in turn is used to heat water vats, presses, veneer dryers and dry kilns.

Wet Bulb - A thermometer that utilizes evaporation of moisture from a water-saturated cloth on its bulb to measure temperature.

X – Exterior glue line.

APPENDIX B

CALENDAR OF SIGNIFICANT EVENTS

1890, April 24 – Birth of Roy Otis Martin, Sr.

1892, February 21 – Birth of Mildred Brown Martin

1914, October 8 – Marriage of Roy O. Martin and Mildred Brown Martin

1923, October 30 – Purchase of Creston Lumber Company, Fenner Street, Alexandria, LA

1923, November 5 – Possession of Creston Lumber Company

1923, November 10 – Organization of Roy O. Martin Lumber Company; Inc.; Roy O. Martin, president

1925 – Purchase of lumber mill at Meeker, LA. Sold to Otis Felger

1925, December 9 – Purchase of Commercial Lumber Company, Alexandria, LA; organized as the Martin-Wilkie-Hopkins Company

1926 – Roy O. Martin Lumber Company of Eunice (LA) organized; sold to May Brothers. Memphis, TN

1927 – Name of Martin-Wilkie-Hopkins Company changed to Martin-Wilkie; Hopkins' interest was bought out

1928 – Martin-Wilkie Company consolidated into Roy O. Martin Lumber Company

1929 – Purchase of 6,560 acres with timber rights on an additional 720 acres from Southern Advance Bag and Paper Company, Hodge, LA; the first major land purchase

1933 - Construction of lumber mill at Castor, LA; Martin Timber Company formed

1933 – Reconstruction of Castor mill after fire

1937 – Purchase of Pineville Lumber Company from E. T. Glankler

1938 – Safetygas Corporation formed; Roy O. Martin sold his interest in six months

1939 – Reconstruction of Martin Timber Co. mill at Castor; Ellis Martin became manager of the Castor mill

1939 - Liquidation of Pineville Lumber Company

1939 – Martin and Sons Chevrolet, Ringgold – opened and closed within six months

LIFE BY THE BOARD FOOT

1942 – Pleasant Hill mill established

1943 – Partnership formed of the five Martin children to own Milroy Mercantile and the mill at Castor

1946 – Howard Lumber Company, Natchitoches, LA established; the first retail lumberyard

1947 – Pleasant Hill mill liquidated

1948 – Martin Development Company formed; merged with Roy O. Martin Lumber Co. in 1988

1952 – Martin Timber Company, Incorporated formed from the partnership of the five Martin children

1952, March – Castor mill burned, then rebuilt; the third mill at Castor

1953 – Vernon Parish Lumber Company bought, then liquidated

1955 – Verneco, Inc. named after the five Martin children incorporated; merged with Roy O. Martin Lumber Co. in 1988

1956 – Colfax Creosoting plant bought from the Edenborn estate

1957 – Martin Timber Company incorporated

1959 – Richard's Ready Mix began operations

1960 – Norman Oil and Gas formed to develop minerals on company land; dissolved a short time later

1962 – Roy O. Martin, Jr., became president of Roy O. Martin Lumber Company; Roy O. Martin, Sr. was chairman of the Board of Directors

1970 – Roy O. Martin, Sr., retired

1970 – Dura-Wood Plant bought from the Koppers Company; sold in 2000 to RailWorks

1971 – Wilmar Plywood, Natchitoches, formed as a partnership between Martin Timber Company and Willamette; Martin Timber Company left the partnership after two years

1972 – Applewhite Mill, a Chip-N-Saw mill, constructed in Alexandria

1973, February 23 – Death of Roy O. Martin, Sr.

1973 – Reorganization of the company into Roy O. Martin Industries, Inc.

1978 – Martin Home Centers (MHC), the operating company for the retail lumberyards, incorporated

1978 – Ellis Martin became president of Roy O. Martin Lumber Company

1978 – Sale of Roy O. Martin Lumber Company mill on Fenner Street in Alexandria and Applewhite Mill to Louisiana-Pacific

1981 – Martco Partnership formed with the Roy O. Martin Lumber Company, Martin Timber Company, and Martin Home Centers as partners

APPENDIX B

1981 – Martco OSB (oriented strand board) plant at LeMoyen construction begun

1983 – Martco OSB plant, LeMoyen, began operation

1984 – Martco sawmill at LeMoyen began production

1987 – Martin Home Center sold its retail stores

1988 – MHC Properties, Inc., a real-estate and holding company, incorporated

1988 – Merger of Verneco and Martin Development Corporation (MDC) into Roy O. Martin Lumber Company

1992 – Martin Timber Company sawmill at Castor sold

1994 – Jonathan E. Martin became president and CEO; Ellis Martin became Chairman of the Board of Directors

1994 – Martin Foundation established

1994 – Heat Systems Limited Partnership formed

1995, October 11 – Death of Mildred Brown Martin

1996 – Roy O. Martin III became executive vice president and CFO

1996 – Martco Plywood, Chopin, LA, began production

2000 – Companies reorganized into limited-liability formats

2000 – ROMEX World Trade Company, L. L. C., formed

2001 – ROMEX World Trade Center, Alexandria, new corporate headquarters

2003 - Companies reorganized, achieving Subchapter S status; Jonathan became chairman and CEO; Roy III became president and CFO; Scott Poole became COO

BIBLIOGRAPHY

Photographs

All included photographs were copied from Martin family files and Martin company archives.

Primary Sources

Minute Book

Minute Book, Roy O. Martin Lumber Company, 1923-2002.

Scrapbook

Scrapbook. ROM 2.

Speeches and Poem

Evans, Les. "To ROM." Employee wrote to Roy O. Martin, Sr., 1954.

Howell, Thomas. Speech at the Golden Anniversary of the Martin Library in Pineville. September 17, 2000.

Martin, Roy O., III. Notes on Address to the Natchitoches [LA] Lion's Club, April, 1996.

Martin Company Reports

"Estate Planning" n. d., n. p.

"General Forestry Facts" n. d., n. p.

"History of the Treating Division of the Roy O. Martin Lumber Company." Typescript. n. d., n. p.

"Innovation" n. d., n. p.

Mitchell, David Lawrence. "A History of the Hardwood Area of the Roy O. Martin Lumber Company." Typescript. n. d., 19 pp.

Martin, Ellis S. "Applewhite Mill." February 5, 1998.

-----------------. "Benefits from Land Ownership." Febraury 5, 1998.

----------------. Handwritten notes. n. d, n. p.

----------------. "Norman Oil and Gas." February 5, 1998.

----------------. "Treating Plants." February 5, 1998.

Martin, Roy O., Jr. Typed notes. n. d., n. p.

"Waferboard (OSB)." n. d., n. p.

Woodard, Zack. "Martin Companies History." Typescript. December 22, 1997. 5 pp.

Martin Company Publications

Employee Focus. A Supplement to ROM Today. Vol. 1-2, 2001-2002.

"Inside ROM". Printed, spiral bound brochure. n. d. 40 pp.

Kerr, Ed. Behind the ROM. Printed, spiral bound in-house advertising brochure for Roy O. Martin Lumber Company, circa 1953.

Ferguson, John L. American Forest Products Industries. Press release found among Martin archives.

Martin, Roy O., Sr. An Autobiography of Roy Otis Martin, ed. Charles H. Jeffress. Printing Department of Roy O. Martin Lumber Company, 1961.

Martco News. Vol. 1. No. 1. July 1993.

The Sawdust Gazette. Vol. 1. No. 2. August 1, 1993-Vol 3, No. 12 December 1995.

"The Roy O. Martin Family Tree." Video. 1998.

LIFE BY THE BOARD FOOT

ROM Today. Vol. 4. No. 1. January, 1996 – Vol. 10. No. 2. July 2002.

Internet Website

www.martinlumber co@martin.com

Secondary Sources

Books

Burns, Anna C. A History of the Louisiana Forestry Commission. Natchitoches, LA: The Louisiana Studies Institute, Northwestern State College of Louisiana, 1968.

Childers, William T. Echoes form the Millpond: A Brief History of the Louisiana Central Lumber Company, Clarks, LA: 1902-1953. Columbia, LA: The Caldwell Parish Library, 1987.

Collier, John M. The First Fifty Years of the Southern Pine Association, 1915-1965. New Orleans: Southern Pine Association, 1965.

Drucker, Peter. Managing in Times of Great Change. New York: Harper and Row, 1995.

Helms, John A. Editor. The Dictionary of Forestry. Bethesda, MD: Society of American Foresters, 1998.

Kerr, Ed. Tales of the Louisiana Forests. Baton Rouge, LA: Claitor's Publishing Division, 1981.

Kellogg, Walter W. The Kellogg Story: Fifty Years in the Southern Hardwood Business. Monroe, LA: Thomas J. Moran's Sons, Inc., 1969.

Lunding, Franklin J. Sharing a Business: A Case Study of a Tested Management Philosophy. Scarsdale, NY: The Updegraff Press, Ltd., 1951.

Martin, Roy O. Roy O. Martin: An Autobiography of Roy Otis Martin. Charles H. Jeffress, editor. Alexandria, LA: Printing Department of the Roy O. Martin Lumber Company, 1961.

Mayor, Archer H. Southern Timberman: The Legacy of William Buchanan. Athens, GA: The University of Georgia Press, 1988.

Recommended Forestry Best Management Practices for Louisiana. Baton Rouge, LA: Louisiana Department of Environmental Quality, 2000.

Thidbodeaux, Joyce Martin. The Browns of Hartford, Michigan. Houma, LA: Professional Printers, 1984.

Articles

Periodicals

Addy, Bobby. "Why We Need the Canadian Lumber Agreement." Forests and People. First Quarter, 2000, pp. 4-5, 7.

Allen, H. Lee, Weir, Robert J., and Goldfarb, Barry. "Investing in Wood Production in Southern Pine Plantations." Paper Age. April, 1998, pp. 20-21.

"Carriage System Offers True Shape Scanning." Timber Processing. September 2000, p. 46.

Davis, Harold. "Roy O. Martin Lumber Company: A Showcase of Perfection." Dixie Lumberman. February, 1964, p. 5-8.

Fandray, Dayton. "Lombardi's Lessons: Leading Well Is the Only Thing That Counts." Continental Magazine. January 2004: 27-28.

Ferguson, John L. "How to Make a Million." Sunday. The Indianapolis [Indiana] Star Magazine. November 20, 1960, p. 30. (Reprinted in Roy O. Martin, Autobiography.)

Flynn, Julia. "The Biology of Business." Business Week. July 14, 1997, p. 11.

"FSC SmartWood Certification." LFA News. Louisiana Forestry Association. July-August, 2000, p. 4.

Griffin, Griff. "Edge Optimization Vital to Hardwood Mill Upgrade." Forest Industries. March, 1989, p. 11.

BIBLIOGRAPHY

Kelly, Tom. "Ellis Martin, Still Active at 80, at Home in the woods." The Piney Woods Journal. October, 1997, pp. 15, 17.

Kerr, Ed. "Success by the Board Foot." Forests and People. First Quarter, 1958. (Reprinted in Roy O. Martin, Autobiography).

"Louisiana: A Peek at Our Future." Brochure. Alexandria, LA: Louisiana Forestry Commission, n. d.

"Martins Give $1000 to Ruby-Wise School." Forests and People. Fourth Quarter, 2000, p. 31.

"Martin Companies Certified by Forest Stewardship." Forests and People. Second Quarter, 2000, p. 29.

"Milestones: Roy O. Martin, Sr. 1892-1973." Newsletter. Louisiana Forestry Association. February, 1973. (Reprinted in Roy O. Martin, Autobiography).

McCrary, Jennifer. "Optimizing the Timber Factory." Timber Harvesting. March, 1998, pp. 14, 16.

Moreno, Kataryna. "On My Mind: What's Worrying Top Executives." Forbes. January 12, 1998, p. 18 ff.

Nelton, Sharon. "Ten Keys to Success in Family Business." Nation's Business. April, 1991, pp. 44-45.

"New Hq. for Roy O. Martin." Building Products Digest. December, 2001, p. 53.

Petree, Jack. "Roy O. Martin Lumber Stays on Leading Edge." Timber Line. October, 2000, p. 7.

"ROM. A Wooden Empire." Esso Oilways. January 1955, n. p.

"ROM Builds New Headquarters in Alexandria." Forests and People. Second Quarter, 2001, p. 29.

Russo, Francine. "Growth Drives Family Firms Crazy." Time. March, 19, 2001, p. B 15.

Skains, James Ronald. "Colfax Creosoting Deals With Environmental Issues While Serving Utilities." The Piney Woods Journal. April, 1998, pp. 3-4.

"South's Timber Basket Under Strain." Random Length Locator. December, 1997, pp. 1-2, 6.

"Tall Timberland Technology." Oilways. Number 1, 1985, pp. 1-7.

Torbett, Melanie. "Higgins Boats: The Wooden Boats that Won the War." Forests and People. Third Quarter, 2000, pp. 4-5, 7.

-------------------. "Made in Louisiana." Forests and People. Second Quarter, 2001, p. 29.

"Wieger Presented La. SAF Award." Forests and People. Fourth Quarter, 2001, p. 20.

Newspapers

_____, Shreveport Journal, February 13, 1950, _____.

Baty, Jann. "Martin Library Turns 50." Alexandria [LA] The Daily Town Talk. September 18, 2000, p. A-6.

Brock, Eric J. "Shreveporter Edenborn Was Among Country's Wealthiest." Shreveport [LA] Times. February 28, 1998, p. A-41.

Camire, Dennis. "Battle for Expiring Quotas Splinters Lumber Industry." Alexandria [LA] The Daily Town Talk. March 2, 2001, p. C-1.

"Classes Set for Workers in Wood Products Industry." The Natchitoches [LA] Times. February 14, 2001, p. 1-A.

Gregory, Melissa. "Mighty Profits from Tiny Saplings." Alexandria [LA] The Daily Town Talk. November 17, 2000, pp. A-1-2, 8.

"Keep Business Going Well with Succession Plan." Alexandria [LA] The Daily Town Talk. ------------------.

"La. Gets High Marks on Forest Management." Alexandria {LA] The Daily Town Talk. November 28, 2001, p. A-7.

"La. Lumber Mill Closing." Alexandria [LA] The Daily Town Talk. November 13, 2000, p. A-4.

"Lost Ground.: Urbanization May Reduce Southern Forests 6 Pct. by 2020." Alexandria [LA] The Daily Town Talk. November 28, 2001, p. A-7.

LTC Hosting of Pre-employment Training Class for Plant Production Workers." The Natchitoches [LA] Times. February 12, 2002, p. 3-A.

LIFE BY THE BOARD FOOT

Manual, Suzan. "Martin Lumber Certified 'Environmentally Sound." Alexandria [LA] The Daily Town Talk. June 22, 2002., p. C-1.

Miller, Robin. "50 Years of Reading: Martin Branch Library Marks a Half-Century of Serving Pineville." Alexandria [LA] The Daily Town Talk. September 17, 2000, p. E-1.

Pinnell, Gary R. "Dura-Wood Treating Sold." Alexandria [LA] The Daily Town Talk. January 1, 2000, p. C-1.

------------------. "Helping Out, Colfax Creosoting Shipping Poles to Ice-Plagued Northeast." Alexandria [LA] The Daily Town Talk. January 13, 1988, p.-----.

Pitchford, Roy. "La. Forests in Good Shape or Danger?" Alexandria [LA] The Daily Town Talk. December 16, 2001, p. D-4.

------------------. "Martin System Growing with Trade Center." Alexandria [LA] The Daily Town Talk. August 19, 2001, p. D-1.

------------------. "Will Treaty's End Hurt U. S. Timber Industry?" Alexandria [LA] The Daily Town Talk. March 30, 2001, p. D-1. "Quality Deer Management Seminar." Alexandria [LA] The Daily Town Talk. August 5, 2001, p. B-6.

"Roy O. Martin Inc. Expands." Alexandria [LA] The Daily Town Talk. January 28, 1973, p. C-12.

"Roy O. Martin, Jr., Becomes President of Lumber Firm." Alexandria [LA] The Daily Town Talk. June 14, 1962, p. ----------.

"Roy O. Martin Makes Wood Plant Official." Natchitoches [LA] Times. June 7, 1994, p. ---------.

Smilie, Jim. "Area Boy and Girl Scouts Receive 76 Acres." Alexandria [LA] The Daily Town Talk. June 4, 1988, p. --------.

Sutherland, Eugene and Jordan, Cerita. "City to Begin Taking Bids on Downtown Art Center. Roy O. Martin Building's Renovation also in the Works." Alexandria [LA] The Daily Town Talk. August 22, 2002, p. A-7.

Interviews

Personal Interviews with Joseph Abraham

Floyd, Esther Martin. January 19, 1999.

Howard, Virginia Martin. May 26, 1998.

Jeffress, Charles. August 4, 1998.

Martin, Ellis S. May 25 and May 26, 1998.

Martin, Roy O., Jr. January 17, 1999.

Personal Interviews with James E. Carter

Alley, John G. September 27, 2000.

Bolton, Robert. September 27, 2000.

Chown, Robert M. January 22, 2002.

Cook, Mr. and Mrs. Cob. June 27, 2001.

Jeffress, Charles. January 19, 2001.

Landry, Jackie. April 2, 2001.

Landry, Richard. March 5, 2001.

Hood, Paul C. May 9, 2001.

Howard, Virginia Martin. July 16, 2001.

Martin, Ellis S. October 26, 2000; February 15, 2001; October 25, 2001.
    Minute Book Reviews: February 8, 2001; February 15, 2001; March 29, 2001.
    Trips to Manufacturing Plants: December 3, 2001; August 30, 2002.

Martin, Jonathan. December 21, 2001; March 1, 2002.

Martin, Norman. November 3, 2000.

BIBLIOGRAPHY

Martin, Roy O., Jr. December 11, 2000; June 11, 2001; June 21, 2001.

Martin, Roy O., III. December 21, 2001; March 5, 2002.

Munsterman, John. September 20, 2000.

Norton, Clyde. January 29, 2001.

O'Quin, Chester. March 21, 2001.

Peterson, Keith. September 14, 2000.

Weems, Charles. July 26, 2001.

Wieger, Bill. May 31, 2001.

Woodard, Zack. June 27, 2001.

Zaytsoff, Rob. March 1, 2002.

Telephone Interviews with James E. Carter

Denley, Wayne. April 16, 2002.

Erdoes, Mary. April 23, 2002.

Floyd, Esther Martin. ------------, 2001.

Fowler, Mary Martin. January 24, 2002.

Kneer, Mike. April 4, 2002.

McNully, Hollis. April 5, 2002.

Moore, Bill. April 8, 2002.

Tudor, Buddy. April 4, 2002.

Personal Notes

Howard, Gene. March 23, 2004.

Woodard, Zack. Notes.

Emails

Email to Jonathan E. Martin

Wagner, Steve. February 4, 2004.

Email to Maggie Martin

Martin, Roy O., III. February 3, 2004.

Martin, Roy O., III. February 4, 2004.